HARRIER BOYS

VOLUME TWO

NEW TECHNOLOGY, NEW THREATS, NEW TACTICS
1990 – 2010

HARRIER BOYS

VOLUME TWO

NEW TECHNOLOGY, NEW THREATS, NEW TACTICS
1990 – 2010

BOB MARSTON

GRUB STREET • LONDON

PUBLISHER'S NOTE

From time to time Bob Marston has written a short introductory piece to the chapter written by the named contributor. Bob's piece has been indented for clarification purposes.

AMENDMENTS TO VOLUME ONE

- Page 11: Bob Heyhoe's rank was chief technician not sergeant.
- Page 46: The picture caption should read XV792 not XV982.
- Page 129 and index: Jim Downey's surname ends -ney not -nie.
- Last page of first photo insert: The top photo attribution should be (unknown) not Jock Heron.

Published by
Grub Street
4 Rainham Close
London
SW11 6SS

A CIP record for this title is available from the British Library

ISBN-13: 9-781-910690-17-8

Printed and bound by Finidr, Czech Republic

CONTENTS

INTRODUCTION
Bob Marston

The first generation Harrier was an exciting seat-of-the-pants, stick and rudder, pilots' flying machine that faithfully followed its Hawker pedigree, with the added dimension of vectored thrust. Bringing the expeditionary air force concept of earlier years into the jet age, it amply fulfilled its role in the Cold War period. Operating from small, mobile, concealed sites near to the battle front, Harriers could support a ground war with impressive sortie rates. While honed for Europe, this concept was proven in national contingencies to protect Belize and the Falkland Islands.

But as the 20th century drew to a close, the Harrier and its world were about to change almost beyond recognition. The second-generation aircraft had a single crew member, a Pegasus engine, and the ability to land vertically. Otherwise, it was more different from the Harrier GR3 than the original GR1 had been from the Hunter. At the same time, the Cold War was won. The Berlin Wall tumbled, Germany was unified, and ex-Warsaw Pact countries defected to NATO. When Iraq invaded Kuwait, the RAF's Harriers were left on the sideline of the first Gulf War, being not yet ready for combat, but significant lessons were evident. While the vulnerability of hardened aircraft shelters supported the Harrier deployment concept, the wide public visibility of the fighting led to an outcry at Iraqi forces dispersing aircraft away from main bases, risking collateral damage to nearby civilians. The old Harrier war plans had to be re-thought.

The GR5 promised significant advantages over the GR3:

- It had more pylons to carry weapons (nine as against five, including the dedicated pylons in front of the outriggers for air-to-air missiles).
- The pylons were wired through a databus, enabling the pilot to communicate with smart weapons, so that they could be best used.
- More of the pylons were 'wet', allowing more external fuel tanks to be used.
- The wing carried significantly more internal fuel.
- Refuelling was facilitated by moving the ground connector to enable use with the engine running, while a retractable probe could be left permanently fitted.
- Fuel flow to the engine was controlled by a digital engine control system, which was easier to maintain and simpler to use than the old hydro-

mechanical system.
- An active electronic countermeasures (ECM) system was built into the airframe.
- The raised cockpit and bulbous canopy gave the pilot a much better view.
- The wing, with leading-edge root extensions (LERX), gave improved turning performance. With its huge flaps and drooping ailerons, it also gave much more lift at low speed.
- Vertical lift performance was enhanced by devices to trap engine thrust under the fuselage.

After the decision to go with the American design as a basis for both AV-8B and GR5, rather than the RAF following the BAe Kingston plan for a metal 'big wing' Harrier II, introduction of the GR5 was far from trouble-free. The wing gave more lift, but the resultant drag, and that from the canopy, resulted in a lower top speed than that of the GR3. While addressing RAF concerns about bird strike resistance and battle damage survivability, many components were also changed in order to increase the UK manufacturing share within the aircraft.

- Extra bird strike tests on the windscreen and wing leading edges took time and necessitated design tweaks.
- Initial bullet impact tests on fully-fuelled wings caused worry, before it was decided that shock-wave transmission through fluid with no air gap in the wing was unrealistic.
- The Ferranti inertial platform took much longer than anticipated to achieve reliability. American Litton platforms had to be used initially.
- The American plan was to use the on-board oxygen generation system (OBOGS) to provide pure oxygen to the pilot. The RAF insisted on a regulated breathing air mix, giving an appropriate partial pressure of oxygen for the environment; this took time to develop.
- The loss of an early GR5, with the test pilot dying and the airframe disappearing into the deep Atlantic, led to a lengthy pause while an explanation was sought.
- The GR5 was to use two guns developed from the Aden cannon used on the GR3, as opposed to the single Gatling gun on the AV-8B. First, a compromise fuselage design was needed to take either the American gun, with ammunition fed from the other side, or the UK pair of guns, one each side. When this had been solved, development of the gun proved difficult. In testing, gun stoppages were frequent. Moreover, it had been decided that, unlike the GR3-era Aden discarding the used cartridges while collecting the spring-steel links used between rounds, in the new gun, the reverse would be the aim. Unfortunately, it was found that the links flew randomly, sometimes damaging the carbon fibre tailplane.

Despite re-designs of the link chute, the problem persisted, along with the stoppages. After considerable development work, the guns were deleted as a cost-saving measure. This was a significant blow for a close air support aircraft, though alternative uses were later found for the gun mounting points, despite the harsh environment in which they were placed.

- The LERX on the wing enhanced pitch rate, but were potentially so destabilising that initially only a 65% size version was fitted.
- Early in GR5 flying, it was found that the skin of the rear fuselage was rippling under the impact of acoustic vibration from the hot nozzles, which were a new 'zero-scarf' design rather than the GR3 type, which gave a less focused efflux. Frustratingly, this was the same problem that had been seen in the GR3, leading to modification in the form of titanium reinforcement. Essential modifications caused further delay.
- Harrier II utilised a technology that had become very popular in civil aviation – Kapton wiring. With its lighter core and insulation, it could save huge amounts of weight in an airliner. Weight saving sounded attractive for the Harrier, but the combination of ultra-thin insulation and a cramped high-vibration environment proved disastrous. If two pieces of the wire rubbed together, the insulation would disappear, leading to short circuits, arcing and sometimes fire. After a major fire in the rear end of a GR5, a mass re-wiring programme became essential.
- As we were bringing in just another Harrier, and we already had a two-seat trainer version, the original plan for GR5 was to buy just single-seaters, plus a state-of-the-art simulator. It soon became apparent that the T4's flying characteristics bore little resemblance to those of the GR5, and that it was more difficult than anticipated to develop a simulator that had full motion and gave realistic all-round visual displays of low-level high-speed flight. The procurement plan was therefore changed, trading off single-seat aircraft against thirteen new two-seaters.
- While a credible night operational capability was an original aim for Harrier II, the necessary equipment and clearances were not available for the early aircraft. The initial production was therefore without FLIR, and designated GR5. The night-attack version, GR7, appeared part-way through the RAF production run, and the GR5s had to be modified later. When the night capability was enabled, it was perhaps the most significant leap forwards in the RAF Harrier, so the process is dwelt on at length in this volume.
- New operational lessons, particularly from the USMC in Gulf War 1, emphasised the high risk of damage from small arms fire to aircraft at low level. The tactical answer was to fly above the level of this threat, but this showed the limitations of the built-in ECM system of the GR5, Zeus. Its antennae were designed to counter threats from above and at small

angles of depression below the Harrier, but not to cover the area directly below. Again, a re-think was needed.

Just as the Sea Harrier FRS1 took advantage of GR1/3 experience to introduce a later, but air defence optimised aircraft, so the updated naval jet, the FA2, took the best features of all versions for its particular role. Utilising the known and trusted main airframe, the RN added an outstanding beyond-visual-range missile, the AMRAAM, a much better radar, an improved cockpit and a digital databus to give them an admirable fighter with very good weapons delivery capability. Political considerations subsequently pushed them towards Joint Force Harrier, with resources shared by the RN and RAF, and then to use of the GR airframes, losing the BVR capability.

The demise of the Soviet Union led to a rapid change of RAF Harrier basing policy. First, they moved back within Germany towards the English Channel, to Laarbruch near the Dutch border. Eventually, the RAF left Germany entirely, Harriers replacing the Tornados at RAF Cottesmore.

While all of this was going on, the demands for air power were multiplying. Though the GR5 missed the first Gulf War, the AV-8B (with one RAF pilot among those of the USMC) was put to good use. From then on, a series of conflicts made the UK Harrier a much-used and well-respected weapons system. In the Balkans, Sierra Leone, Iraq and Afghanistan, every new demand was met by an innovative solution. By the end of the commitment in Afghanistan, Harrier GR9, flown by RAF and RN pilots, offered a terrific capability to support troops on the ground. Withdrawn to the UK in 2009, and able to regain currency in skills such as embarked operations, the Joint Force Harrier was retired with indecent haste barely a year later. Ironically, the next conflict in which UK air power was needed was in Libya in 2011. With a long Mediterranean coastline, Libya was obviously suited to carrier-borne air operations, as demonstrated by France in spearheading operations, but also by USMC Harrier AV-8Bs. The UK effort had to fly from much further afield, with complex AAR support.

The assembled talent of the Harrier Boys took on many challenges over the years, rapidly developing new ways of using a swiftly-evolving aircraft to serve with distinction in a series of operations that would fill their lives. Some of those operators share their experience in this book, giving an impression of what it was like to have been a member of this august company, working with such a remarkable aircraft. Their contributions cover varying time periods, starting with some background stories from the Cold War years. Rather than artificially dividing them to give a strict chronological narrative, I have added my own explanations of context where they might help to guide the reader. Each chapter is a stand-alone narrative; together they outline the history of the second half of the UK Harrier era.

CONTRIBUTORS
(in alphabetical order)

Jim Arkell

Wing Commander Jim Arkell OBE flew the GR3 on IV(AC) Squadron, 1(F) Squadron and 233 OCU. On exchange with the USN, he flew FA-18 and A-7E. He was OC Ops Wing in Laarbruch, flying Harrier GR7. He filled several Harrier-related staff posts. Upon retiring from regular service, he served as a squadron uncle on IV Squadron.

Stuart Atha

Air Vice-Marshal Stuart Atha CB, DSO, ADC flew the GR7 on 1(F) Squadron, was a flight commander on IV(AC) Squadron, and then OC 3(F) Squadron. Subsequently, he was the station commander at RAF Coningsby, flying Tornado, Spitfire and Hurricane, and later AOC 1 Group.

Dave Baddams

Lieutenant Commander Dave Baddams MBE was an A-4 pilot with the Royal Australian Navy until the Skyhawk was taken out of front-line service in 1982. He transferred to the RN to fly Harriers, and commanded 800 Squadron.

Jonathan Baynton

Squadron Leader Jonathan Baynton flew the GR3 on 3(F) Squadron after a first tour as a flying instructor. As a QFI on 233 OCU, he was promoted to become a flight commander, and then led the GR5 conversion team. He subsequently became an airline pilot.

Chris Benn

Wing Commander Chris Benn flew the Hunter in Oman before joining the Harrier Force. He was a GR3 pilot on 3(F) Squadron in Germany, then a flight commander on 1(F) Squadron in the early days of the GR5.

James Blackmore

Commander James Blackmore flew the Sea Harrier FA2 on 800 Squadron, and as an instructor on 899 Squadron. In Joint Force Harrier, he was a GR9 pilot on IV(AC) Squadron and 1(F) Squadron. He also flew the F/A-18 on exchange with the USN.

Chris Burwell

Group Captain Chris Burwell MBE, MSc flew Harriers on 1(F) and 3(F) Squadrons, and was OC 1(F) Squadron. He was the station commander of RAF Scampton. Later, he managed a commercial flying training school in Spain.

Jon 'Dog' Davis

Lieutenant General Jon 'Dog' Davis USMC was an exchange pilot with the RAF in Germany from 1988 to 1991. A long-time Harrier pilot, flying AV-8A, AV-8B, GR3, GR5 and GR7, he rose to become the deputy commandant for aviation of the Marine Corps at the time of writing.

Don Fennessey

Captain Don Fennessey USN was an exchange officer on 3(F) Squadron. He later commanded an F-18 Squadron and retired as a navy captain, to teach at a university.

Heinz Frick

Heinz Frick qualified as a test pilot while serving with the RAF, then became a company test pilot with Hawker Siddeley, later British Aerospace.

Marc 'Rambo' Frith

Captain Marc 'Rambo' Frith USAF flew A-10 attack aircraft before becoming an exchange Harrier pilot on IV(AC) Squadron. Later, he became an airline pilot.

Keith Grumbley

Wing Commander Keith Grumbley flew GR3 Harriers on 1(F) Squadron, 3(F) Squadron and Air Commander Belize, and commanded the SAOEU flying the GR7.

Tony Harper

Wing Commander Tony Harper flew GR3 Harriers with 20 Squadron, 1(F) Squadron during the Falklands War, and GR5/7 as OC 233 OCU. After retiring from regular service, he served as a squadron uncle on 1(F) Squadron.

Mike Harwood

Air Vice-Marshal Mike Harwood CB, CBE, MA flew GR3 Harriers in Germany and GR5/7 on the SAOEU and as a flight commander on 1(F) Squadron. He commanded 20(R) Squadron and RAF Cottesmore.

John 'Jock' Heron

Group Captain John 'Jock' Heron OBE flew Harriers as a flight commander on IV(AC) Squadron and as OC Ops Wing at RAF Gütersloh. He was the station commander of RAF Swinderby. After retiring from the RAF, he was the military representative at Rolls-Royce. His full story is told in his book *From Schoolboy to Station Commander.*

Gerry Humphreys

Squadron Leader Gerry Humphreys flew the GR3 in the UK and Germany. He was a flight commander on 1(F) Squadron during the introduction of the GR5/7.

Brian Johnstone

Warrant Officer Brian Johnstone was an RN aircraft mechanic who first worked on the Sea Vixen then Phantom. In 1980 he started a 22-year association with the Sea Harrier which ended when he left the RN. He was awarded the MBE for services to the Sea Harrier force. After leaving the RN he worked on the JSF programme and then for Saab on the Sea Gripen programme. He is the chief engineer for Sea Vixen XP924.

Mark Leakey

Air Commodore Mark Leakey flew the GR3 as a junior pilot, then GR3/5 as a flight commander on 3(F) Squadron. He commanded 1(F) Squadron in the GR7 era.

Steve Long

Flight Lieutenant Steve Long flew the GR7 on 3(F) Squadron, then the AV-8B Plus on exchange with the USMC. Having qualified as a test pilot, he flew the F-35 before becoming a civilian test pilot.

Keith Marshall

Squadron Leader Keith Marshall flew GR3 Harriers on IV(AC) Squadron and as a flight commander on 3(F) Squadron. He then followed a career in civil aviation.

Art Nalls

Lieutenant Colonel Art Nalls flew the AV-8A Harrier with the USMC before becoming a test pilot. He then flew many AV-8B development trials, including ski-jump take-offs and airborne engine relights. On retirement from the corps, he went into the real estate development business before founding Nalls Aviation and displaying his Sea Harrier. http://www.artnalls.com/pilots/art-nalls-ltcol-usmc-ret/

Roger Robertshaw

Flight Lieutenant Roger Robertshaw was a GR3 pilot on 1(F) Squadron, then a Hawk tactical-weapons instructor. He again flew the GR3 on IV(AC) Squadron in Germany, and 1417 Flight in Belize, before becoming an airline pilot.

Bernie Scott

Flight Lieutenant Bernie Scott flew the GR3 on 1(F) Squadron before joining the Red Arrows flying the Gnat and Hawk. On exchange with the RNLAF, he flew the F-16. After qualifying as a test pilot, he flew early GR5s, before transferring to BAe, where he worked on GR7, GR9 and Sea Harrier as well as the Hawk. He was also an airline pilot.

Andy Sephton

Flight Lieutenant Andy Sephton was on the same advanced flying training course at Valley as the author; he then flew the Jaguar. He became a test pilot, and qualified to fly the Harrier for trials work. As a Rolls-Royce test pilot, he conducted Pegasus engine development flying. He was later the chief test pilot for Marshall Aerospace, and chief pilot for the Shuttleworth Collection of historic aircraft.

Keith Skinner

Wing Commander Keith Skinner was an air defence pilot flying the Lightning and Phantom, and a TWU instructor. He served on the UK Taceval team, with the MoD team in Saudi Arabia, and as wing commander RAFAT, before becoming a Harrier squadron uncle.

Simon Turner

Squadron Leader Simon Turner flew the Harrier GR3 on IV(AC) Squadron, the GR5 on 1(F) Squadron, then the AV-8B with the USMC. He was a 1 Squadron GR7 pilot before becoming a flight commander on 20 Squadron, then OCU. He then retired from the RAF to fly airliners.

Gary Waterfall

Air Vice-Marshal Gary Waterfall CBE flew the GR3 on 3(F) Squadron, and the Hawk with the Red Arrows. He commanded 41 (Test and Evaluation) Squadron and was the final station commander of RAF Cottesmore and force commander of Joint Force Harrier. At the time of writing, he was AOC 1 Group.

Mitch Webb

Squadron Leader Mitch Webb flew the Hawk on 100 Squadron before becoming a Harrier pilot. She flew the GR7 on 3(F) Squadron, IV(AC) Squadron and as a QWI on 20(R) Squadron. She was squadron leader Ops at Wittering before becoming a school teacher and mother living in France. She runs ultra marathons "because everyone needs a challenge".

Graham Williams

Air Vice-Marshal Graham Williams AFC*, FRAeS was one of the first Harrier development test pilots, and later commanded 3(F) Squadron at RAF Wildenrath.

He was the station commander of RAF Brüggen as a Jaguar station. A full account of his RAF career is in his book *Rhapsody In Blue*.

Mark Zanker

Flight Lieutenant Mark Zanker began his flying career as a Jaguar pilot. After converting to the Harrier, he flew the GR3 then GR5 on 3(F) Squadron and 233 OCU. After a tour on the Red Arrows, he flew the GR7 on IV(AC) Squadron and 1(F) Squadron before becoming an airline pilot.

CHAPTER 1

THE THICK OF IT

During the 1980s, most of the RAF's Harrier Force was based at Gütersloh in West Germany, just minutes of flying time from the inner German border, which marked the start of Warsaw Pact territory. The two squadrons, 3(F) Squadron and IV(AC) Squadron, were each bigger than 1(F) Squadron in Wittering, having incorporated the assets of 20 Squadron on moving forward from Wildenrath. Life on the Gütersloh squadrons was dominated by the Cold War and the proximity of the perceived threat. When the border between the two parts of Germany was opened up in November 1989, and all of Germany was reunified in October 1990, that was all to change.

Having developed from the Wildenrath days, the Harrier concept of operations in Germany in the 80s was based on dispersal of the aircraft to temporary sites spread over a wide area, making them difficult to locate and to attack. Each squadron had three flights, each of which had its own flying site. In addition, there was a logistics site for each squadron, supplying fuel, weapons and spare parts as necessary. The sappers (Royal Engineers) who did the site preparation had their own resources park where they stored the materials to build operating surfaces, fuel storage and aircraft hides. Providing control and coordination for all of these was the Forward Wing Operations Centre (FWOC), giving ten active sites at any time. The sappers would normally have two more flying sites ready for use in case a site became compromised. It was anticipated that sites might need to move as often as every 48 hours. Ground defence was provided by an RAF Regiment field squadron, while all deployed personnel were armed for self-protection. The second vital army asset to make the concept workable was the Royal Signals, who provided communications between the sites and out to the tasking agency. Generally, tasks would come from the NATO HQ in the caves at Maastricht in Holland, though this function could be delegated to HQ 1 (BR) Corps, for whom the Harriers mostly provided support. Air traffic controllers also deployed to each site, but their job was unusual in that flying operations were conducted in radio silence, to avoid revealing site locations, unless flight safety required an intervention.

On each flying site, there were eight hides, able to accommodate the six aircraft of the deployed flight, plus two spare hides to be used by aircraft diverted during a site move. Each time a new flying site was activated, a modified air traffic plan was issued from the FWOC, showing departure lanes, initial points (IPs) and sites. For a pilot, recovering to a field site was always a challenge. All military pilots are taught to find a target by flying accurately from an IP, which would be chosen as a feature easily identifiable from the air, to a target at a constant speed. However, for recovery to a field site, a Harrier pilot would start the run at 420kts and end it in the hover over the pad. With the site camouflaged to make it difficult for enemies to find, and operating in radio silence, this was a tricky procedure.

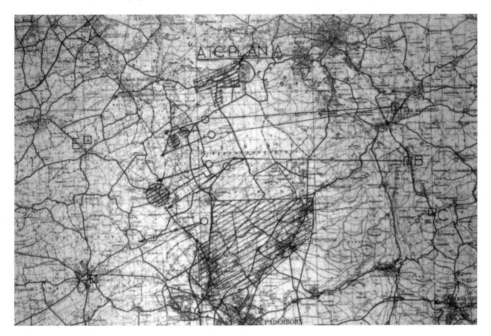

Simple air traffic plan with just five flying sites. (Author)

Identifying potential sites was a continuous process carried out by the Harrier Plans staff. The prime requirements for a flying site were fairly level and firm surfaces for a take-off strip of some 200 metres, a square landing pad, and the aircraft hides. The pad would be a MEXE pad constructed by the sappers using PSA1 material. The strip would often be made of this same material, necessitating the sapper ritual of 'kicking tin' to go on for rather longer, or for a short period, the natural surface could be used, if its hardness (CBR) was sufficient, as tested by the 'pogo stick' or cone penetrometer. Any local deficit in hardness would often lead to the Harrier 'bogging in', typically with the nosewheel sinking in far enough to prevent further movement. Ground crew became very skilled at extracting jets from such situations, digging a ramp in front of the wheel before as many people as possible climbed onto the tailplane while a Unimog, or if more weight was needed for grip, a three-ton Bedford truck, pulled on the towbar. In extreme situations, usually after heavy rainfall, a metal skid device could be attached to the nosewheel to prevent it sinking beyond the axle while it taxied to the take-off strip. The skid was removed before departure. The potential bog-in embarrassment factor for the pilot was increased by a design feature of the GR3, whereby a footstep to assist access lowered as the canopy opened. However, if the aircraft bogged in far enough, the canopy could not be opened until a hole had been dug for the footstep to go down into. To maintain the necessary level of expertise, field deployments were usually practised three times a year.

The qualities of sites varied a lot, from a new autobahn in one case, to the trickiest of grass strips. Often, the strip length was such that there was no option to abort the take-off on the strip once the engine had reached full power; if anything went wrong after that, ejection was the way out. One strip that sticks in my mind was in the Bergen-Hohne training area. We had moved site overnight, and after diverting to other sites, I and five other pilots flew into the new site early in the morning. We had a look at the take-off strip, which was not very long and pointed towards tall trees, and were reassured that all the calculations showed that it would be safe. However, the standard calculations appeared not to make sufficient allowance for gradient, and this strip was distinctly downhill. With a new task planned, I was the first to take off. I was told later that my jet blast parted the tree tops sufficiently for me to miss them. The next pilot out was not so lucky. He collected some foliage in his undercarriage, which he left down as he flew to the diversion airfield. All further tasking was cancelled, the remaining jets were defuelled to a light weight, and the site was abandoned.

The challenge of a first field deployment is described below by Keith Marshall. Keith Grumbley admits his error in the account that follows, as does Gerry Humphreys in the third story.

KEITH MARSHALL

It was my first deployment with 4 Squadron. I was an experienced pilot with more than 2,000 hours but very new on the Harrier and what I am about to tell you does me no credit, but exemplifies the complexity of the aircraft I was now assigned to fly and the equally demanding environment in which to operate it.

I was not trusted to fly in with the big boys and instead went to our operating base, Eberhard in the Sennelager military training area, with the ground party. The weather was very poor for the first five days with thick fog preventing the arrival of the jets and I kept thinking how nice it must be to still be on base, going home each night to a warm cuddly wife instead of enduring the joys of a damp 'green worm' sleeping bag. Sometimes life gets unbearably tough so we, the boss, the engineers and several of the lads sought solace in the local strip club (funny how these things always pop up around barracks) which was quiet at the time and more than happy to give us its undivided attention and lots of excellent beer.

On the morning of the sixth day the fog cleared enough to allow the jets to fly in and so with a splitting head I watched with awe as they arrived; then the fog came mockingly back, preventing any more activity that day. The flyers were most impressed with our thorough reconnaissance of the local locales and insisted that we take them for a personal look, and so it was that when the next day unexpectedly broke crystal clear, the last thing we really wanted was to put a bone dome on our aching heads. But queen and country call, and we briefed, grabbed our kit and I set off for my first flight from a deployed site.

This particular site had a stretch of road (open to traffic except during take-off or landing) of about 300 yards for take-off with what looked to me like extremely tall and hard pine trees immediately off the end of the runway. The normal procedure was to use water, injected into the rear of the combustion chamber to give an extra boost for take-off and for the vertical landing. A full tank was enough for 90 seconds and weighed about 500 lbs. On arrival at my jet, the crew chief told me that the water system was unserviceable; no sweat, I'd been briefed that a waterless departure was perfectly OK at this particular location provided, of course, the water tank was empty. I'm sure you know what's coming; the tank was not empty and I was so nervous of making a mess of things that it was precisely what I did. The water contents gauge was right in front of my face and indicating full but I did not see it. In mitigation, everything was a bit rushed and in what seemed like seconds I was out of the hide and onto the road.

The usual checks were completed and off I went for my first deployment take-off, which came uncomfortably close to being my last. Even without water flowing and with an extra 500 lbs of weight, the Harrier acceleration is pretty impressive, but not impressive enough for my liking with those big, hard-looking trees getting ominously close. It was beginning to dawn on me that something was not quite right but it was too late to abort, I just had to hang in there and hope. At the pre-computed speed I rotated the nozzles and the nose at the same time but those trees were still filling an awfully big part of the forward cockpit window. I kept rotating, probably exceeding the recommended angle of attack limit, but as I went past the trees there were still some branches above the level of my head. I'm not sure, but I think I felt a bump somewhere on the underside of my aircraft.

Surprised at still being inside this tiny cockpit, I lowered the nose with much relief, raised the gear and flaps and scanned the horizon for my leader. There was no time to reflect on what had just happened as in moments the lead and I were engaged by two RAF Phantoms that had been sneakily waiting for us. We managed to shake them off and then flew through the surface-to-air missile (SAM) zone with lots of avoiding action to break the locks as indicated on the radar warning receiver (RWR). Lead called us over to the Forward Air Controller frequency and we started our attack runs. The target was an inflatable rubber tank which when fully erect (so to speak) looked like a Russian T62. On this morning however, it was looking much as I felt, half deflated, with its protruding rubber gun barrel drooping like a sad little worm hanging over the edge of a table.

Back through the SAM belt to find the Phantoms still lurking on the other side, we quickly saw them off and headed for our temporary home. Now comes the tricky bit: trying to find one's site when it is specifically designed not to be found from the air. I decided to follow my leader and started the deceleration about two miles in trail. He made it look easy and I was feeling pretty confident that I could accomplish a vertical landing onto the pad with every bit as much panache as he had done. There was just one small problem: to hover, the Harrier needed to be below a certain fuel weight and the trick was to get below that weight but still have enough fuel to divert if necessary. (As experience and expertise grew, most Harrier pilots would start their deceleration above that critical weight and arrive above the pad, in the hover, fractionally below it.) It usually meant getting into the hover with about 600-800 lbs of fuel. Now, remember that extra 500 lbs of water that I did not think I had?

Everything was going fine until I realised I had the nozzles down with full power and still some wing lift. I decided to go round again to burn off a bit more fuel, thinking that my hover weight calculations must have been a bit off. It would mean going below fuel minimums but I was the last airborne and there was therefore no reason to have to divert. I figured that if I was going to crash, it might as well be on my own site.

The next approach got me into the hover with just about enough fuel to land. The only problem now was that I had full power on the engine and the jet was going down. There was nothing left, I was sinking into the trees but luckily somewhere over the pad. There was no chance to do the customary pause at 50 feet and make corrections. I was committed for better or for worse. Lucky for me, it was for better. I taxied to the hide and at last had a chance to think. It was then that I saw the water contents gauge and cringed inside my shell.

KEITH GRUMBLEY: JÄGERGRUND (LOOKING AFTER THE LAWN)

Harrier operations off grass-field sites were not uncommon during the halcyon years of the RAF Germany Harrier Force. We did them for three reasons: the aircraft could do it, there were seldom enough conventional field sites (either road or metal alloy 'tin' strips) and it was

Grass runway. (Dave Morgan)

another challenging dimension to the force's capability. Let me explain.

Rules of thumb came into play when selecting a grass site. The surface smoothness was deemed OK if you could drive a Land Rover over it at 40 mph and maintain control. The surface hardness was measured by a spring-loaded pogo stick jabber which gave a reading at various depths. For us a reading of three at six inches was generally OK although heavy rain degraded the soil structure leading to much effort and swearing when the site had to turn out to extricate bogged-in Harriers. One became pretty adept at eyeballing the length of strips and the 10° obstacle clearance criterion, but these were confirmed by the Harrier operating manual.

Take-off and obstacle clearance assumed that the engine was performing at full poke, that flaps were down and that the correct climb-out angle was achieved by easing back on the stick at lift-off. Regardless of the Land Rover check, the vibration during take-off rendered the instruments an illegible blur. The take-off, or nozzle rotate, point was therefore marked with an orange peg at a position calculated to take account of aircraft weight, engine thrust rating, wind, ambient temperature and pressure. The marker would be moved during the day as conditions changed, but for simplicity the heaviest site aircraft and the worst site engine were used in the calculation.

Harrier exhaust eroded and burnt grass surfaces very quickly so special techniques were applied. These involved some changes to normal procedures to minimise time on the ground and so everything from engine start-up onwards was done at the double. If the field was big enough, the start point for the take-off roll would be moved around to spread the wear. If you failed to keep the site operational for the full two weeks of the deployment, you were automatically the poor sods nailed for a site move. Thus it was up to everyone to facilitate a highly slick operation.

The short time from start-up to take-off necessitated the quickest romp through the checks to get out of the hide without blowing all manner of dust and crap into the site, and over your colleagues' jets. Out of the hide you raced through the pre-take-off vital actions and did a quick acceleration check to ensure that the engine was going to wind up as advertised. During this run up to 55% you needed to check that the engine inlet guide vanes were operating correctly, and pull in a quick dab of nozzle to check that reaction control ducts were pressurizing to give you control between the 70-odd knot lift-off speed and reaching conventional flying speed. These two gauges were inconspicuous little blighters, adversely commented on early in the jet's life, but never improved.

Check instruments: reaction control duct pressure gauge. (Author)

Finally, as you turned onto the strip for the rolling take-off it was essential to select the flaps down. Air traffic control was always situated to give a good view of the take-off and they were under no illusions about their responsibility to break radio silence should they doubt the flap selection. The engines were reliable and would respond willingly, which left the human action of selecting flaps down at a time of great distraction as the weak link in the chain. Flapless take-offs could have serious consequences.

In 1981 I was site commander at Jägergrund, one of our grass sites in the Sennelager training area. There were some tall trees in the climb-out, but no problem according to the calculations. They were brought to pilots' notice before we started flying when we walked the site. Early one morning I observed one of our newer pilots conduct a flawless flapless take-off. Instead of crisply adopting the climb-away attitude the jet mushed sluggishly into the air and climbed reluctantly at a shallow angle. I could see that he was concerned at the proximity of the trees as he dropped a wing, which helped with clearance. As ever in these situations, a sequence of small events conspired to very nearly cause a big one. ATC were late with their call as the dust made it very difficult to see the flaps clearly and I think there was some other needless R/T chatter going on. In any case by the time the pilot realised the error, the last thing he could do was take his hand off the throttle and grope for the flap selector. On the turnround I think I went over and had a word along the lines, "You won't do that again will you?" "No," he said, "that is a very big tree indeed." Later I had a trip myself, and bugger me, I went and did exactly the same thing.

At cease flying we always had a wash-up before relaxing or heading off to get a shower. This was no holds barred time and I think I opened proceedings with a statement of the blindingly obvious along the lines that that was a very big tree and no more flapless take-offs please.

GERRY HUMPHREYS: SMILE... CHICK'S LAST TRIP

Chick Kirkham was one of our most experienced Harrier simulator instructors. A charming man and somewhat of a legend in the RAF, he first retired from active service in 1976 and at that time was the oldest known practising Hunter pilot in the service. He then served as a 'retired officer' finishing on the Harrier simulator at RAF Wildenrath. It was a delight to discover from Chick when we first met in 1982, that he and my dad had flown photo-reconnaissance Mosquitos on 81(PR) Squadron in Borneo in the early 1950s. My dad hardly ever mentioned his time in the RAF so I found it fascinating to chat with Chick about what life was like in the old days.

I always enjoyed flying the simulator with Chick as instructor; everyone who flew the Harrier in those days learned from his vast store of experience – often without realising it until much later. One of his favourite tricks towards the end of a busy 'mission' was to introduce pressures and minor emergencies to the point where one was almost overloaded, but not quite. Then he would introduce a catastrophic control or engine failure from which it was only possible to survive if one ejected immediately... I certainly had reason to thank him personally for this in my future career on the Harrier, as did many others. At one stage in the mid-1980s approximately one out of three Harrier pilots had ejected at least once.

Towards the end of my first tour on 3(F) Squadron, Chick and I found ourselves manning the ops wagon for a few days during a field exercise at Geseke, one of the many Cold War deployment sites from where we practised off-base operations. I was the auth and Chick was ops officer; we ran the site from a small cabin on the back of a truck. This site was particularly tight, the standard strip length was 747 ft long; there was little to spare off the end of this one, in fact there was a nasty ditch in the over-run which would probably swallow a Harrier whole. The standard brief here was to eject rather than abort if the engine failed late during the take-off roll. Each day during my site inspection I noticed a possible escape route along a short track at around 45° to the right just before the end of the strip. It led through a gap in the hedge alongside and seemed like it would fit a Harrier, but it led to a ploughed field, so not ideal.

This was to be our last field deployment; Chick was finally retiring after over 40 years of continuous RAF service. I had been posted to the other Germany Harrier squadron, so someone decided it would be nice if we flew our last trip together from the site in a T4. A little publicity was always good for morale and so we 'suited up' and had our photos taken.

We lined up at the beginning of the strip, lots of photographers were about so we posed; TV wanted a different angle so we posed again, then we were off. I carefully briefed Chick: "Make sure your seat is live, if we have an engine failure we will eject, ready? Let's go."

Chick Kirkham, Gareth 'Bones' Jones and Hum, 3(F) Squadron site ops control July 1985.

I put on full power and immediately realised something was wrong... the RPM was 3% low and the green water flow light was not on. I'd forgotten to turn it on! I reached to flick the switch on the right side of the instrument panel... it was not there. This can't be... then I remembered this was one of the first jets with a new 'improved' water switch location down by the throttle on the left side. By now I realised we would be in trouble if we kept going as we were in a seriously limited performance situation. We needed full power immediately after brake-release and all through the ground roll to get off before the end of the strip. In fact we had de-fuelled the jet to give ourselves adequate take-off performance. I immediately pulled the HP cock to shut down the engine... DON'T EJECT CHICK! I have a

plan... max wheel braking and total concentration on that farmer's track now. We shot through the gap with inches to spare and came to a gentle halt in the beginning of the ploughed field. I'll never forget that moment's silence, broken only by the clanking of the Pegasus fan blades and Chick, cool as a cucumber saying, "Nice abort Gerry".

Hum and Chick.

BOB MARSTON

Dispersed sites were sometimes in interesting places. In exploring around a site located on a big grass gliding site at Borkenberge, I found an old man in a workshop making a huge wooden framework for a wing. He showed me the plans for an assault glider, explaining that he was building it for display in a museum in Munich. Asked why he had this job up in the north of the country, he said that he was chosen because he had flown this type in WW2. I thought that he wouldn't have many hours on type, but he said he had flown 400 hours, mostly being towed from Italy to North Africa laden with Jerry cans of fuel to keep Rommel's tanks going, then being towed back if unbroken. The intended operational assault profile involved the glider being towed to near overhead the target carrying ten troops. Having cast off from the towing aircraft, the pilot would put the glider into a near-vertical dive with airbrakes out, the gunner would put his head and shoulders out of the top hatch and fire his aimed machine gun (there were also fixed forward-firing guns) to deter ground defences, then at the last moment the pilot would pull back hard, pop the brake 'chute, and fire the retro rockets. He had, of course, never actually done that. He also showed me a photo of himself as a young student glider pilot at Borkenberge in the 1930s, proudly wearing his Hitler Youth uniform. At another site on a former military airfield, where grass had grown all over the rather thin tarmac runway surfaces, two more veterans turned up, introducing themselves as the last jet pilots to have used those runways – flying Me 262s.

Overshadowing all of this high readiness was the spectre of the NATO Taceval. All air assets would be assessed each year by a permanent team, augmented by drafted-in subject matter experts. Evaluations were of two types: part one – readiness and generation, part two – operational effectiveness, including weapons delivery. Both were also practised through Maxeval, run by HQ RAFG, and Mineval, generated at station level. For part one, the assessors went to great lengths to achieve surprise. At some stage, an evaluator with a little learning must have noted the average circadian rhythm, as 0430 became a fairly standard time for the hooter to sound after the short delay that followed the incoming alert message. I still wake at that time most mornings, just in case. One of the more imaginative Gütersloh call-outs came on a Sunday afternoon. I was flying a display at Bergneustadt auf dem Dümpel, and quite a few Gütersloh personnel were there as spectators. Ops staff telephoned the organisers, who put out a message over the PA system telling all Gütersloh personnel to return to base immediately. I phoned back to query this, and was told to fly the display, then return, cancelling the post-show entertainment and hotel booking. Back home, I found that this was all generated by the station commander, who, during a lunchtime drinks party with his executives, had nipped out to tell the duty operations staff to initiate the recall. Another time, the NATO Taceval team, based at Ramstein in southern Germany, arrived in the early hours on 1 November. This being All Saints' Day and a religious holiday in northern Germany, the officers and SNCOs had taken advantage of the opportunity to hold a games night in the sergeants' mess, starting on the previous evening. When the call-out started, I was on my way home; many others were still at the party. I was the first to arrive at the squadron, and as more soon gathered, the evaluators issued modified instructions to the effect that anyone who had reached home from the games night must not attempt to drive to work, and under no circumstances must any aircraft engines be started. Fortunately, part two Tacevals had to be pre-programmed, and were usually during the third field deployment of the year.

Occasionally, other special events were superimposed on the training deployment cycle. One such was Trial Arbitrator, an evaluation of the effect of fighting a war in NBC kit. One flying site spent a week in July in the Bergen-Hohne training area in such conditions. They were at NBC High, wearing charcoal-impregnated suits in addition to normal clothes, or NBC Black, with respirators, hoods, overboots and gloves as well. Pilots had to wear the AR5, a rubber hood with attached visor and oxygen mask, with a neck seal to ensure that air could enter only from the aircraft's oxygen system or a portable electric fan unit driving air through filters. With this and the additional layer of clothing, in the July heat, body temperature was a particular area of interest. The pilots slept in a Porton liner, a pressurised chemical-proof fabric chamber inside a tent, and were monitored at every step. The first action of the day was to fit a core temperature sensor. As modern swallowable RF transmitters were not then available, this involved (self-) insertion of an anal-thermistor with wired connection to a remote monitor. For safety, pilots flew in T-birds with a safety pilot in the rear seat wearing normal summer kit who could monitor performance and temperature. One pilot, having performed the dressing ritual, attended the morning briefing, received a task, planned and briefed, finally strapped into the aircraft and prepared to start. At this point, the safety pilot intervened, pointing out that the pilot was too hot, and so the sortie was terminated. This was the only occasion of which I am aware when a Harrier flight was cancelled due to a 'bottom over-temp'. Probably the most stressful task was loading heavy weapons in high temperatures, but that continued up to the point of collapse. At the end of the week, personnel of Site 6 looked shattered but distinctly relieved.

Another memorable event was the firepower demo during a major NATO exercise to which Soviet observers were invited. All of the deployed Harriers took part, as well as those of 1(F) Squadron operating from Gütersloh, giving a total of forty-two aircraft. The plan would have been ambitious on a good day, but in fact the notoriously poor low-level visibility in Germany that day was a real challenge. At the designated first take-off time, 3 Squadron launched an aircraft from each of its sites to form an escort formation. Thirty seconds later, 4 Squadron did the same from its three sites, and so on until all were airborne. 1 Squadron joined on to the back of the Balbo. So far, so good. However, having managed to get to the target, the first few aircraft dropped their practice bombs, and on the ground the army set off explosive charges to simulate HE weapons. The smoke from the explosions considerably reduced the already limited visibility, leading to some very close shaves among the following Harriers. It was with great relief that we all landed safely, but when the message came down that the demonstration had been so impressive that the general would like to repeat it the next day, trepidation resumed. Fortunately, the weather was so bad in the morning that the task was cancelled. Another firepower demo flown from Sennelager involved some exploration of take-off and landing planning data. Four aircraft were each to fire four full pods of the operational version of SNEB, which fired all of its rockets before the pod itself was jettisoned. The pods and the HE rockets were fine, but the frangible fibreglass nosecones through which they fired had been declared a FOD hazard, so we flew with the rockets projecting beyond the front of the pod. No take-off performance figures existed for this configuration, so the site commander took off first; seeing him safely over the trees, the others followed. Then, in the demo, one of the pods failed to fire all of its rockets, so did not jettison. The pilot thus had to do his vertical landing back at Eberhard with half a pod of rockets on an outboard wing pylon. But again, all was well.

In the UK, the national Taceval team once arrived at Wittering at 1900 hours on a midweek day. I was on the OCU, where we were declared for a low level of readiness that required us just to call out all our personnel and to show that we had sufficient aircraft. Soon, the evaluators became uneasy at the lack of reaction from the high readiness squadron, 1(F) Squadron. They were assured by ops staff that 1(F) Squadron were all ready, and arming their aircraft, but they were in Lossiemouth. As they were required to verify this first hand, I ended up launching at 2300, after a normal day's work, in a T4 with an evaluator in the rear seat. It was a dark and stormy night, and I suffered an unusual aircraft fault. When the undercarriage was raised, the airbrake remained in its normal gear-down position, extended to 25°. The extra directional stability this gives is useful at low speeds, but not so good when cruising at high speed. So we rode on through the dark and the weather with a strange Dutch rolling motion up to Scotland. There the weather was worse, and the strong wind required landing on the shorter runway with less good approach aids. Having taxied to the line of armed 1(F) Squadron jets in the pouring rain, we were greeted by the rather wet OC and even wetter engineers. After a cursory check of readiness, the evaluator cleared the engineers to unload the weapons, while we went off in search of an open bar. He seemed unconcerned about his popularity, or lack thereof.

The complexity of the support organisation for deployed Harrier operations was reflected in the staff I commanded in my tour as OC Harrier Plans. They included officers representing the RAF Regiment, RAF Logistics Branch, Royal

Engineers and Royal Signals. So, while the most visible feature of the Harrier Force was the flying of the few aircraft by the slightly larger number of pilots, each squadron also needed some 100 engineers to support on-base operations, while all the external agencies listed above would be needed for flying from a typical austere site. In Germany, Harrier Plans coordinated all of this for the traditional three annual training deployments, and also maintained plans for wartime deployments within the anticipated area of operation. Some of these sites were similar to those used for exercises, but others were planned utilising roads and existing buildings, minimising build times but relying on a relaxation of peacetime constraints. In the divided Germany of that era, exercises could, and did, utilise some such assets, but the cost of the compensation that had to be paid to owners limited their use. When a reunited Germany lost its appetite for such overtly martial activities, and events in the first Gulf War led to a public perception that military activity could and should be segregated from civilian areas, a major re-think became necessary.

The planned locations of war sites were known only to those that needed such knowledge. There had to be co-ordination with HQ 1(BR) Corps, because a huge number of military units needed dispersed bases, while movements into and out of the area had to be maintained. Within the Harrier Force, the planners had the big picture, but down at flight commander level, each flight commander was briefed only on his initial site location. Jock Heron describes below his own introduction to this covert practice.

JOCK HERON

As the squadron executive officer it was my responsibility to carry out periodic surveys of the squadron's proposed war sites and, with the Harrier Force planning team, to ensure that their characteristics had not changed materially. We were always on the lookout for significant road improvements or new construction development in our potential area of operation in an attempt to increase the number of site options. These ground-reconnaissance visits were conducted very discreetly in groups of two or three in civilian clothes and invariably we travelled in a variety of private cars. We would rendezvous with our sapper and signals colleagues and drive in one vehicle to the appropriate grid reference. No photographs were taken during the ground recce to avoid compromise and detailed measurements of strip length, width and hide access were noted mentally and committed to paper in the vehicle afterwards. It was an elaborate subterfuge and I well remember taking measured strides along and across potential strips, dressed in a sports jacket and tweed hat, while engaged in earnest conversation with my sapper colleague about widening the access to car parks and potential aircraft hides or demolishing advertising hoardings. In the event that we might be challenged while exploring a light industrial estate we always had a brief question in German to protect our motives, such as "Wo ist der BP Tankstelle bitte?" which broadly translated meant "Where is the BP petrol station please?" We were never challenged but we shall never know how successful were our attempts to keep secret our clandestine duties.

Comprehensive dossiers were held for each site and on our return to base after these war site ground recces, we added our findings to the information which was secured in the wing operations centre in locked cabinets. Airborne reconnaissance photography of the sites was handled very carefully to guard against compromise and the sorties were flown only by the site commander who had conducted the ground recce. These pictures were essential to enable each site to be documented faithfully. Operation Warlock existed for over 20 years and although we knew that the reconnaissance expertise of the Warsaw Pact was formidable and that we risked being compromised by satellite imagery and by other clandestine means, we were confident that by moving our sites periodically the Harrier Force could survive and make a substantial contribution to NATO's offensive air effort.

CHAPTER 2

EACH TO HIS OWN

The adrenaline-pumping excitement of Harrier life did not appeal to everyone. Some people did one tour of high drama and low flying, then went off to do something more sensible. Others didn't even go that far; one member of my OCU course quit before the final operational phase. A pilot whose first tour would lead to nightmares in later life describes some incidents below. Despite his efforts never to return to Harrier flying, he eventually did, and came to enjoy the life in Germany and Belize.

ROGER ROBERTSHAW
"BACK ON THE SQUADRON"
It was nearly twenty-five years ago that I placed some memories into that dark corner of my mind, in the padlocked suitcase under the bed with the devils and all, never to be opened again.

23 JANUARY 1981
On an OCU course solo I foolishly set the nozzles to 60° rather than 20° on a radar approach and being heavy, had insufficient vertical thrust to hover, insufficient horizontal thrust component to maintain speed for full wing lift to fly, and was therefore descending slowly with maximum thrust and decreasing airspeed, losing wing lift as time went on. Suspecting something was 'not right' early on, I started to overshoot from the approach rather early at about 1,000 ft, but the beast had other plans and continued down. The PAR controller's voice went up an octave on each subsequent call after "*going below the glide slope*" to "*well below the glide slope*". I knew I was in trouble when he stopped talking altogether. I figured he had given up on me, but he was actually scrambling to contact the duty pilot in the tower for help. The duty pilot broke onto the controller's frequency and we had a lengthy discussion on the wireless as to possible reasons why I was about to join some of my anatomy cadavers from my university days. Believe me I was very interested as I slowly headed towards mother earth with only a Martin-Baker letdown option available, speed decaying and some red lights flashing on the CWP (I think it was the 'limiters' telling me I was melting the engine).

During training you rapidly learn that amber warnings (cautions) are bad, real bad in a fighter, but a red warning equals a 'balls-up'. The conversation went something like this: "*Duty pilot here, overshoot,*" I replied, "I am, it isn't working",

"Full power" "Yes it is," *"Got the gear up?"*, "Done that as well", *"Flaps?"*, "yep, they are up as well" – no idea what was said next, as the fence and trees were getting rather large, and I was thinking, 'I have done so much to get here, I have only just got onto the Harrier, it was my dream, now I am going to lose this beautiful aircraft and splat it slowly into the ground short of the runway – it's going to make the headlines and also a mess on the ground, and I will be in the shit again and end my career in a fireball – I have two options, stay longer and risk being part of the wreckage, or pull the handle – which will it be?' It is amazing what goes through your head in these situations. If I close my eyes now, I am back there, the devils chewing at my heels. It was slow, surreal, and almost a dream. Sun, blue skies, the lovely English countryside around, large (getting larger) houses and fields (getting much bigger now) down there ... erm, *here*; they weren't down there anymore! Just before I disappeared from view of the tower, the duty pilot screamed, *"Nozzles"* as he astutely realised my error (his next order was going to be *"eject"* he told me afterwards in the bar) so I slammed the nozzles aft. Bad move ... I just killed all the vertical thrust and plummeted closer to the grass as the aircraft accelerated forward rapidly with a huge kick in the backside. Fifty to 150 in seconds was only just fast enough and I was lucky, and got away with it. If I had to put a number on it, maybe 100 ft from the deck. This whole event left two or three very distinct, red-hot branded impressions on my subconscious peanut-sized brain forever. Firstly, the Harrier was dangerous as it didn't fly like a normal aeroplane. Secondly, it was dangerous and I got away with it. Thirdly, and most importantly, the Harrier was dangerous and had to be handled rather carefully as there were going to be more dangerous situations ahead of me and *oh yes*, the Harrier was rather dangerous (period, full stop).

20 NOVEMBER 1981

Having achieved my life's ambition, I was a 1(F) Squadron Harrier pilot. I was tasked to fly into a small clearing in the wooded tank range on Salisbury Plain, VL, simulate a weapon upload, get airborne vertically on minimum fuel, fly on to Boscombe Down to refuel, then back to Wittering at low level. This was all to be in front of a contingent of army officers to demonstrate the Harrier's capability. No-one on 1(F) wanted to do it, and being the junior pilot, the job came my way. The approach to the site was to be straight in at low level using a 50,000:1 map, with no prior recce of the area, just appearing 'out of the blue'. Simple enough, but I missed the pad (being a camouflaged site in the middle of a wood surrounded by more woods in a wooded range) and found myself flying past some 200 yards south of the pad, at 75 feet, doing 80 kts or so. The RAF controller on the pad heard me (courtesy of high-power Pegasus) and said, *"You missed the pad* [thanks], *turn north, we are only a short way away"*. Which I duly did, raising the nose to slow down (high angle of attack) to about 60 kts (in the 30-90 kts range) and put a boot of rudder in to help the turn (sideslip). POW

... POW, POW. I thought I had been hit on the side by a runaway truck as the aircraft jarred violently sideways and I guess, began to flick. I hit the power to full, dropped the nose and straightened the rudder (as we had been taught) to go around for another shot. There goes another life. That's number two so far and I am not even halfway through my first tour. I was very lucky that day, far luckier than many, and what hit me the most, was the violent reaction of the aircraft. If it had fully departed and rolled over, I would not have been able to control it.

THE FALKLANDS

I arrived in theatre after several weeks on Ascension Island (carrying out air defence – and dare I say it – first-ever night-vision goggle trials), and after a quick week back in the UK honing more skills and then flying back to Ascension (tanking a Harrier from the UK) followed by four weeks on a gutted ferry troopship, with the aircraft on a cargo ship where we had flown them the day before. After a week of going around in circles just offshore from Stanley, we finally sailed into Stanley Sound the day after the shooting war stopped, on 25 May 1982.

Once we had settled in, QRA consisted of two pilots on 'Alert 2' (two minutes to airborne), sitting in the aircraft in sub-zero conditions in the South Atlantic winter with no heaters. I did a six-hour stint like this and had to be lifted out of the cockpit as I was so cold and couldn't move – so the boss cut it down to four hours a go in the 'freezer'. Thanks boss.

17 JULY 1982

On QRA sitting in a shot-out abandoned shed someone had liberated, next to the runway at 0500 hours local time. Dark, cold and windy outside. We were the QRA team – a radar-equipped Sea Harrier and a GR3 each with two x Aim-9 and several hundred rounds of HE 30mm cannon shells. It was common to set up the aircraft 'hot to go', that is all weapons live except the final master arm switch. There were four of us in the shed, two pilots and two engineers nodding off in the warmth of a stolen paraffin stove hissing away – someone had finally seen sense and decided QRA 2 in the aircraft seat could not be carried out due to the weather after I had to be lifted out, and QRA 5 was adequate. Inside the shed was the warmest place on Stanley airfield, but the carbon monoxide levels were probably slightly higher than recommended

Falklands QRA. (Dave Morgan)

as all the shed's bullet holes had been taped up to stop the cold wind blowing through – it looked like mom's kitchen sieve with plasters on it.

Red phone rings: "Scramble, Scramble, Scramble. Vector west, inbound raid, picket ship will give details, call ZZZZ on xxx frequency, good luck." Two minutes later we were screaming down the runway, and away as a pair, all weapons live. I remember some white fluffy stuff going between me and the leader's wingtip, and it was dark. WHOA! Hold on a minute – dark? We don't fly in the dark. We just didn't fly in the dark ... no radar on a GR3 and no letdown aids ... so I guess it must be important and the sun was about to come up soon anyway. We broke cloud tops around 12,000 ft and headed west at full power as the sun slowly rose behind us. We tested the guns with a two-shot burst as we coasted out, checked we weren't leaving contrails that might give us away, and the adrenalin started to kick in. We were a pair of fighter pilots looking for a fight, dare I say it, *wanting* a fight, and we had the edge with the Aim-9L missiles.

The picket ship was about 100 miles west of land, and they told us fast moving targets 200 nm west, so vector west. We looked at our maps. Err, hang on a minute, that's pretty close to the Argentinian coast which would put us in heavily-defended Argentinian airspace with no back-up and a bunch of angry fighters, no air-to-air refuel capability, middle of winter, no real radar cover and 20,000 other good reasons that this was not a good idea.

"I say old chap, bit far to go" – i.e. we needed fuel to get back to Stanley, or our short back-up strip on the side of a mountain, and we didn't have enough fuel right then ... "Set up a CAP in your current position," was the reply. After only five minutes (it seemed like an eternity) we were running really low on fuel and told the picket ship we needed to leave very soon, so they had better scramble another pair to replace us. Ten seconds later and the voice came back, "Vector south immediately, multiple bogeys coming in, angels 100, range 60 miles, high speed". Holy shit, this was it. Years of training about to be put to the test. Full power, dive-off height down to 10,000 ft, cross-check all weapon switches live again and let's get in there.

Eyes on stalks – straining to see the wisp of an enemy trail. Fast-moving so probably Mirages – they will be in burner so not much time to fight and they will use the vertical – which we couldn't use so well. How the hell did they outflank us? Keep them low and turning and the missiles will do the rest. We needed to get below them for the initial engagement so we went lower, maybe 8,000 ft, and stayed in wide line abreast formation ('battle' about 3 nm split) so we could cover each other's six o'clock, as briefed before getting airborne. "40 miles, 20 miles, 10... merge" from the controller. Nothing, not a dicky bird, not even a speck of fly shit on the windscreen. 'Merge' when you don't see the enemy is death – 99.999% for sure. It means the controller's 'blips' have merged to one blob.

We blew through the fight, decided we would turn back for another go to see if we can put them out front, have a quick shot and then bug out fast if nothing was seen, always leave the fight heading home, and today it was a good idea to do just that as we had no fuel. Hi 'G' turn back and we were in again with the controller telling us targets 15 miles, 10 miles, 5 then "merge" ... Again. Now we were in serious trouble as we couldn't see them and didn't have any fuel. We decided to run out at full power. "Bingo, bugging out" to the controller, meaning no fuel and going home, fast as we could. The reply echoes in my mind to this day; I will never forget it. Someone opened the cupboard and let a devil out and it had me by the throat. "OK, thanks for the training, have a good one". There is that long, pregnant pause when you know, just know, there has been an almighty balls-up and someone is going to be in serious trouble. A fraction of a second later you realise that someone is you. We didn't have enough fuel to get back to Stanley, but we could just make San Carlos airstrip if we were lucky. We had our own pilot there (Ada), with a hand-held radio, some engineers, and some fuel. That was it. No instrument let down aids, no nothing. The strip was halfway up a mountain and hard to see. The boss had crashed there during the war so there was still debris around, and it was a known bad place to be, but nevertheless it had fuel.

We throttled back, climbed, and said a little prayer. Looking down from 30,000 ft, I could see that all the Falklands was out in weather. This will be fun, NOT. We finally got hold of Ada, comms were poor, and he told us the strip was out in fog, so bad in fact he couldn't see it and he was only 100 ft from the strip. The strip was 'cumulo granite' (land in cloud). His wished us good luck and said he would try and alert Stanley. We climbed to max altitude around 42,000 ft. We weren't going to make it unless we saved gas. Eighty miles out we radioed Stanley ATC for a weather update. Nothing. We tried a dozen times or more. Not a thing. Our only means of a let down below cloud on the GR3 was a barometric altimeter to 300 ft or whatever you dared, then fly in under the cloud. There were no let down aids for the airfield, the original Argentinian radars having been 'tweaked' by Johnny Paratrooper, and the RAF radar sent south going to the bottom of the sea with the *Atlantic Conveyor*. So we couldn't self let down easily unless the weather was satisfactory.

An army chopper pilot breaks in on guard (emergency frequency) and in a broken chopper-sounding voice, *"Harriers calling Stanley. They have a power failure. I am in the bay at 5 ft and can't get in because of the weather. It's bad. Thick fog. If I can't get in, you don't stand a chance so forget it,"* or words to that effect. This was not what we wanted to hear. Fog you can only ever get under once, then you 'push up daisies' forever, so we flew higher – higher than I had ever been and way outside the flight envelope of the Harrier, to save some gas. We had a chat on the radio and decided to head out to sea and see if we could find the fleet. We knew where it was yesterday, but overnight it could sail 200 miles, or more, and we weren't going to make it anyway.

It was a long shot, but better than a Martin-Baker let down. Way below us, 20 to 40 ft sea swells, freezing Antarctic Ocean, no rescue helicopter, no ideas, no chance – not good. Fighter pilots do not get heart attacks under such circumstances, you tend to have an 'oh well, not my day' kind of approach and get on with it. So we headed out to sea, with no gas and my leader working his radar into a lather. We both knew it wasn't going to work unless Andy found the ship. After some time watching the fuel gauges edge towards 'empty' a call comes "*I got them, follow me*" – some 100 miles or so out to one side he spotted the fleet as a small blip on his air-to-air radar, so we turned towards, and set up a 'glide' approach. Shortly after he gets them on the radio, and tells them to launch the helicopter, because "*we aren't going to make it*". "*Negative, turn back, all flying is cancelled due fog*" was the immediate reply.

Did he just say that? Fog. Yup F-O-G with a capital F, "*OK launch the helicopter because we will be ejecting shortly, we can't make the ship anyway*" from Andy, provokes the irate schoolteacher response, "*Didn't you hear us, we can't launch, we are in fog and all flying suspended. You are not cleared the approach so go back to Stanley.*" F no longer stands for fog. We decide to go for it anyway. Another memory burnt so deep in my brain, as if cast in stone, as we break into a lucky hole in the fogbank at 2,000 ft, a dark distant toy ship sails out of the bath bubbles and into the hole, then another appears from out of the murk just like being in the bath as a kid. From the fog and murk the whole fleet slowly emerges, but immediately ahead of them more fog, so we throw the jets onto the deck amid a flurry of deck personnel and flashing lights. I never, ever landed so quickly, ever, never ever. A chopper is winding up on the deck. They must have hit the crash button. A few seconds later and we can't see the end of the ski jump as it is in fog. I climbed out with less than 200 lbs of fuel, which is less than one minute to flameout, and shaky knees as the adrenalin rush hit again. Getting to be a habit this. Andy had zero fuel on his gauges and was living on borrowed time. That was the last of his nine lives – he died shortly after the Falklands in an air crash doing what he loved best: flying fighters at an air show. We were stuck in fog for two days onboard the ship. We were launched in fog for a navy exercise and some idiot in ops didn't check the weather or tell us it was an exercise. We were airborne for 1 hour 45 minutes on 100-gal drop tanks (6,600 lbs of fuel), with half that time being at pretty much full power. We had been 200 miles to the west of the farthest of the Falklands Islands, and then ended up over 150 miles to the east. That was the third of my nine lives blown away. The next one was just five days later.

22 JULY 1982

This was my one morning off for the month, so I decided to lie in bed an extra hour or two and have a slow start to the day. I hated this place beyond belief. Around 0800 hours, the familiar roar of engines as the QRA pair scrambled about 500 yds away from my tent – again. The thought ran through my head, 'getting to be a habit, hope they will be OK'. Within a minute the ops corporal appeared inside my tent, yelling for me to "*get out now, report to the ops tent*". Bit cheeky I thought, he didn't say "Sir", as I threw on a goon suit and ran towards the ops setup. The airfield air raid siren was wailing again, so probably time to get a tin hat on and dive into a slit trench 'tout suite'. Squadron Leader Pete Moules (Squadron Exec O) saw me running towards him and hanging half out the caravan he yells, "*No duff. Air raid 60 miles out to the west. Get airborne NOW there's an air raid coming in!*" Anyone else and I might have said hold on a minute, just done that, but after my earlier incident, there had been a change of thinking and no scrambles were to be called unless confirmed targets and good weather (meaning no thick fog rolling over the airfield, and no false scrambles). I ran past him straight to the tent containing our flying gear, stole someone's jacket, found my helmet and raced to the line. Everyone was going 'weapons free' diving into slit trenches, cocking their weapons, and those with a job on the line were pulling blanks off aircraft, getting chocks out, and scrambling around.

The first jet I got to had someone in it, which I found annoying at the time. Their engine howled into life before I even reached the aircraft next to it. This jet was empty so I yelled at the ground crew to remove the missile caps and engine blanks immediately, leant over the side and hit the gang bar (turns on all the electrics) and hit the engine start whist strapping in. Within a minute I was taxiing out, luckily without anyone sucked into the intake in my haste to go. I knew we were vulnerable, all the jets cleverly parked in that straight line next to the runway. All the time I was looking skyward expecting little black dots to appear from the cloud with napalm or cluster weapons falling from them.

The cloud base was solid at around 900 ft, with the surrounding hills and mountain tops in thick cloud. Onto the runway, thankful I hadn't been strafed yet, or worse, only to find a Sea Harrier just in front of me some 20 yds away, carrying out flight control checks as if he was on a summer's day jolly. "*Get airborne NOW*" I yelled over the radio, and a second later he was doing 100 kts, with me close behind him. He turned east downwind, and I paired with him, both of us heading east at 800 ft and 500 kts, me slightly in trail. East? The raid was inbound from the west. I quickly asked where he was going and he said "*Back to the carrier*" which was lurking out at sea well east of the Falklands. I sure as hell didn't ever want to see another flat-top as long as I lived, despite the 'going to protect mother' attitude of the Sea Harrier pilot. What about protecting our guys on the ground at Stanley Airfield? There was some high octave chatter on the radio about targets to the west above cloud, and I thought why would anyone head east if the fight was to the west. That was all the incentive I needed, so I pulled away up into cloud, to quickly get above it, and join the rapidly developing dogfight to the west. That was Plan A all thought through and executed in the blink of an eye.

Speed washing back, altimeter climbing, head-up display straight and level and VSI showing a climb. Let's try that again, altimeter winding up, speed is decaying, VSI off the clock 'up', that means I am climbing, HUD straight and level. For the life of me, I couldn't figure it out. Downwind a few seconds ago the HUD was working fine, straight and level, airspeed, altimeter all OK. One more time, still straight and level, still climbing with airspeed rapidly washing off, I topped at about 12,000 ft, IMC in cloud, still trying to figure it out as the altimeter began to unwind at first slowly, with the airspeed starting to increase, VSI showing a shallow descent, and the HUD still straight and level. I looked for the standby artificial horizon, something we never used, so it took about one millisecond to find it (time does slow down when you are having a life-threatening moment) and there it was. All bright and shiny, with the biggest red and white chequered flag right across the face that I had ever seen. I mean it was huge. This meant the standby artificial horizon was about as useful as a condom in a convent. Since it felt like I was upside down in a shallow descent with no instruments, I rolled and pulled to what I thought was level, and the altimeter began unwinding so fast it was a blur, VSI went 'off the clock', and the speedo wound up 'rapidly'.

Oh shit, another balls-up but this one is a huge one, even by my standards. My thought process went along the lines of this: 'I don't have control ... I can't do anything else ... I went IMC at *about* 1,000 ft in the climb, I am on the way down I think, so if I don't break cloud by *about* 1,000 ft, I will bang out'. Everything felt smooth like a shallow descent, but that wasn't what the instruments were telling me. Everything had been silky smooth and I really couldn't assimilate it or understand what was going on. Mountains nearby, but I have to be in the bay so I will stay with it till 1,000 ft? Those QFIs out there will be wondering about the turn and slip. It was never taught, never used, and someone had stolen the bubble from it a long time ago!

At *about* 900 ft I broke cloud. That was a relief. But what is that huge boat in the 12 o'clock high position (that is, if you look up 45 degrees, it was there), along with a world full of sea in place of the sky. Being both upside down and some 45 degrees nose down going like a train, I instinctively rolled and pulled. I think I even got a hand on the nozzles at some point to help with pitch, and with both hands full and pulling like a bastard, came within a few feet of hitting the sea and the boat. I hadn't even gone for the handle, and would probably not have made it, leaving it so late. Thank you Lord, now if I could ask just one more favour please.

I had no IFF and was in an active Blindfire Rapier fire zone with trigger happy RAF Regiment operators keen to add an airframe to their scorecard and blasting out of cloud at 500+ kts upside down one mile north of the airfield didn't leave Johnny Rock Ape much 'trigger finger thinking time'. No call sign either, so all that came to mind was "*Don't shoot, it's me*" at about three octaves higher than my normal voice pitch.

I found the standby AH switch, turned it on, erected it, then climbed through cloud on standby instruments getting clear on top at about 15,000 ft, headed west with a gallon of adrenalin rushing through my veins and both missiles ready to go, listening to the ensuing chatter on the radio with eyes on stalks scanning for targets. I recall other Harriers popping out of cloud ahead of me, so the odds were getting better in our favour.

Then a "*No Duff, everyone come back and land*" over the radio. But ... "*No buts, come back immediately and land. We will explain later*". I recognised the voice as Pete Moules and let myself down over the sea to the east of the airfield, 'schneebled in' below dank clouds and landed. I signed for the jet (noting it was red lined for the standby AH not turning on with the gang bar switch) and walked towards the ops tent. I met Pete just outside the tent, and then I started shaking uncontrollably. "*I just nearly crashed, what happened out there?*" When he asked about what happened to me I told him, trying desperately not to have a meltdown. I didn't need to remind him this was the second time in five days I had used up another of my cat's lives. He wasn't happy, and said we nearly just lost three aircraft in the space of a few minutes. The QRA pair intercepted the incoming targets at a distance, had growling missiles and were going to fire, when they decided to close in and visually identify the targets (smelling a dead rat – or in this case, rotting fish). Delaying a shot could have cost them their lives in combat, but it was a good thing on this occasion.

Two Sea Harriers had decided to fly a practice airfield attack in a 'war zone'. They had been at low level, hit bad weather and pulled up. To be on the safe side, they had called, "*FAKIR 60 miles out for an airfield attack.*" Unfortunately the radio operator in ATC hadn't a clue what "FAKIR" meant, and the ops clerk didn't either, so ops commander had hit the airfield air raid siren sending the entire RAF airfield contingent from 'weapons tight' (safe) to 'weapons free' (meaning it is now *war* and *shoot anything you think is the enemy*) in the space of a nanosecond. Good old navy again, but since they didn't hold a monopoly on idiots, the RAF ATC/OPS all had a finger in the 'balls-up' pie this time.

My story, and I am sticking to it, is we scrambled the entire squadron in less than sixteen minutes. I was in bed 400 yds from the line when the hooter went up, and wasn't the last one airborne. I hadn't signed for the jet, had no idea about its state, and certainly wasn't aware of the red line entry. When you taxi onto a runway with a whole bunch of people out there you think are trying to kill you with HE and napalm, you don't tend to look inside the cockpit. The INAS wasn't in align to prepare the HUD, which was the primary attitude information for flying in cloud. With the aircraft straight and level on the ground, the HUD showed straight and level whether in alignment or not. Straight and level flying down wind, it showed straight and level, and all the pitot and barometric systems (like airspeed, VSI, and altitude) worked normally. So I had flown into cloud with no instruments, gone all the way to 12,000 ft and fallen out upside down, climbed back up on standby instruments, and managed to walk away from it at the end of the day. Thank you Lord. I am not worthy of your graces. I was running out of cat's lives, as this was my fourth.

I spent another few months in the war zone, witnessed stuff you only read about from 'juicy' war books, and then came back to the UK. A few weeks later I found myself back in the Falklands for another tour (albeit only three months this time). I spent nine months away from home that year, averaged just nine hours flying per month, was lucky to be alive, and hated the Harrier. I went back again to the Falklands the following year to help on a BoI (Harrier crashed in the circuit). The boss decided I was the perfect man for the job, so screaming and yelling I went back to hell.

Yes, I still have occasional nightmares thirty years later that I am tasked to do the seemingly impossible .... in full Technicolor, with the squadron mates, the TOT tasking with minimum time to plan and brief, the fear of a 'balls-up', and trying to find a camouflaged pad in the middle of nowhere with no gas. I even see my fellow pilots' individual faces in my dreams; such was the powerful force that branded my brain, leaving indelible impressions. My wife understands immediately when I wake up in a cold sweat and say to her I was 'back on the squadron again' that night, but she doesn't really know what happened.

CHAPTER 3

LOOKING AHEAD

Like all defence equipment, the Harrier went through a continuous process of evolution. Military kit is very expensive, but, there being no silver medal for coming second in a war, you always want the best. Knowing that something even better is always just around the corner, it is tempting to delay procurement. However, even if the risks posed by gaps in capability are accepted, there comes a point where commitment is necessary. So it was at the start of the Harrier story that, despite a Royal Navy and indeed RAF preference for the bigger, faster, P1154 project, the P1127 was developed into the Kestrel and then the Harrier GR1.

The GR1 soon gained INAS, then a more powerful version of the Pegasus, becoming the GR3, then the LRMTS that so changed the appearance of the aircraft. The RWR further modified the profile of the tail fin, while new weapons and defensive measures vied for position on the five pylons.

But even in the 1970s, thought was being devoted to what would be the next major step. Jock Heron offers a fascinating insight into that process from the viewpoint of a desk in the MoD.

JOCK HERON

When I arrived in the office on the fourth floor of the Whitehall main building I knew many of the personalities in the Air Support branch. I replaced a test pilot who was being promoted to take up another MoD PE flying appointment at Bedford and I had first met him several years before when he had been a few entries ahead of me as a flight cadet at Cranwell. He had flown the Harrier and its P1127 predecessors at Boscombe Down but having been away from front-line squadron duties since his Hunter days his judgement and priorities for the Harrier, understandably, were influenced by his experience as a test pilot. I saw things from a different standpoint because my background principally was as a front-line pilot but my position in the MoD command chain was fairly low down the pecking order. My wing commander boss was a seasoned Hunter man, our group captain deputy director had been a Vampire and Hunter pilot earlier in his career and our new director who had arrived shortly after me was a young, charismatic air commodore. He had completed a tour as a station commander in Germany only a year earlier and was widely experienced on several aircraft roles and types, including the Phantom and Buccaneer. However, none had flown the Harrier so I was considered to be the branch 'expert'.

The arrival briefings were straightforward and my terms of reference were to manage the operational aspects of the Harrier fleet and to ensure that the aircraft remained capable of performing its task for the foreseeable future. It seemed to me therefore that my first task in the office should be to ascertain the existing MoD air staff policy for the aircraft by meeting the air plans staff and agreeing with them an order of priority for the Harrier and its development. The next step, in consultation with my colleagues in the MoD PE project office in St Giles Court and the RAF engineers, was to achieve a sound working relationship with the designers and manufacturers at the Kingston factory of Hawker Siddeley Aviation (HSA) and with the test pilots at the Dunsfold aerodrome, to determine how best to enhance the Harrier's operational capability.

Although these steps sounded fairly simple in principle, it was less easy in practice to prepare a suitable outline plan of action. I was a member of several committees which were responsible for Harrier aircraft modifications, trials priorities and project reviews and there was a need to pay regular visits to the RAF headquarters and front-line stations. The in tray was always threatening to bury me in staff papers on matters which were very relevant to the job so I was not in control of my own diary. Nevertheless I began to understand where the Harrier fitted into the long-term plans for the RAF front line. It became evident, but only indirectly, that the Harrier was not seen in a good light in the MoD at senior levels due partly, I suspect, to the cost of the deployed concept of operations, its apparent unreliability and its limited performance. Although its status in 1975 seemed reasonably secure, with an attrition buy of fifteen GR3 and three T4 aircraft being assembled at Dunsfold for delivery the following year, it was apparent that the long-term prospects for the Harrier were bleak.

The loss of twenty-four aircraft and several pilots in aircraft accidents since its introduction in 1969, together with the apparent high cost of ownership and its short range and limited payload, which were significant operational limitations, had damaged the aircraft's reputation. So the Harrier supporters in the MoD were faced by substantial and well presented but ill-informed prejudice against the aircraft. In 1975 the threat from the Warsaw Pact was real and very capable and it was my view firstly that there was a need to retain operational flexibility by protecting the future of the Harrier Force and secondly to enhance significantly its operational capability. But to gain such improvements meant considerable investment and there was the problem. After the previous year's election the new Labour government had inherited a significant overspend, funding for defence was tight and other projects took priority. Also, aircraft fuel was being rationed to save money and it was another of my tasks to argue the case for a sensible allocation for the Harrier Force.

In 1975 the planning assumptions for the RAF offensive support forces were to buy twenty-four more Jaguars and extend their service life to 1995 while allowing the Harrier Force to run down by about 1985. My argument to retain operational flexibility by extending the life of the Harrier instead of the Jaguar was not palatable to the MoD hierarchy, but fortunately world events helped to promote the Harrier's cause. In late 1975 the newly-independent Belize, formerly British Honduras, was under threat from Guatemala, its bigger Central American neighbour, whose armed forces were deployed along the border between the two countries. Britain had a commitment to protect Belize so, in the deteriorating political and military situation, troops and helicopters were despatched quickly in transport aircraft to the small airfield at Belize city to support our treaty obligations. The only combat type which could operate safely from the short runway was the Harrier, so within a few days six aircraft were deployed from RAF Wittering to Belize, using air refuelling for the lengthy transit, to provide offensive air support and a limited air defence capability. Although they never saw active service this commitment was to last almost continuously for the next eighteen years, until the GR3 finally was withdrawn from service in 1993. The Belize operation confirmed the unique operational flexibility of the Harrier and its advantages were recognised, perhaps reluctantly by the disbelievers. Gradually the mood in the MoD began to change in favour of the little jet.

In 1976 the first battle in the campaign to protect the Harrier Force was won when the MoD acknowledged the Harrier's special capabilities by reversing the policy for the acquisition of new offensive-support aircraft. Twenty-four Harriers were ordered as a long-term attrition buy and the Jaguar Force was frozen at its initial level. Also relevant to this decision, I suspect, was the Labour government's wish to balance work between the British Aircraft Corporation at Warton and its satellites in the north against a diminishing workload at Hawker Siddeley in the south at Kingston and Dunsfold. Preparations were underway to amalgamate and nationalise the two companies and in 1977 British Aerospace was formed as a state-owned company. The order book was thus better balanced and more healthy at both groups of sites with substantial numbers of Jaguars and Tornados being produced at Warton and Hawks and Harriers being manufactured at Kingston and assembled at Dunsfold.

The MoD's long-term planning assumptions dictated that there was no budget to acquire a new aircraft type, other than the requirement for an agile fighter known as Air Staff Target (AST) 403 which was planned to replace the Harrier and the Jaguar by the 1990s. However, to sustain the capability of the current offensive support front line in the shorter term, there was some money to pay for improvements to our existing inventory, so I began to explore the possibility, with the HSA Harrier project team, of designing a new wing for the Harrier GR3 which could improve its payload and performance and extend its range. Because the wing assembly was removed as a single item for routine engine changes, my proposal was that a bigger wing could be fitted as a replacement and that this modification could provide these improvements. Wing loading would be reduced, manoeuvrability enhanced and the greater area would allow more fuel to be carried internally and provide the space for additional underwing pylons. It seemed to be a simple proposal although I acknowledged that matters wouldn't be that straightforward. The late Dr John Fozard and his Kingston team were supportive and by early 1977 I had drafted the first air staff papers for circulation within the MoD to justify a feasibility study for a much modified GR3, which we designated the GR5, the 'Big Wing' Harrier.

I was encouraged to promote my ideas by my old station commander at Wildenrath who had returned to the MoD as the RAF director of public relations and both the MoD PE project director and my air staff director supported the work. However as there was no funding for a new aircraft type it was important to describe the GR5 as merely a major modification of the GR3 which could be introduced as a retrofit to existing aircraft. Because the Harrier was a 1965 development of the Kestrel which itself was a development of the original P1127, only the minimum of changes to the Kestrel were introduced to contain costs and development timescales. The design aim in 1965 had been to offer a credible operational capability with the little aircraft and the wing area, only marginally larger than that on the prototype, was constrained by weight and therefore size. The original Harrier wing had an area of 200 square feet and contained some of the aircraft's internal fuel which totalled 5,000 lbs. To achieve an acceptable performance for take-off and landing and manoeuvring in conventional flight, the wing section and area were defined to offer the most suitable compromise between all the requirements and was as light as possible so that performance in the hover with the original Pegasus Mk101 of 19,000-lb thrust was not unduly penalised.

By 1976 the Pegasus Mk103 offered substantial improvements in hover performance so there was a strong argument to trade some of this extra thrust for an increase in all-up weight which would have permitted a bigger but slightly heavier wing to be retrofitted to the Harrier. The original proposal from HSA for the big wing had an area of about 250 square feet plus leading-edge root extensions and was equipped with six underwing pylons. Considerably more internal fuel was carried in the wing which raised the total internal fuel capacity to 6,700 lbs and our outline specification required the Harrier to manoeuvre like a Hunter and to have the same radius of action with six bombs, two air-to-air missiles, guns and ammunition as did the GR3 with two external fuel tanks, two bombs and guns but without air-to-air missiles. More thrust from the Pegasus and a digital avionics suite were also desirable features and on paper the promising

HSA design met these aspirations.

From a different standpoint, by 1976 the US Marine Corps had lost several AV-8A aircraft apparently due to pilot error and I was one of the RAF team who visited Norfolk, Virginia to compare notes on concepts of operation, pilot selection and training standards. Several presentations were given by the RAF and by the USMC mainly on the cause and analysis of Harrier accidents and the need to select high-calibre pilots in the first place. However one of the presentations from the marines was on the improvements which would be sought to the STOVL handling of the AV-8A's successor, the 'AV-8B'. This was the first time I had heard of the USMC's aspirations for such an aircraft, which had emerged as an affordable option for the USMC STOVL attack aircraft requirement, after the cancellation of the AV-16 programme in 1975. It seemed that the marines wanted similar improvements in the AV-8B to those which we had specified for the HSA GR5 although we had not sought improved STOVL handling as a key characteristic. The detailed performance and design parameters were not defined but the 'B' was to be a new airframe with a thicker composite wing of increased area and it had several features which could not be incorporated as modifications to the existing aircraft, the option which we had been forced to pursue for the HSA GR5 Harrier.

After our return to the UK I asked the HSA design team about Kingston's involvement with the AV-8B and they acknowledged that several of their people were working with McDonnell Douglas on the details of the design and that HSA hoped to gain a contract for major airframe assemblies. Their view was that although the AV-8B and the HSA GR5 might share certain features, the need for enhanced manoeuvrability had not been addressed by the USMC who placed greater emphasis on the requirement for longer range while carrying bombs at medium altitude. Senior MoD OR and PE staffs had been briefed on the AV-8B earlier in the year but because it was a new aircraft and therefore a 'procurement' programme there was no provision in the long-term

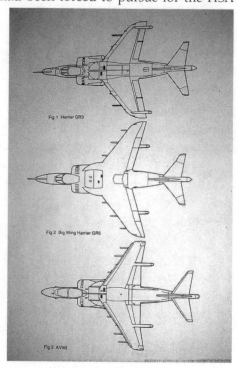

Comparison of options. (Jock Heron)

costings for such a proposal so MoD involvement had been rejected. However, subsequent events were to change this situation.

Throughout my tour, which was at the height of the Cold War, the draft papers from the operational requirements branch on future equipment policy saw the need for an agile fighter to replace the Harrier and the Jaguar by the 1990s. AST 403 was the basis for the aircraft which, many years later through several iterations, became the Eurofighter Typhoon. In the Harrier office we were convinced of the need for a STOVL capability in a new aircraft and our views were endorsed by the branch director. The studies which were being conducted by the Defence Operational Analysis Establishment at the time did not acknowledge the validity of our arguments and official MoD policy directed that the airfield performance criteria were to be based on a STOL requirement with the assumption that in operational circumstances there would always be short runways available. For several years the Harrier lobby aspiration was for a supersonic STOVL multi-role fighter and to reflect this need an outline AST 396 had been drafted as early as 1970. Although stealth as a design characteristic was not specified in the AST, today's Joint Strike Fighter performance requirements are close to those which we had expressed several decades earlier for a 'Harrier replacement'. Hindsight is a wonderful attribute but I still have a slide which I composed to promote the Big Wing Harrier in 1977 which stated: 'The Harrier today is where the helicopter was thirty years ago; limited in range and payload, misunderstood by many and opposed by men without vision, but it is a new dimension in tactical air operations and its versatile capability must be recognised.'

Long after my time in the MoD, the record shows that after submission of the feasibility study on the big wing retrofit option in 1980, the tide of opinion had moved progressively in favour of the Harrier and the attractions of the improved 'GR5' version finally had been accepted by the doubters in the MoD. Because of delays in other aircraft projects, particularly for the agile fighter, the MoD decided in 1981 that funding should be split between the AST 403 project studies and the procurement of a new and much more capable variant of the Harrier, rather than pursuing the original modification package. Prolonged debate took place on the development costs, performance comparisons, the political and industrial attractions of a joint programme and the relative merits of the two designs. The HSA 'GR5' with its metal wing offered an all-British aircraft with a higher top speed and superior manoeuvrability whereas the slower AV-8B 'GR5' with its thick composite wing gave access to a much bigger production run, the fully developed digital avionics suite adapted from the F-18 and a commitment to a collaborative programme with shared development costs. It was decided in late 1981 that the UK would become involved fully in a joint BAe/McDonnell Douglas AV-8B programme and that the RAF would acquire sixty GR5 aircraft for delivery in 1986 although additional GR7s (a modified GR5 with improved avionics) and T10 aircraft were delivered in the early 1990s. BAe became a sub-contractor to McDonnell Douglas for the manufacture of the rear fuselages for the entire AV-8B programme and the Harrier GR5 became an anglicised version of the aircraft, with final assembly of the RAF aircraft being carried out at Dunsfold. Although the AV-8B wing area was increased from that of the original Harrier, it was not quite as large as the Hawker Siddeley big wing but it was thicker and contained more fuel raising the total internal capacity of the 'joint' GR5 to about 7,600 lbs. It was designed more for the bomber role than as a fighter and as a result the GR5/7 has more drag and is about 60 knots slower than the GR3 in conventional flight. Neither can it manoeuvre like a Hunter. Nevertheless the RAF GR7/9 was a fine aircraft which remained popular with its pilots in the tradition of the unique STOVL Harrier family powered by the Pegasus. The rest is history.

CHAPTER 4

ACROSS THE POND

Perhaps surprisingly for such a short-range aircraft, the Atlantic features a lot in the Harrier story. Graham Williams and Tom Lecky-Thompson participated in the Transatlantic Air Race at the start of its service life. 1(F) Squadron took the aircraft across the Atlantic to enhance the defence of Belize in 1975, and then down to the South Atlantic in support of another British outpost, the Falkland Islands. The USMC's whole-hearted adoption of the aircraft led to a manufacturing facility at McDonnell Douglas's factory in St Louis[1], Missouri, and a UK Harrier office in Washington DC. UK Harriers have regularly crossed the Atlantic for Flag exercises in the USA and Canada.

Above all, the exchange programme between UK and USA armed forces has led to a tremendous enhancement of knowledge and experience. Engineers take part in the programme, and exchange pilots fly various types of aircraft. UK Harrier pilots that have flown in the States were selected for their high quality, and have tended to go on to greater things on their return. On the formation of the RAF Harrier Force with four front-line squadrons, four exchange posts were established: two USAF, one USN and one USMC.

This chapter contains the reminiscences of three American exchange pilots. Don Fennessey USN adopted the Harrier lifestyle to the extent that he married an RAF officer. Marc 'Rambo' Frith USAF brought his American wife with him, but thoroughly enjoyed the experience of RAF life, not least socially. The third is Jon 'Dog' Davis, who at the time of writing had risen to the rank of lieutenant general, in the post of deputy commandant for aviation of the corps.

DON FENNESSEY

I wasn't a Harrier boy yet, but I was coming closer. Ever since I had gotten my orders to be an exchange officer, I couldn't wait. Leaving the USS *Enterprise* as an A-7E Corsair pilot, I spent time in Florida learning how to hover in helicopters, and then to RAF Brawdy for the UK Orientation Course to learn how to speak properly

---

[1] At Wittering, we had a modest note at the bottom of the entrance board; I was a little taken aback when I first saw the phrase echoed in huge letters on a hoarding spanning a highway in Missouri reading, 'Welcome to St Louis – The Home of The Harrier'.

on the radio and get lost buzzing around Wales in Jet Provosts and Hunters with Standards Squadron. I was even scheduled for a hop in the Meteor with the world famous Flight Lieutenant 'Puddy' Catt. It really was a lot of fun and the fun hit its peak at my first RAF dining-in. However, the mess games ended my course prematurely. After a trip to Haverfordwest hospital and a full-length heavy leg bandage, my flying days at Brawdy were over. I do regret not having been able to fly that Meteor trip with Puddy. I was unfit to take the train to get to Wittering, so I bummed a ride with the very kind Squadron Leader Steve Jennings.

On arrival at Wittering, I was quickly introduced to the other resident Yank, Captain Chuck DeVlaming USAF, on 1 Squadron. He was loud and fun and had the biggest 'shit-eating grin' in the RAF. He enjoyed firing a small-scale brass cannon on the front lawn of the mess. One day he got a bit overenthusiastic with the gunpowder and it blew up, fortunately missing all spectators, but one piece of shrapnel lodged in a tree. Chuck placed a commemorative plaque there stating that the tree had been damaged by American cannon fire on 4 July 1977.

During the OCU ground school the bandages came off and I gradually gained flexibility in my leg while doing leg curls and wrist curls on the bar stools in the mess. When flying started I could just manage to get myself into the cockpit but was pretty stiff getting out when the trip was over. Three weeks later I had my solo hover flight and survived the ritual with the hover pot. Now I really was a Harrier boy.

While going through the OCU, three of us, Flight Lieutenant Simon 'Woody' Woods, Flight Officer Pete Cockman and I, lived with Chuck DeVlaming in a house in Ketton. We softened up the neighbours by inviting them to a fancy dress party, but I'm glad the house owner, Group Captain Ord, never knew all the details of what went on there.

Happy hours on Fridays at Wittering were wonderful. Sid the barman pulled a great pint and the curry was excellent. There was always a darts game on and the most entertaining player was Dave 'Soaks' Oakley. He could stand totally focused on his target despite the ever-present cigarette smoke curling up past his eyes, pint glass expertly curled into his chest, never spilling a drop and always good for double one to go out.

The Schnapps Patrol at Wittering was a little known but highly colourful group led by Flight Lieutenant Brian Draper (simulator), his wife Joyce, Roger Mathew (supply), Charlie Clayton (admin), and Mike McGinty (security). On my 27th birthday, my buttocks were painted with shoe polish and pressed against the ceiling of the back bar at the mess, where the imprint remained almost three years later.

LEARNING THE HARRIER

The Harrier cockpit was particularly befuddling to me. After the A-7E cockpit, which was designed for a human, this was very strange, but my first car as an ensign in Pensacola had been an MGB (SU carburettor and Lucas electrics), and the Hunter cockpit at Brawdy was even more confusing, so you can forgive my conclusion that this was just another quirky aspect of British engineering. Who in their right mind would put a TACAN indicator with a fixed north-up dial between your ankles behind the stick? Fortunately the TACAN approaches to RAF Gütersloh were 090 and 270° so figuring out which way to push the head of the needle or raise the tail wasn't as impossible as it was for approaches to other stations, but it led to stiff necks from turning your head sideways trying to suss out which way the compass card was supposed to move.

Programming the waypoints seemed particularly British in its clunkiness. I had come from the 1970s state-of-the-art A-7E with a magnetic drum computer-driven inertial measurement unit and a projected map display system, so I understood the theory behind the Harrier's system, but was amazed at the Heath Robinson multi-step process for entering waypoint: Select, fix, lock, ackle (slew) the map to the desired point, fix, unlock, reject. If you got any of those steps wrong, the map slewed right back to where it started. This was especially frustrating if going from Gütersloh to Wittering. Slew west across northern Germany, across Holland, over to England, there's London, up the A1 to Wittering, click, damn! Map slews back to Gütersloh.

The INAS in the A-7 was quite reliable, being twenty years newer than that of the Harrier, and I had become spoiled by it and was a system cripple, but I always had faith in the Harrier system. The map display just looked so right, urging you to believe it. My rusty map, stopwatch and compass skills could get me from Wittering to the Duddington roundabout and into the first link route on the way to LFA 5. From there I was usually lost. At least the moving map advertised two map scales – 1:500,000 and 1:250,000. The second was just a magnified version of the first so you could still be lost, but with the same map effectively closer to your face.

The HUD wasn't too much different from that in the A-7, but it was not good for bombing accuracy. Hit the IP, pop up to the roll-in point, roll over, put the crow's feet offset into the forecast wind, guess at a 10° dive angle, wait for the release cue to appear and stabilise, compare it with the crow's feet (right!), flip up the cover over the bomb release button, pickle at 200 feet (with no radar altimeter), pull off, flip the cover back and proceed. Gun camera film usually looked pretty good, but the debrief from QWI Flight Lieutenant Henry 'DEC' de Courcier was usually: "Can't explain the score. Hard luck, mate."

Strafing was even worse. Those 30mm guns were so inaccurate unless you fired inside the minimum range. Flicking up the pickle button cover was easy compared to pushing a sliding release on the top of the stick to release the trigger as it flopped forward. Then you had to carefully move your index finger around it to get into position for firing. Same drill with dive angle and airspeed, drive in until the target banner filled the aiming circle – theoretically representing the size of a Russian tank – squeeze the trigger, pull off target to avoid any ricochets, try to raise the trigger and snap it back into place while pulling 6 Gs. Film debrief was the same. "Can't explain the score. Hard luck, mate."

GÜTERSLOH AND FIELD OPS

I was amazed at how good Harrier pilots were at planning for low levels. I was used to painstakingly making perfect strip charts from several big charts in preparation for a flight the next day. In the Harrier world, you even planned while sitting in the cockpit, on an acetated map using a protractor and a chinagraph. Figure out the headings using the protractor, add minute marks every seven miles, then someone delivered the 1:50,000 IP-to-target map to you in your camouflaged hide. Fold everything to a handy size and Bob's your uncle. After the flight, wipe off the chinagraph with your handkerchief, clear your kneeboards with your elbows, thus explaining some of the odd stains on your flight suit.

Mornings in the field were heralded by the sound of the generator starting at 0600 hours. The duty officer fetched a bucket of hot water from the mess tent. It was poured into a big plastic bowl and we all shaved while standing around it, flight suits unzipped to the waist, our legs spread wide so they wouldn't slide down to the ground. Breakfast was eggs cooked in grease and odd not-100% meat sausages. I usually opted for the oatmeal, which was a safer bet. There was always a big urn of well-sugared tea. A gourmet delight.

Six flights per day was the limit for each pilot, each one lasting about thirty minutes. No more than five flights before lunch. Quick trip, back to the site, stay strapped in the cockpit or stand up and take a leak over the side, slam down a Kit Kat and a Coke, refuel, get a new mission and off you go again. Wow!

We enjoyed a Taceval team visit to us in the field. We had the usual 700 feet of steel planking and a Land Rover with a radio in it to 'control' the flying. A USAF officer from Ramstein in her crisp blue uniform asked where flight clearance was; we pointed to the Land Rover. She asked where approach control was; we pointed to the Land Rover. Another officer asked where we kept the camera film for German F-104s. We said if they could land one at the site, we'd figure out how to change the film.

Woody and I were usually assigned to the same site. Our job was to make sure we had the stuff for the Saturday barbecue – usually nicely smoked pork chops. Dessert was bananas flambéed with Grand Marnier. Rough life in the field. Cabarets in the field were something I had never seen except in the movies. The ones we had were just as silly, performed on a stage near the beer tent. Proving that there is no accounting for taste, everyone liked my rendition of *Alice's Restaurant*, an American anti-Vietnam War folk song by Arlo Guthrie that lasted 18 minutes and 23 seconds. "You can get anything you want at Alice's Restaurant." Ever courteous, no one threw any rotten cabbages.

I really enjoyed taking ground crew up for a trip, especially in the field. My favourite time was when my back-seater was Corporal Jim Yorston, our army NCO. He was so excited and could hardly stand still as he was being fitted with his G-suit and torso harness, nattering to our ops clerk, SAC Jenkins. "Hey, Jenksie, we're going out to get some T-72s and then we're going to get some MiGs, and then we're going to..." What a hoot. We still talk about that flight.

The Harrier simulator at Wildenrath was remarkable. It was run by kindly Flight Lieutenant Chick Kirkham. A surprisingly good visual display was provided by a tiny camera which moved across a large table modelled like northern Germany. We also did our annual water survival training in the Wildenrath pool. Put on your dry suit, jump in the pool, climb into your dinghy, swim ashore, and have a cup of tea laced with rum. The British way.

As we flew at low level so much, bird strikes were common. Some we didn't even notice until the ground crew discovered the fact by smelling inside the intakes. One sunny day 25 miles south of Gütersloh there was no doubt for my Harrier. I was out on a low level just rolling out of a turn, still in a left wing down bank looking over my left shoulder for my wingman Flight Lieutenant Paul 'Hoppy' Hopkins. As I rolled wings level I hit a flock of birds. Bam! One hit the outer windscreen, cracking it and shattering the inner windscreen. There was a loud buzzing sound coming from the right intake. Procedure was to set the throttle at 85% and use the nozzles to control airspeed. It worked. I landed safely and shut the aircraft down. I then saw that the buzzing was caused by a strip of metal that had torn loose from the intake. Several corners of the tips of the first-stage fan blades were gone, their exit path shown by chip marks on the underside of the wing. One bird had hit the starboard gun pod, one had scraped across some rivets in a patch on the top of the port wing, one had hit just forward of the canopy release handle on the left side of the nose, cracking the metal rib underneath and causing the handle to pop out partway. There was even one still in the lower laser eyelid. SEngO said the jet might have flown another five minutes. Thanks to sturdy British engineering I never did get a Martin-Baker tie for having ejected.

GR3 minus mainwheel. (Hoelscher)

Once while doing circuits at Gütersloh, the main wheel undercarriage indicated unsafe. What aircraft could be more versatile than a Harrier, being able to land gently on the nosewheel and outriggers? The landing was routine and the jet settled nicely without touching the ground. I will be forever grateful to Wing Commander Jock Heron who advised me to not put the nozzles aft because the brakes didn't work without main wheels. I later received a 'Good Show' award from HQ. I was hoping for a knighthood, but I guess the paperwork got lost.

THE END OF THE DREAM

Sue, whom I met as the RAF families officer at Wittering, and I were married at Wittering church on 26 April 1980, my last week with the RAF. I think I had come to England with the intent of bringing back a war bride, maybe even a princess. I succeeded in both as Sue's maiden name was Tudor. The wedding was attended by more people than could fit into the church and comprised members of the RAF, Chuck DeVlaming as my best man, US Marines, army, and four F-100 pilots from the Danish air force who had been our hosts for an exchange at Skrydstrup. The organist was the officers' mess manager, the flowers were done by the mess gardener, and she knew someone who did wedding cakes, so it was very much a family affair. Of course the reception was at the mess, and my family was most impressed by my butt prints from October 1977 on the ceiling of the back bar.

Don and Sue Fennessey's wedding.
(Don Fennessey)

Next thing I knew I was on my way back to America and the relatively mundane life of a US Navy carrier pilot. I had experienced something only a handful of navy guys have done. The stories I told my new squadron mates of my Harrier days were absolutely true, but no one could believe them. Can't say that I blamed them. They really were the most outrageous and wonderful three years of my life. The more I look back on those times, and especially when visiting England, the fonder I become of that part of my life. It has taken on a much greater proportional significance of my past than just three years. I get very emotional seeing the Wittering church, looking at the class photos at the Heritage Centre, and having a pint at the George or the Haycock, all holding such special memories. I treasure the extraordinary friendships that remain, especially with Major John Hickie, our GLO, and Jenny Green, who looked after us knucklehead singlies in Ketton and Gütersloh so well. I am forever grateful that I was welcomed into the RAF brotherhood and had the privilege of being a Yank in the RAF – and a Harrier boy.

MARC 'RAMBO' FRITH USAF

I volunteered for the Harrier Exchange post because I really wanted to do the job, and it was a highlight of my military career. At Wittering I joined 49 Course, a unique Harrier course because there were more 'colonials' than British officers. Our class included myself, going to IV(AC) Squadron, Lieutenant John Carver, USN, going to 3(F) Squadron, Captain Dave Wallace, USAF, headed for 1(F) Squadron – three 'Yanks' – then we had our 'token' RAF officers: Simon Turner and Tim Ellison going with me to IV Squadron and Terry Parker going to 3 Squadron. They were all brand-new flying officers. Finally, we had three Aussies join our course for initial Harrier training on their way to the Royal Navy to fly the Sea Harrier. I'm not sure the instructors on 233 OCU were ready for this onslaught.

My RAF training included ten hours on the Jet Provost to teach me to speak 'English' and forty hours on the Hawk at Brawdy to learn RAF low level and gunnery tactics. There I flew with the infamous 'Puddy' Catt, a dinosaur of instructors, but a superior aviator. I learned about the 30mm Aden cannon flying with Puddy. After my first strafe pass, he commented, "I say Marc, you are firing much too far out of range". Thus, I learned to get hits firing this gun: press the foul line – breathe – shoot – PULL! Then on the low level back to Brawdy I had my eyes watered as we got the met report and Puddy stated, "The weather is much too bad for a PAR. I have control". We flew along the sea until he found his cottage on the coast, pitched over the cliffs and called to 'join the low circuit'. We pitched out and landed at 500 feet max altitude with barely a 1,000-foot ceiling. Welcome to the RAF, Marc. I got six hours on the Gazelle at Shawbury to build confidence in going straight up and down. The confined landing sites in those forests were indeed confidence building. Finally, the Brits made the Yanks do the whole life-support training. They were over the top as we did the decompression training three times: once for the Hawk, once for the Harrier and my favourite, decompressing in full AR5 chemical protection kit. I felt like Darth Vader wearing that full head mask. Additionally, the Brits threw us in the pool (twice) with AR5 on. We finally met the young flying officers of 49 Course in Portsmouth for sea survival training.

The exploits of 49 Course were indeed spectacular. I got my call sign 'Rambo' because *Rambo II First Blood* had just come out in England. It was my new custom to tie my cummerbund around my head as the dining-in nights wore on; it was a natural extension of fact/fiction. Additionally, it was there that an instructor wrote about me: "He flies the Harrier like a multi-gym". I remember

Tim Ellison walking to his jet for his first solo hover of our class. I thought it was strange that instructors and students stood by the windows with our coffees, watching. Then we learned about the 'horror film', a compilation of film from the pre-T-bird days. They didn't show you the film until *after* you solo hovered.

Flying the Harrier was a blast. Sitting right on top of the fan blades in that tiny cockpit was intimidating. British 'kit' took a bit of getting used to. The fact that the ejection sequence blew the canopy around you with MDC required you to wear the friggin' equivalent of an American heavyweight football helmet. I learned about 'flaps on your boots' as a way of determining who the Harrier mates were. When you went to the bar with RAF pilots in flight suits you first looked to the floor to see who had flaps on their boots as a badge of honour. The flaps were required to keep your shoe strings from getting entangled in the instrument panel on ejection and ripping your boots off – obviously learned the hard way.

Harrier pilot's boots. (Author)

As an American I was impressed with the aviation skills of the young flying officers on the course. They were indeed impressive compared to the new lieutenants I flew with in the A-10. 233 OCU graduated real flight leaders and not just proficient wingmen like they did in the USA. Our graduation deployment to Lossiemouth was the culmination of all the training we had done. To pass, you had to lead a pairs Harrier flight, 'survive' a Harrier bounce, and bogey after the evasion in the hills of Scotland to join Tain Range for a timed scored bomb pass: a real challenge to any fighter pilot, let alone a new Harrier pilot.

I am proud to have won the coveted 'Player of the Course' award. The instructors told me I had a 100% vote for this prize. Part of being a good exchange officer is to assimilate the culture and social activities of the host country. Well, I could always drink and sing with the best of them. This would follow on to IV(AC) Squadron where I became the best entertainments officer – ever – on the Harrier Force.

Flying in Germany with the Brits was a blast. After my A-10 tour at Bentwaters, I was somewhat familiar with low flying in Europe. On one of my first low-level sorties in Germany in the T4, I was flying the grease pen line on my map at 480 knots and 250 feet. A large town was at my 12 o'clock. I started to turn and go around as we did in the USAF. From the back I heard, "Whatcha doing mate?" "I'm missing the built-up areas so we don't get a complaint." He responded, "Nah, press on". So as I felt the apartment buildings going by in my peripheral vision, I learned how to fly low RAFG style. We needed 5 kilometres visibility to fly low level. As Gwyn Richardson said on one of my T4 sorties, "I've got 2½ km visibility on the left and 2½ km visibility on the right ... Press on!"

Once, we flew against the American F-15s from Bitburg. We had escorts of Dutch F-16s from Leeuwarden. On day one we had the standard eight-ship Harrier freight train with F-16 outriggers. We got schwacked by the Eagles pretty good. On day two, we mixed the F-16s in with the Harrier freight train and put Harriers as outriggers. We waxed the Eagles' asses! As I was hanging up my G-suit I had the American F-15 commander get in my face and he shouted, "You can't do that. That's mixed-force tactics!" I looked at him and stated "Welcome to NATO," and walked off.

The exchange tour was a great time in my family's life. My boys learned to talk with an accent, and we made lifelong friends, I flew with great pilots both young and older who became wheels in the RAF, airline pilots, Red Arrows and lords of retirement. We won the Cold War and the Harrier Force was a big part of that team. As I say, "If you can't do 540 on a low level and come back to hover, you ain't shit."

JON 'DOG' DAVIS USMC

In late 1987, I had just checked out of a WTI (QWI) tour with our Harrier training squadron (VMAT-203) and had begun a follow-on tour with VMA-223 as their squadron WTI. At the prompting of my wing commander, I applied for a USMC FA-18 exchange tour, and was accepted. We were scheduled to upgrade our Harriers to a radar configuration and we wanted to get a couple of Harrier men checked out in radar-equipped aircraft to ease the introduction to the rest of the fleet when they arrived. In late November I was called and told the exchange was cancelled due to fiscal reasons, but was then asked if I was interested in going on exchange with the RAF instead. I didn't hesitate and said yes. I had quite a few senior leaders tell me not to do the exchange and that it was 'dead time' for my career and would probably 'hurt' my chances for successful career progression. Luckily, I respectfully didn't listen to them.

I had started flying Harriers right out of our training command in 1982. I wanted to fly the Harrier because the marines had them, and the Royal Navy and RAF had just fought them so well in the Falklands campaign. I can't say it was an 'easy' transition to a VSTOL AV-8A, but I made it and had a blast flying in my first gun squadron VMA-231, then as an instructor in VMAT-203. My first introduction to an RAF Harrier pilot was meeting Chris Moran (on exchange with our sister squadron VMA-542). He was impressive, and even as a new guy, I could tell he was something special. We had two former UK exchange officers in VMA-231 (Majors Willie McAtee RN Sea Harriers, and Charlie Davis of 4 Squadron). They checked into the squadron about the same time, decided I was 'way hosed up' and turned to 'fix the damage done'. I can say honestly that I really looked up to these two leaders and started putting 'RAF or RN exchange' on my dream sheets. They worked me up for my MAWTS-1 instructor certifications and helped turn me from a bottom feeder into a better STOVL strike-fighter pilot. After a deployment on the USS *Inchon* where we flew with the RN Sea Harrier guys off *Ark Royal*, I transferred to VMAT-203 and transitioned to the AV-8B. While I was an instructor at 203 I attended the WTI course at MAWTS-1 and served as our OCU's WTI. During this tour we had the first three RAF officers come to 203 to transition to the AV-8B. Squadron Leaders Pete Walmsley, Andy Golledge, and Jonathan Baynton showed up ready and knowledgeable and I was assigned to give them all their weapon and systems briefs. They were superb and a joy to work with.

For all the above-mentioned reasons, I was really excited to be selected for an exchange tour. I was a captain, had about 1,000 hours in the AV-8A, 700 hours in the AV-8B, and thought I had 'done it all'. I hadn't, but the exchange tour was one of the things that kept me in the USMC. If I hadn't gone to the UK then Germany, I might have left the corps in 1989.

I left the States in early January 1988 and brought my wife Carol and our four and two-year-old sons (Jeffrey and Eric) a week later. We made our way to RAF Brawdy in Wales and checked into 79 Squadron. Our first night, we met our neighbours (the Dudleys) and they were wonderful to us. Matt was a flight lieutenant Jaguar QFI and since that day in 1988 has been a close friend of our family. While my eldest learned Welsh songs in the school in Haverfordwest, I flew the mighty Jet Provost (about 12 hours) then the Hawk (about 30 hours). I learned to understand what I was being told on the radios, what to tell the others when I talked on the radio, and how you made the best of weather and terrain to employ the Hawk in the air-to-ground role. Flew with a guy they called Uncle Ray – who had more days on the Hawk than I had on earth and only had to apologise a couple times for exceeding 9-Gs. A fantastic couple of months in a great part of the world.

I checked in at Wittering that April. The three RAF pilots I had trained on the AV-8B were on the staff of 233 OCU, and all welcomed me warmly. Since I was the high time AV-8B guy on duty with the RAF, they gave me a modified OCU syllabus. Did most of my intro work (four sorties) in a T4 with Jon Baynton (QFI). On 13 April, on my instrument check – while 'under the bag' – and doing the unusual attitude part of the check Jonathan was flying and getting me set up to take and 'recover' the jet, when he said, "we have a problem, the stick is jammed". I hadn't seen that technique before on a check like this – but thought it might be part of the British way. I said, "Roger, I've got it". And he said, "No, we have a problem!" He told me to tighten up my straps and prepare to eject. I asked if I could remove the instrument 'bag' and he said yes. I pulled the bag and did notice that the stick was jammed fore and aft. We could move it laterally. We discussed the problem, discovered we could get some tailplane authority with the trim switch, and with trim, aileron and nozzles we set up for a long straight in (in IMC of course) to recover at Wittering via GCA. Landed and PNB-ed (stick still stuck when we shut down), went in, debriefed, had a cup of tea then I went off to attend ground school with the 3(F) guys who had started their ground training for the GR5. The squadron boss came in to the classroom about an hour later and showed me a handle from a TRU (I think) that had come off and lodged in the tailplane jack. That's why we couldn't move the stick. Really glad my Harrier tour with the RAF didn't start out with an ejection. In my logbook it reads: 'XW265 Baynton/Self INST/PANIC …50 minutes.' Flew my check ride the next day and moved on.

I finished up the T4 syllabus pretty quickly and transitioned to the GR5. It was a superb step up from the day attack (early model) AV-8Bs we flew in the corps. An onboard EW system, moving map – really a nice system. I started training events with the 3(F) Squadron guys and got to be close with Andy Golledge and Andy Dakin who were either members of or on their way to 3(F) Squadron in Gütersloh with me. We also had a USN exchange guy on the unit, Lieutenant Joe Capstaff (an A-7 man). We got to be close with him as well. Since the US Marine normally was assigned to 4 Squadron, Joe did a fair bit of work prepping the lads for what they could expect from me (to include how marines are a little 'tight' when it comes to uniform violations – i.e. stealing my cover or ripping it from my skull in the van on the way back from the Met brief – both of which the lads experimented with on my tour). My eldest son attended the local school at Wittering, my youngest had a slew of like-aged almost three-year-olds to play with and Carol and I enjoyed what I learned to be a rare perfect spring and early summer in East Anglia. I had my first flight in the GR5 on 18 April, and finished my conversion on 4 July. I really learned a lot in those first couple of months flying with the OCU instructors and my new squadron mates. I flew with Mark Green to Gütersloh in a T4 to do a Germany 'checkout' so I could be a full 'up' upon arrival in July. I had one more rather too interesting flight on 30 June. I was dash three on a four versus one SAP up north when I had a flickering oil light. Initially I thought it was a light problem, but I aborted regardless and soon the light was on 'full time'. I had already set the throttle at 85% and flew a straight-in fixed power SL to Leeming, where after landing we learned that a plug on the tank had come loose in flight and there was no oil in the engine. Just proves the procedures do work and the engine is pretty tough. After I finished the GR5 training, my 3(F) Squadron boss asked that I get a quick checkout on the GR3, so I did in pretty short order. The GR3 was very, very different to an AV-8A. Many more systems and switches than our 'stripped down' AV-8A (GR1 without a map), but it was nice to screech around the UK with an additional 60 knots over the GR5.

We packed up, booked a ferry, and checked into 3(F) Squadron in Gütersloh in mid-July 1989, and got right to work. I soon learned that flying in Germany was very different than the UK. Gütersloh was the closest jet base to the then East German border. I studied our mission taskings and operational concept, learned about briefing timelines, expectations and to never leave your viewgraphs in a spot where Charlie McIlroy could get his hands on them. Always a surprise when his 'art work' popped up in the middle of your brief.

I also learned that I was now the 'new guy' in Germany. While I had a lot of time in Harriers I didn't have RAF Germany time and I threw my rattle out of the crib early on when I had to re-earn the qualifications I had in the UK and graduate from Tower SOF as a primary duty. As I said, my initial take on the backwards progression was to think poorly of it, but I learned over time that in order to lead in an RAF squadron, I had to know everything about what could happen on a not-so-great peacetime or wartime day in Germany. The summer 1,500 ft cloudbase over three miles visibility in haze transitioned to the autumn 700 and one and then worse for winter. The good news is the RAF planned to fight good weather or bad and if you followed the rule set and flew in a standardized and disciplined manner – you could fight and thrive – and surge fly even in the crappiest of northern German plain weather. With the help of my flight commander, Squadron Leader Mark Leakey, I got my attitude 'right', learned what I needed to do as an RAF flight leader, then pretty quickly advanced in the squadron flight leader roster. For my last year on the squadron I was our representative for NATO War Plans, and was one of the Zulu leads, which meant I could lead the first eight-ship strikes of the big fight (if it ever came). Never achieved a qualification in any service that meant as much to me as that one.

Operating out of RAF Gütersloh was exhilarating. I'd ride my bike in from our house at 33 Frankestrasse (about two-and-a-half miles) and be ready for first go. I learned to be qualified for about everything, ready for anything and be near the SOF as he crafted the schedule in the early morning. I had a boss in the States who said that he thought I'd rather fly than eat – and that's true. I flew about 550 hours in two-and-a-half years – and had a blast.

My first deployment with 3(F) Squadron was to Lisbon to fly with the G-91s of the Portuguese air force. We came in on the heels of 1(F) Squadron who left in a bit of a rush, but we had a pretty solid deployment. The squadron made me the ACI standards officer so I was able to help run the next deployment to Akrotiri to fight RAF F-4s in December 1989. I wasn't able to spend my time off in town due to US security concerns – but I did get to spend time up on the mountain with the radar operators. Learned a great deal and probably saved some brain cells. We came home in time for Christmas and a group of us rented chalets in Austria to take our kids skiing. Both our sons learned to ski on Austrian snow (ice) at Alpbach. In late January, 3(F) left for Deci. The flying was a balanced mix of ACM and air-to-ground. The squadron had been flying the new jet for about seven months and everyone was finding new ways to make it perform a bit better every day. To me the combination of the QFI and QWI helped the RAF make the most out of every training opportunity. Each instructor attacked every problem and task in great detail, and their professionalism and attention to the details helped all of us learn faster than we would have normally.

In March 1990, we went to Leuchars for OLF. I flew my first 100' flight in a T4 with the squadron boss, Wing Commander Pete Moules. The OLF programme was exceptionally well structured and executed. I really felt that if we had to, we could go very low (USMC minimum tactical employment for defensive purposes was 100 ft AGL). The RAF ran divisions at 100 ft in the attack mode. I'm still not convinced it's the best move from a weapons effect or survivability standpoint, but the RAF was the best in the world at low flight. I finished up my OLF qualification in Scotland in late May with an eight versus two SAP bounced by F3s. Amazing flight, solid execution – and we killed the target.

In July 3(F) Squadron deployed to the field for the first time as a GR5 squadron, then again in September. Of all the things I saw on my RAF tour, the field deployments were the most impressive. We really made the Harrier be the force multiplier we needed it to be in a big fight – and we were in our element. I remember the mass briefs (you always wanted to be on the first wave in the morning since they tended to keep you in the jet – for up to six sorties). I had deployed to the field multiple times with the marines – but it was nothing like what the RAF did. In the RAFG scheme, the Harrier was employed in a highly agile and survivable mode (what the USMC is now calling Distributed STOVL operations for its F-35s and AV-8s). It was on field deployment that I first understood the power of a high level of standardisation and professionalism. I believed I *could* fly six combat sorties a day – never seeing my wingman face-to-face except for the first mass brief and last debrief of the day, operate out of several extremely austere field sites (roads and pads in woods) I had never been to before – and do it with zero mishaps. When I returned to the USMC, I fought for three years to get the Harrier Force to adopt a common TACSOP – all the time telling the 'doubters' how well it worked for the RAF. The USMC Harriers were the first to have a common TACSOP. The rest of the USMC TACAIR followed suit several years later. I admit that my first task on my first field deployment was to camouflage the pallet of beer and port we had sent to the field so that the IR cameras wouldn't pick it up. Thought it was hokey until after a long day (and the days in the field were very long), when we popped the top on the first can of wobbly in the mass debrief.

One other thing I thought the RAF did very well was the dining-ins and mess nights (both in the field and in garrison). My first Gütersloh dining-in featured my Marine Forces Europe boss, a USMC infantry officer colonel (a serious man). The squadron wanted to fly him in a T4 and then 'entertain' him and his wife as squadron guests for the dining-in. Needless to say I was 'worried' on a couple of fronts. The colonel had flown as an OA-4 observer in Vietnam but that was very likely *very different* than flying in the back of a Harrier in Germany (every day was like a Red Flag). On the dining-in side of the ledger, we had been 'counselled' several times about 3(F)'s and 4 Squadron's animal acts in the mess, and thought that it might not be in my best interest to show that side of RAF squadron life to my boss. Pete Moules had me in his office and *promised* me that the lads and lassies would behave and that the unit would be on its best behaviour. The last time, the JOs set fire to the floral arrangements and we got counselled for not being creative enough. My colonel and his wife arrived and he went flying with one of the squadron QFIs and a friend of mine, Mark Green. I saw them take off and beat up Gütersloh a bit on the return, followed by a slow landing in the grass section of the airfield. I helped get my colonel out of the jet and he didn't look too great. We took him to flight equipment in 4 Squadron, where he asked for some quiet time and for the shades to be pulled down. I left him alone for a while and asked Mark what he had done to him. Mark said they did a two-target SAP at 250 feet and 480 kts and threat reacted a couple of times to 'Red Air'. My colonel didn't get sick but we did give him a 'bog standard e-ticket ride'.

That night, we dressed in our service best, my colonel and his wife (a very nice lady with silver curled hair) sat at the head table with Pete Moules and his wife. We hadn't been sitting down for more than five minutes when the rolls started to fly and the patties of butter too. Molly got things back in order (but did have a big smile on his face). Think my colonel had fun and his wife calmly picked the patty of butter from her hair as dinner was served.

In August of 1990, Carol and I took the boys down to Bordeaux (rented Dave Walker's farmhouse) for what was probably my family's favourite vacation of all time. Saddam Hussein decided to invade Kuwait as we arrived back at Gütersloh. 3(F) Squadron had not 'declared ready' to NATO – so we sat out Desert Storm. Andy Dakin, who was now on exchange with VMA-542, a USMC AV-8B squadron, did get to the fight and passed what he could.

We were in Deci at weapons camp when the air war started. Several of us were advocating for employing medium-altitude tactics and even though the GR5 weapons computers didn't have a computed solution for high-altitude deliveries we improvised and in a couple of weeks had developed a reasonable medium-altitude tactics capability. I think that the RAF Harrier Force was able to flex as quickly as they did because of their very strong baseline of operational competence and standardisation. On the way back from Deci, Paul Hackney, myself and a couple of others executed a ranger deployment to Aviano. From there we skied Cortina for three days. Exceptional skiing and fellowship.

I was made a Zulu lead and OLF instructor for my last OLF to Kinloss. At this point in my exchange tour I was collecting my lessons learned for an AAR to the RAF and more importantly what I'd take back to the USMC. The Harrier shop head at our weapons school (MAWTS-1 in Yuma) called and asked if I wanted to serve at MAWTS after my exchange tour. I jumped at the chance, especially since it would give me a prime spot to help influence and change USMC tactics and standardisation.

My last big event as an exchange pilot was a squadron deployment to a Green Flag at Nellis. The new squadron boss, Richie Thomas, let me lead one of the RAF's turns at running the entire strike package. It went well, and more importantly the RAF Harrier Force showed that it 'had some serious game'.

My last flight in the unit was on 12 June 1991, an air-to-air event above a cloud deck that topped at about 7,000 ft over Gütersloh. I think Sean Bell was my dash two. He did well, and we recovered via a GCA to VLs and champagne with my bride and the rest of the unit.

Jon Davis (centre) after his last RAF flight, with Mark Zanker (left) and Richie Thomas. (Jon Davis)

I can honestly say that serving with the RAF in the UK and Germany was a high point in my career. As a young captain, I thought I knew it all. Some very talented (and spirited) RAF pilots and maintainers taught me that I had a lot to learn about flying and myself. I left the RAF in June of 1991, but the RAF experience is still with me. My eldest son is a second tour Harrier pilot in Yuma, and my youngest flies FA-18s in Beaufort. The USMC is a better service for my experience with the Brits. On my desk is a set of RAF wings Paul Hackney gave me when I left the squadron. If we ever fight again, I'll be ready to wear your wings or mine to defend our countries from any foe. *Semper Fi.*

CHAPTER 5
UNRELATED UNCLES

Tony Harper was on No 14 Harrier course (with a future CAS), two courses ahead of me (with another future CAS), but served in various Harrier roles right into the 21st century, latterly as the uncle on 1 Squadron. Keith Skinner was also an uncle, on IV Squadron, his first Harrier Force job. Harps explains the variety of experience open to pilots of that era, and the changes brought in with Harrier II. While most Harrier pilots might be too modest to explain the career challenges they faced (or might not be believed if they did), Keith gives an objective insight into the quality and progress of Harrier mates (notwithstanding the two x CAS mentioned above, who made their early career moves before flying the Harrier).

TONY HARPER

I joined the RAF, aged 19, in 1970, as an officer cadet on the last Cranwell cadet entry before the change to the graduate entry system. I was commissioned in 1973 as a pilot officer. My first exposure to the Harrier was when I arrived at Wittering in late 1974 to fly the Hunter on 58 Squadron. The Harrier OCU was on full song on one side of our hangar and 1(F) Squadron lived in the hangar to the east. Until that point I had been through the training system and had flown the Jet Provost Mks 3 and 5 at Cranwell, the Gnat at Valley and had completed the first quarter of the Tactical Weapons Unit course at Chivenor on the Hunter. Four of us were posted to 45/58 Squadrons at Wittering as an experiment to see if the unit was capable of training us 'abos' up to form a pool of single-seat pilots to feed the Jaguar and Harrier OCUs. It obviously worked since I went from being 'unfit single-seat, unfit ground attack', post my Gnat course, to being a student on the Harrier OCU in just seven months. (Most of this success was due to sage advice from my flight commander, Callum Kerr.)

We all wanted to fly the Jag as the Harrier had a reputation of being difficult to fly and easy to crash (occasionally with fatal consequences). The Harrier 'mates' had also acquired a not very flattering reputation as poseurs. However, in those days, there was no discussion and you went where you were sent. I was encouraged to accept this move by Ian Stewart (later air vice-marshal) who was on the Harrier course ahead of me and, sure enough, after just one trip in the 'bona jet', I was completely sold. Even the early Harrier T2 set off down the runway like a scalded cat. The handling, as I quickly discovered, was very like the Hunter in conventional flight, and even in the hover, the jet did what it was told. Provided one stayed firmly within the handling boundaries during the transition from conventional flight to the hover, all remained in order (well most of the time). I did struggle at the latter end of the 'operational' phase of the course but some one-to-one tuition with Steve Jennings sorted me out.

I joined my first 'real' squadron, 20 (AC), at Wildenrath in January 1975 and spent three exciting years flying the jet around Europe, operating out of field sites, doing weapons training at Decimomannu in Sardinia and testing other pilots in my role as an instrument rating examiner. Around all this professional activity was a pretty hectic social life. The bachelor members of the community made the most of opportunities to visit the Oktoberfest and other similar well-lubricated events around Western Europe.

During that tour in Germany I had a few close scrapes. We did three field deployments each year when we deployed forward and provided close air support to, often multi-national, army exercises. The sites varied from roads in military training areas to farmers' fields where the REs would build 50 ft square landing pads for us which were often connected to a metal runway. On my first attempt to land on one of these, I decelerated along the side of the strip aiming for a hover over the pad at the end. It did not go well. My jet efflux got under the edge of the strip and I turned it over along its whole length. Needless to say I was warned off and ended up landing at Gütersloh, about 30 miles away. The following day I had my second attempt which was successful. However, the action was not over. On emerging from the cockpit I was invited for 'a walk in the grass' with the boss (Wing Commander David Brook) who, in no uncertain terms, told me where my future lay were I to make a habit of wrecking his airfield. The incident also had some financial impact as I felt compelled to buy the sappers (a tough TA unit from Newcastle) a few slabs of 'Wibbly-Wobbly' (a nickname for a particularly fine German brew from the Warsteiner Company). to make up for the extra effort they had to put in repairing the damage.

Field deployments had their own characteristics. If you were unfortunate enough to deploy by road rather than by Harrier, it was essential to ride with the ground liaison officer (an army major). He didn't travel in convoy and his Land Rover was by far the fastest on the squadron. Post-flying debriefs were held at the end of each day after we had eaten the excellent food provided by the deployed caterers. On 20 Squadron, the debrief was washed down with a healthy dose of Stilton cheese and vintage port (preferably Graham's '66). After the conclusion of the evening's events one would retire to a 12 ft x 12 ft tent (put up by ourselves) seeking a good night's sleep. This was often interrupted either by the loud snores (port has that effect) or the grinding of teeth by one of the team who shall remain nameless. We rushed to not share a tent with him.

The field trips were normally two weeks long, with no flying on the middle Sunday to avoid upsetting the locals. Therefore, it seemed a good idea to have a 'wing-ding' on the Saturday evening; these were momentous social events. Somewhere there is a legion of war-stories about 'wing-dings' which are probably best left untold.

Away from the field, routine training consisted of air-to-ground weapons training dropping 4 kg practice bombs, firing SNEB 68mm rockets and the 30mm Aden cannon. We did lots of low-level navigation and off-range simulated-attack profiles, routinely at 250 ft or 500 ft above ground. On bad weather days we conducted air-to-air combat training. Life was pretty much spent at low level and we were quite good at it. The early Harrier had an analogue INAS which was basically that designed for the TSR2. It was not very good and it paid to cross check one's location against an old-fashioned paper map and we referred to it as 'Basil', after Mr Ferranti whose company had designed it. On most Fridays, weather permitting, we would arrange our sorties to transit via the Möhne dam where the Lightnings from Gütersloh would set up combat air patrols (CAPs) to intercept us. This generally resulted in a 'furball' or 'knife fight in a phone box', below 3,000 ft which continued until one side ran out of fuel and had to go home. It was huge fun but really rather dangerous given our proximity to the ground and the number of aircraft involved.

The weapons training was normally done on Nordhorn range on the Dutch/German border. We transited to and fro (about 15 minutes each way) in tactical formation at low level. This was fine on a nice day but when it was misty, you often would not see the formation ahead returning from the earlier range slot until they rushed past in the murk. We used to refer to stumbling around in that kind of weather as 'flying Brit VFR'. The other range we used was called Helchteren, in the Belgian Ardennes. From the air the Ardennes have few distinguishing features and the only way I ever found Helchteren was to route via the motor-racing circuit at Spa Francorchamps whose grandstands stood out as a landmark.

All this excitement led to much letting off of steam. This normally meant attending 'happy hour' in the officers' mess which lasted considerably more than an hour. 20 Squadron had a jazz band which had two or three competent musicians to try and overcome the discordant noises produced by the remainder. The annual '20s 20s night' would start at 2020 hours and was an event not to be missed. I think everyone probably has the fondest memories of their first squadron tour and that is definitely my experience on No 20.

After three years in Germany I was posted to instruct at the TWU at Brawdy then Lossiemouth. After some 900 more hours of Hunter flying and qualifying as a QWI, I returned to the Harrier with 1(F) Squadron at Wittering. 1(F) had a different role to the RAFG squadrons. It was part of NATO's Allied Command Europe (ACE) Mobile Force and as such, was on call to deploy forward to areas of trouble at short notice. We trained routinely in the UK in the close air support (CAS), interdiction, reconnaissance and air-to-air refuelling roles and deployed each year to the Northern Flank (Tromsø, Norway) and to Vandel airfield in Denmark, as well as supporting the RAFG squadrons.

Tromsø was lovely. We were normally there in March which meant we operated off a snow-covered airfield and flew over the snow and ice some 300 miles north of the Arctic Circle. Operating off snow had its challenges but the Harrier was generally OK provided you moved slowly (with the throttle set below the normal idle rpm) until you were dead straight and pointing down the runway before opening the throttle. The flying itself was magnificent. The fjords are spectacular, the snow lovely and the blue ice of the glaciers stunning. The weather at that time of year was either awful (so we did not fly), or beautiful, when we flew as much as possible. We were normally part of a Royal Marine

A nice day in Norway. (Chris Rayner)

Arctic Warfare exercise on these occasions.

In Vandel we lived in tents much as we had done in Germany. On one exercise in November the chap next to me woke up in the morning with frost on his head. This was to be good practice for the events soon to unfold in the South Atlantic. The flying from Vandel lacked the scenic beauty of the Norwegian exercises and the low flying was restricted to 500 or 1,000 ft which we considered rather simple. As in Norway, the beer was horribly expensive but the locals seemed less friendly.

1982 started in the normal fashion with a March deployment to Tromsø. We then ferried aircraft to Canada in preparation for Exercise Maple Flag. We were back at Wittering when we heard the Falkland Islands had been invaded by the Argentinians. Like most people we had to go and get an atlas to find out where the Falklands are. We could not see how we could be involved as there were no airfields available within range of the islands so what good would our GR3s be. Then the decision was taken to recover the islands. Still no airfields for us. The RN Sea Harriers would obviously deploy to provide air defence for the fleet and we quickly learnt that we would be going as casualty replacements for the Sea Harriers. This would mean flying from the carrier HMS *Hermes*. Perhaps more significantly, it would mean living on board with the navy.

We flew from St Mawgan to Ascension Island (9 hours 15 minutes) on 3 May and a few days later flew the aircraft onto the container ship *Atlantic Conveyor* for the trip to the South Atlantic. (So in the space of a few weeks we had flown the Atlantic east to west and north to south.) Having reached the South Atlantic and rendezvoused with the carriers, we took off from the *Atlantic Conveyor* and landed on HMS *Hermes* to a mixed reception from the ship's company. The story of our activities has been relayed in a very accurate and readable way by Jerry Pook in his book, *RAF Harrier – Ground Attack Falklands*, which I highly recommend, and by Sir Peter Squire in *Harrier Boys Volume One*. Rather than repeat their words, I shall just add a few impressions of my own.

I was flattered to be included in the team taken south by OC 1(F) Squadron, Wing Commander Peter Squire. The other members of the team were, in my eyes, the 'A-Team'. I was not particularly close to anyone but we soon got to know each other well as we spent most of the day together and then shared 'dossing' space on the floor of the wardroom which was our bedroom (at least it was once the first lieutenant had finished playing bridge). No one was allowed to sleep below the waterline in case we had to abandon ship in a hurry.

The flying day seemed very short as we were operating in autumn in the southern hemisphere. Two trips in a day was unusual. The other strange effect of the southern hemisphere was that the sun was always to the north of us. This was initially very disorientating as we had always had the sun to our south when flying in the northern hemisphere. As a pilot you do not realise how much you use the sun as a basic orientation aid until it is in the wrong place. The challenging bits were finding the targets and then finding 'Mother' afterwards. Although the ship would give us its intended position before we launched, it was not uncommon for it to be somewhere other than where we expected it when we returned. The feeling of insecurity was increased by our lack of knowledge of our own position over the South Atlantic. This was often quite tense as we rarely had much fuel left to hang around.

It was quickly apparent that Sea Harrier losses were less than feared so the RN chaps carried out their primary role of fleet defence and achieving a measure of air superiority over the ground forces ashore. We were then free for our normal role of interdiction and CAS for the army and Royal Marines on the ground. We did fall foul of the Sea Harrier combat air patrols once or twice which led to some expletives over the common guard frequency to make sure they did not launch a Sidewinder in our direction.

Falklands low flying: recce photo of Argentinian troops. (Peter Squire)

Once the ground forces had established a bridgehead at San Carlos, the sappers constructed a strip for us at Port San Carlos so that we would be closer to the action and be able to react faster to calls for support. The strip was a typical RAFG tin affair with a couple of extra loops to provide access to refuelling bunds. It worked well except we found ourselves out of communication rather too frequently. We were billeted at the Davis' farm and ate wonderful fresh lamb which Ellen (Mrs Davis) casseroled for us. My lasting memory is standing in a slit trench during an Argentinian air raid brandishing my 9mm pistol hoping there would be something to shoot at (nothing came close enough). We took it in turns to spend days and nights ashore until the conclusion of hostilities on 14 June.

A few days after the surrender a couple of us were sent ashore to make room for relief pilots who had arrived from the UK. We spent our days walking around Port Stanley (much smaller then than it is now), looking at the captured air defences which had worried us so, seeing the piles of abandoned Argentinian small arms and spending a lot of time chatting to the local people, who were wonderfully welcoming. During this period we had bunks in the bowels of RFA *Sir Tristram* which had been tied up alongside to provide extra accommodation.

My war came to an abrupt end in early July when we were flown out of Port

Stanley airfield on a C-130 bound for Ascension Island and then onto a VC10 for the final leg to a very warm reception at RAF Brize Norton and, subsequently, a real welcome at RAF Wittering.

I have been back to the islands three times since 1982 and I have been delighted to see the way they have developed thanks to the income from fishing licences, tourism and hopefully, in the future, oil extraction. I am often asked if I think it was worth going to war in 1982. My answer is a resounding yes. The islanders are British through and through and if they wish to remain British then we have a duty to them to keep the islands under the Union flag.

After another year or so on 1(F) Squadron, I was moved to 233 OCU as a weapons and tactics instructor. This was an opportunity to spend much more time at home and we were only on the road for a month or so each year.

Then in 1985 I was promoted to squadron leader and moved back to 1(F) Squadron as a flight commander. It was back to the same routine as before with lots of deployments around Europe, plenty of air-to-air refuelling practice and routine UK training. A couple of things stick in my memory from that tour. One of my chaps managed to do a touch-and-go without lowering the undercarriage. He went around the circuit and then landed on the wheels without further incident. The only damage was to the two gun pods under the fuselage. On the second incident my number two's canopy opened itself at 400 kts. The normal speed limit for opening the 'lid' was 40 kts. Again, once he had got over the shock, a normal landing was carried out.

In the summer of 1987 I was detached to Belize for six months to command 1417 Flight, probably the best tour of my career. We had four jets, three pilots plus myself and fifty ground crew. It was all rather basic but all the better for it. The flying was excellent with a token low-flying minimum of 250 ft, no controlled airspace and virtually no air traffic control other than that at Belize International Airport. We had access to an air-to-ground range for practice weapons and occasionally got to drop 1,000-lb bombs in the mountains and fire the guns against splash targets towed by visiting RN ships. We normally stopped flying at 1330 hours (too hot/too humid and limited flying hours permitted) and returned to the mess for lunch. The resident REs were from the Ghurkhas during my stay and every Thursday they produced the most wonderful curries for lunch. The social life was pretty busy with lots of self-created entertainment, trips to the off-shore cayes for sailing and swimming and trips to the jungle to look at Mayan ruins. I was joined by my wife for my mid-tour leave which we spent touring the Yucatán region of Mexico.

Finally the system caught up with me and I was sent on my first ground tour at Upavon. This was the HQ of No 1 Group where I represented the interests of the UK Harrier units to the higher chain of command. After all the flying, this was fairly mundane and only lasted about eighteen months but, on reflection, I was probably ready for a break. A very pleasant six months at the Joint Service Defence College at Greenwich doing the 'Joint Service Drinking Course' followed. This was a national tri-service course and we were privileged to be given access to some significant military and political leaders, under Chatham House Rules. The experience was very interesting and I learned a lot. I was then elevated to the dizzy heights of wing commander and despatched to the 'mad house' (MoD) in Whitehall for eighteen months. This was as the Harrier desk officer working for the assistant chief of the Air Staff. In simple terms, the main task was linking the MoD to British Aerospace in terms of procurement timing (often frustrated by the bureaucracy of the Procurement Executive), modification states and keeping the Harrier Force informed of progress. It was an interesting time with the introduction of the Harrier GR5 underway and the subsequent GR7 modification being planned. I finally learned why equipment procurement takes so long but I am ashamed to say that I was unable to speed up the process in any way during my time in MoD. Overall, a very frustrating experience.

I completed the escape tunnel and returned to the Harrier Force as OC the OCU which was, in my opinion, the best of the available wing commander flying tours. Lots of aeroplanes, lots of keen students, instructors who were the cream of the crop and some very experienced ground crew. To top it off, the Harrier GR5 had recently arrived. This was a very different aeroplane and I found it a challenge. Driving the aircraft was easy as it was almost the same as the older Harrier. However the navigation and weapon aiming system was something else entirely. It was a modern digital system which actually worked so the aeroplane knew where it was and the weapon aiming system was also very good. I confess that I really enjoyed flying the GR5 and GR7 but that I was not any good as an operator as I struggled to master the modern digital avionics. The students coming through onto the new aircraft were digitally capable and took to it like ducks to water.

I left the OCU in 1994 and was fortunate to have a series of interesting ground tours including four years on exchange with the USAF (including some A-10 flying) and three years as Air and Naval Attaché in South Africa. The circle was finally completed for me when, following my retirement from active duty in 2005, I was employed, as a full-time reservist, as the 1(F) Squadron uncle. This enabled me to resume flying with the local Air Experience Flight on the Tutor aircraft and to pass on some of my hard-won experience to the next generation.

KEITH SKINNER

After nearly thirty years serving on the front line of the Cold War, RAF Harriers, specifically 3(F) and IV(AC) Squadrons, finally left Germany in 1999 and headed to Cottesmore, formerly the home of the Tri-National Tornado Training Establishment (TTTE) for eighteen years, which had settled into a comfortable non-operational routine with few budgetary constraints. All that was soon to change dramatically.

Our two Harrier squadrons left not only duty-free perks and local overseas allowance (LOA) behind in Germany. The numbers of aircraft on both squadrons had recently been reduced along with pilot and ground crew establishment figures. However, what was not reduced was the flying task and associated operational commitments (stats). The achievement of these performance indicators has always tended to define the success (or not as the case may be) of the careers for peacetime squadron commanders.

The net effect was that squadron executives were having to devote a higher proportion of their time to administrative tasks, often to the detriment of their flying currency. This may not have been a show stopper on a squadron flying more conventional aircraft. But the Harrier was always an unforgiving partner requiring total focus by the pilot from engine start to shut down.

In an effort to reduce the administrative burden on the single-seat squadrons, the relevant staff officers at 1 Group and Strike Command conceived a plan to fund the creation of an additional support post. To the surprise of many the plan was approved and the concerned stations were asked to define job specifications as a prelude to recruitment.

In general terms the post holder would be a FTRS (full-time reserve service) squadron leader and a member of the squadron executive. His/her title would be flight commander operations. The job would include day-to-day supervision of the CO's outer office including adjutant and registry staff; dissemination and collation of officers joint appraisal reports (OJARs); responsibility for devolved budgets; squadron IT infrastructure; F540 quality and timeliness; representing the CO at station meetings when the squadron was deployed; and providing general service advice to junior pilots if requested. In reality, although the job developed slightly differently on each squadron, the guiding principles held firm.

But where did the term 'uncle' come from? Most historians point us back to the days of the Royal Flying Corps when pilot life expectancy was measured in days and turnover was such that only a 'grounded' officer could possibly carry corporate squadron knowledge from one month to the next. It was felt that such an officer was better able to act in the best interests of all if he was himself a flyer – and ideally with fairly current experience. This led to the adjutant (always an officer in those early days) perhaps being a pilot or observer whose injuries or medical condition kept him grounded. This was probably the genesis of the 'squadron uncle'. The man who had been there before and knew the score.

So jumping forward again to 1999 we find Cottesmore trawling for two uncles, one for 3(F) and one for IV(AC) Squadron. As the post was FTRS there could be no resettlement fees paid nor home to duty travel paid and so the expected applicant would be a retired Harrier pilot from the Stamford (Wittering) area. Unfortunately, those ex-Harrier pilots not enjoying their retirement freedom on the local golf courses seemed to be flying large aeroplanes from Hong Kong. There were no takers for the 'uncle' posts, and the trawl was widened.

Enter the author of this piece, recently retired from the 'real' air force and beginning to wonder why the public schools and golf clubs approached were not clamouring to recruit such obvious talent in the bursar/club secretary role. Something to do with a lack of formal accountancy or business qualifications... What's wrong with a decent golf handicap, a Barbour jacket, Volvo estate and a black Labrador? I was tempted to ask.

And so when the Officers' Association advertised the Cottesmore post I never doubted that I could do the job – and more importantly would really enjoy seeing it evolve. And as my last flying post with the RAF had been as wing commander Red Arrows at Scampton I was reasonably up to speed with senior Harrier personalities – many of whom had flown with the Reds.

And so late in 1999, Ken McCann (OC IV[AC] Squadron) and Ashley Stevenson (OC 3[F] Squadron) were the joint interviewers of myself and one Squadron Leader (rtd) Bob Wilkey – whom I had never met before even though it transpired later that we lived 300 yards apart in Warwickshire. We were both successful and started work early in 2000. I was lucky enough to get the slot on Happy 4 where I got to know my office quite intimately over the next seven years.

Some names to conjure with: station commanders were David Walker, Mike Harwood, Andy Golledge and Sean Bell. Squadron commanders I worked for started with Ken McCann followed by Andy Suddards, Andy Offer and Ian 'Squid' Duguid. XOs whose office I shared were Squid (to start with); Sean Perrett, Al Pinner, Andy McKeon, Jamie Hunter and Damian Killeen. These squadron executives were supported by some of the most talented junior officers I have had the pleasure of working with. And perhaps I can even quantify that statement.

Back in the day, I instructed for four years on Hunter aircraft at the TWU at Brawdy. Our job was to train embryo RAF fighter pilots for onward posting to Buccaneer, Lightning, Jaguar, Phantom (air defence and ground attack) and Harrier. If those pilots selected for Harrier had not graduated in the top twenty percentile of their TWU course then there was an inevitability that they would fail the Harrier OCU at Wittering. As a result, the Harrier Force was staffed with the crème de la crème of the aviation fraternity.

But in some ways, that grouping of skills generated a built-in headwind for individual progress by Harrier pilots in the RAF. Our service has always required its general duties (GD) officers, comprising in the main pilots and navigators (WSOs), to 'perform' in areas other than their primary flying duty. But when the whole flying team is 'Premier League' quality *and* everybody within that team is a 'striker' *and* there are no substitutes on the bench *and* your primary role takes you away from your home base for six months in a calendar year, it is quite difficult to stand out against your peers in the promotion stakes. And as 'uncle' I saw the frustration that this policy could engender amongst pilots who might have swept to the top much more quickly in another, perhaps less demanding flying role.

Did the 'uncle' post add value? That is for others to answer. But I do know that I would not have stayed at Cottesmore for seven years unless I personally felt that I had a contribution to make as well as enjoying the diverse nature of the job. One of the most satisfying periods came during the Iraq War of 2003 when all the Cottesmore Harriers deployed to the Middle East. The only squadron officers left behind were the uncles, who served as the link between the deployed men and women and their families back in the UK. I realise that function normally falls on a station admin team – and we worked closely with them – but there was something more personal for the families at home dealing with people they knew.

Another area where the deployed squadrons (in peace and war) benefited was by retaining representation at weekly station executive meetings in their absence. The uncles had the time to consult their respective COs and take a considered view back to the station thus negating controversial decisions being taken in absentia. Recently there has been a tendency for the 'uncle' to have more of a role on the ops and mission-planning side of squadron life to the extent that requires them to deploy with the squadron. I suppose you put the incumbent to work where he makes the greatest contribution but I think we lose a key benefit of the post if we simply make the uncle in effect an ops officer. Interestingly, what was conceived as uniquely a GD post has been successfully filled by officers from the admin branches on at least two occasions. Any skill set will do just as long as there is mutual respect between the aircrew and the uncle (or auntie).

Highlights of my long tour of duty? Being on an active airfield again; being able to cycle to work; running the station golf club (as officer I/C), working with all sections of the station – including civilian staff – to better the lot of Happy 4 – something I never seemed to manage when working as a line pilot. Then there was seeing Joint Force 2000 morph into Joint Force Harrier with the arrival of our RN colleagues. Our station commander became a force commander and the concept of the Expeditionary Air Wing resurfaced – what goes around... But by far the greatest pleasure was working alongside some of the sharpest and most professional aviators and engineers in the business. I have missed the buzz of life on a Harrier squadron and returning to Cottesmore in December 2010 to see the final fly-pasts was an incredibly moving experience. We may not see their like again. *In Futurum Videre.*

CHAPTER 6
BRIDGING THE GENERATIONS

On the OCU course ahead of mine was a pilot who went on to fly only one Harrier squadron tour, but whose name became legendary, and who contributed to Harrier development right up to the GR9 and T10. In between, he did lots of exciting stuff, including ejecting from a GR3 and setting world time-to-height records in a GR5. His witticisms also live in my memory. During a boring period of an exercise at Wittering, several of us junior pilots sat in our simulated NBC shelter. Having worn respirators for a long time, due to the simulated contamination, we had taken advantage of the absence of observers to take a rubber-free breather. As the first to see the approaching senior officer, Bernie quickly donned his S6 respirator, replacing the traditional 'gas, gas, gas' call with one of 'boss, boss, boss'.

BERNIE SCOTT
To get through training was something of a miracle, but then to find myself on 1(F) Squadron flying the Harrier was a dream come true. Not naturally gifted, I often struggled both on the ground and in the air but thanks to incredible dedication, determination and a willingness never to give up on a lost cause, I made it. Those were all shown by my brilliant flying instructors, not me.

RAF Wittering was a very busy place when I arrived in September 1973 to fly Hunters on 58 Squadron, with the possibility of a posting to Jaguars. BAe Warton planned a production rate of twelve per month and a pool of pilots would be needed to meet the demand. After my thirteen months flying the immaculate Hunters of the sister squadrons 45 and 58, Lossiemouth was the proud operator of just two Jaguars. Out of the blue, I was posted to 233 OCU to train on the Harrier. I was over the moon.

My time at Wittering prior to the course meant that I already knew a number of the personalities in the Harrier world and I shared a house in Stamford with Paul Hopkins, who was on 1 Squadron and was not only a great friend but a hugely talented pilot. The OCU was amazing for its quality of instruction, especially so after my experiences at Chivenor where I had trained with 79 Squadron, a unit geared to re-training experienced Hunter pilots rather than first-tourists. That said, I did get to fly Rod Dean's spare display aircraft and enjoy some summer weekends at places such as Manston and Thorney Island; the latter allowing me to pop over to see my parents on the Isle of Wight.

Despite the tension inherent in training, there was a huge amount of laughter and banter throughout the course. It is bizarre the things that I remember though, for example, the food. The flying rate determined the amount and quality of aircrew rations that were available in the crew room and the OCU did a lot of flying. Culinary highlights included 'Donkey Knob', pork luncheon meat not from a standard tin but rather a 4-inch-diameter tube at least a foot long. Such delights in a sandwich could be enhanced by additions such as crushed crisps, all cemented with gobs of tomato ketchup. So healthy when accompanied by a cup of NAAFI Nescafé and a fag.

It was all a whirlwind of activity and it seemed that no time had passed before, in May 1975, I was having my introductory chat with Pete Taylor, the boss of 1 Squadron. Because of a string of aircraft losses and tragedies in RAFG, the UK and Cyprus, he was, like all Harrier squadron commanders at the time, under enormous pressure from above. I know that I added my fair share for him to worry about during my pre-operational work up and for some time after.

I had only been out of the country once to the winter survival course, so going to 1 Squadron was an amazing eye-opener with frequent detachments to Norway, Denmark and Sardinia plus two deployments to Belize. It was there, during the first deployment in December 1975, that I managed to get home for Christmas by ejecting after an engine failure.

F95 shot of Bernie's ejection by 'Bomber' Harris. (Bernie Scott)

Pete Harris was leading me on an FAC sortie with Dougie Gibbons as the controller. Luckily I was going like the clappers trying to restore some semblance of a position in battle formation abeam Pete when the engine quit with an almighty bang. It relit three times but into surge. Pete gave me a timely reminder that coincided with my decision to get out. I made a quick call to Pete, did all the visor lowering and posture stuff then pulled the handle. It was an amazing transition from short-lived explosive noise and power to the silence of hanging in the parachute with the seat going down and the aeroplane hitting the sea. I lowered my dinghy just before hitting the water. So warm and so full of sharks and barracuda. The dinghy inflation handle wouldn't pull so I had to dismantle the packing and flick the lever on the gas bottle. I was sure that the sharks were closing in. Once in the dinghy, I was able to wave to Pete and very soon after a customs boat came to offer me help. I stayed in the dinghy rather than complicate things for the Puma rescue helicopter which arrived with Stan

Smith at the controls. They did a great job but the winch on the Puma was very harsh and I swear that the entire combined, saturated weight of the crewman and me was supported by my left testicle as we rose into the helicopter. The boss, Pete Taylor, was smiling but a very worried man when he met me from the Puma. I think that he was much happier when he heard my account of how dramatic and obvious the engine failure was.

I was checked over by the RAF doctor and taken to Belize Hospital for x-rays, with plates provided by the military, then back to the bar. As dusk approached news came that an army Sioux helicopter was heading for the airfield but was in danger of running out of fuel before making the field. Just as everyone was wondering what to do, the suspension in drinking was brought to

Bernie returns. (Bernie Scott)

an end by the news that the helicopter had landed very heavily and with much damage, but that everyone was ok and on their way to the bar. The final twist came when we heard that the RAF doctor and the RN doctor had driven off at speed towards the helicopter pad and had both been injured in a head-on crash with a lorry. They were the only casualties of that day and were flown to the US hospital in Panama the next day. Funnily enough, I found my flight reference cards from the ejection in with some old memorabilia and it was open at the engine malfunction page, so I must have checked my actions whilst sitting in the dinghy.

Detachments were an excuse for serious undertakings such as moustache-growing competitions and seeing how long people could go without washing their flying suits. There was also a concert night where any act or turn was welcomed as long as it wasn't too serious. Back at Wittering, we staged a version of the Deci concerts for the families. This was, of course, a hugely distilled version of what would have been seen in Sardinia where much of the inspiration and talent was enhanced by the consumption of duty-free liquids.

Pete Day instructed me in post-maintenance air tests, which provided a great source of extra flying. This also brought me into regular contact with people like John Farley, Dunsfold's chief test pilot. Without his detailed explanation, I don't think anyone would have understood how to conduct the ritual of the pressure ratio limiter that had the potential to take up the majority of an air test sortie.

Dudley Carvell joined the Red Arrows from No 1 and I remember him coming back in the Gnat for his dining-out and leaving a smoke trail at ground level past the squadron. What is the chance of ever doing that? Well, thanks to him, my application, late, due to my being away in Belize, was not only allowed but accepted. I was offered to join the team in September 1977. So, off to the Red Arrows and, incredibly, another dream come true. Two years on the Gnat and the first year of the Hawk in the 1980 display season were packed with terrific flying and a chance to represent the RAF and the UK all over Europe. It really was an honour and a privilege. I often see the Red Arrows and can't believe that I was once allowed legitimately to tear around the sky like that; absolutely brilliant.

Bernie flew the Gnat with the Red Arrows. (Bernie Scott)

From the Red Arrows, I was posted to fly the Starfighter with the Royal Netherlands Air Force at Volkel. Knowing that the F-16 was being introduced into service with the RNLAF it was a sensible choice to take a gamble. Three months of intensive language training which involved a leisurely train ride into London and a couple of hours tuition, each day, near Piccadilly, set me up to speak only in Dutch at work during the entire tour. It certainly helped gain the Dutch pilots' respect not least because they all spoke perfect English and most were amazed at my command of their language, so was I. Dutch lager served in the squadron bar always helped though. I was just at the end of the Starfighter ground school when my request to convert to F-16s was granted. This meant a move to Leeuwarden in Friesland but it was well worth it.

The tour, which was essentially re-establishing an exchange post at Leeuwarden that had not been filled for decades, was hard work both domestically and professionally. The aircraft were all brand new and maintained in immaculate condition. The operational attitude of the RNLAF was excellent and they always worked hard and effectively to procure the best available weapons and equipment within their budgets.

The F-16 was brilliant with a design that set out from the beginning to allow growth; so it was fitted for, but not with, systems and equipment under development and planned for fitment in the future. It had tremendous performance and such a high power-to-weight ratio that it could be loaded up with a serious fuel, bomb and defensive-aids load.

From the Netherlands, I returned to the UK in February 1984, in order to learn French during a few months ahead of training at EPNER, the French Test Pilots' School. This was tantamount to torture in that the whole course was in the French language and it took place at Istres in Provence. So, whilst the family was enjoying the amazing lifestyle, culture and climate, my head was in the books.

August 1985 saw me back at Boscombe Down, on A Squadron. I was lucky enough to enjoy a four-year tour during which new aircraft were being introduced in the form of the F2 and F3 Tornado, Harrier II, FA2 Sea Harrier, the Tucano trainer and even a new motor-glider for the air cadets. Additionally, the TriStar was going through its conversion and testing as a tanker. New guided weapons and fuses were under development together with electro-optic systems under test in prototype form on development aircraft and being quickly integrated into every type of front-line aircraft.

It was a brilliant but sometimes frustrating job in many respects as virtually all the problems cited in reports as needing to be addressed were often ignored on the grounds of cost rather than risk. Without going into details, failure to address some problems found during testing led to the loss of at least one Tornado, a Tucano and a Harrier II in service.

The Harrier II was a great leap forward in capability, with increased internal fuel capacity and external stations that allowed, for an aeroplane of its size, remarkable combinations of fuel, weapons and pod-mounted systems. I loved flying it more than any other aeroplane. The cockpit design was influenced by a large population of experienced pilots and would have been familiar territory to any F-18 pilot. The early testing was progressing well until the tragic loss of Taylor Scott on a production flight test due, for whatever reason, to an ejection problem.

The ejection seat was introduced as a UK fit, along with many other items such as the inertial navigation set, radios and the gun. It was frustrating, in the early days, to be testing substitute equipment that was often less capable than the original AV-8B fit. This was going on whilst the USMC were already well advanced in planning and forging ahead with their future enhancements and capability growth.

I left the RAF at the end of 1989, having accepted a post test flying the Harriers at Dunsfold. Absolute heaven with GR5s, GR7s, RN and Indian navy Sea Harriers, T10s, Hawks and Tornados at Warton. Some epic deliveries to India in the FRS51 Sea Harrier and Hawks to South Korea, Malaysia and Indonesia. Hawk demonstrations in Brunei, Australia, Malaysia and India and a month developing Hawk weapons in South Africa provided hugely enjoyable flying. All this in addition to the development testing and production testing that was the bread and butter of the job.

The only fly in the ointment was ever-increasing problems with my back and especially my neck when at about 4 to 5 G I would find my chin on my chest and no apparent way of raising my head. In mid-1998, I flew my last Harrier trip having lost my medical category to fly on ejection seats. I remained at Dunsfold until its closure in 2000 when I had the chance to fly Airbus A320, A321 and A330s with Airtours. There was a good smattering of ex-Harrier and ex-RAF people with Airtours which was great for breaking the ice. I was really impressed with the initial and ongoing training and the competence of the training captains was remarkable. A very different world from the RAF and BAe though.

In mid-2003, I accepted the offer to rejoin BAE Systems at Farnborough to help with the development of the GR9 with its new mission computer and the start of a whole new chapter in the life of this amazing aeroplane. Even though

Test pilots – TriStar 'plugged in' to Buccaneer tanker. (*Bernie Scott*)

it was a 'ground tour' it was terrific to be so involved in aircraft and systems development again.

After eighteen months at Farnborough the opportunity to test-fly on the Nimrod MRA4 came up and I spent five professionally satisfying years at Warton helping to get this aircraft into service. At the stage it was cancelled it had surpassed any other new aircraft on which I'd worked in that it had a useful, and immediately employable, operational capability. The 2010 SDSR cancelled and destroyed not only an aeroplane but an incredibly powerful, long-range weapons system and lost the expertise of some highly skilled operators. To compound this decision by taking out the only other strategic, worldwide capability in the form of the Harrier and *Ark Royal* was beyond common sense.

I remain immensely proud of my time on the Harrier and feel incredibly privileged to have worked at all levels with some wonderful people. I miss the power and awe that I sensed when watching the 'Jet' come to the hover and dip its nose to the crowds at an air show; I always felt compelled to say to someone close-by, "I used to fly those".

CHAPTER 7

ANOTHER RACING START

ANDY SEPHTON

It was the summer of 1989. I'd just left the RAF and joined Rolls-Royce as a test pilot to carry out the testing of the new Pegasus 11-61 engine for the US Marine Corps. The testing was progressing well when the company marketing people decided to look for a way of showcasing the engine. Their solution was to demo a VTOL with a fully-bombed aircraft at that year's Paris Air Show. I made a couple of throwaway lines about what happened in the 60s when a Harrier was demoed at Paris[2] and made a tongue-in-cheek suggestion that they should consider breaking a world record instead. A few days later, I learned that they had taken up the suggestion.

A search of the rules for such things showed that we might have a chance at beating Bernie Scott's recent time-to-height records for Class H, VSTOL, aircraft. The Rolls-Royce computer model for the aircraft performance with the new engine suggested that the required margin of +3% over existing record times could be exceeded and so planning commenced. There were several Class H records that could have been attempted, some had not even been set at that time, but a stab at Bernie's time-to-climb achievements was chosen, as better publicity would be had by beating a record rather than setting one.

It has to be said that there were many dissenters to the attempt. The time taken to modify, fly and de-modify the aircraft was the reason most often cited for cancellation. Personally, although 'for' the idea in principle, I had some doubts as to the outcome. Bernie had used a stripped-down development batch Harrier, and had made the attempt in very cold conditions – a January day at -10°C if I remember right. We would be using a heavy, instrumented GR5 in the middle of August with expected temperatures in the high 20s.

For non-Harrier operators to understand the problem, one must appreciate that for the Pegasus, thrust falls off with ambient temperature increase at about 100 lbs for every degree Celsius. As the thrust increase of the 11-61 over the existing engine was only about 1,000 lbs in the 'flat-rated' area and our aircraft was some 2,000 lbs heavier than Bernie's, it didn't take much analysis to suggest that we didn't have a hope. On the other hand, one can only increase thrust to a certain point as temperature falls before the engine surges (about +5° C for

---

[2] In 1963, the first P1127, XP831, broke its undercarriage, blocking the VTOL pad for the French rival, Balzac.

Bernie's aircraft) and we had a computer model, which together with the advanced aerodynamics of the Harrier II wing, said we could do it.

As the day approached, several data-gathering profiles were flown at the end of normal test flights in an attempt to prove or disprove the Rolls-Royce computer model. Power used in these attempts was up to the normal limits of the engine, i.e. short lift wet (SLW) or dry for take-off, leading to max thrust for the climb. All took the form of a vertical take-off followed by an acceleration in a slight climb to about 1,000 ft and then a pull, at a predefined G, into a steep climb. Different climb angles were assessed, accelerating or decelerating to a predefined height and/or speed for a final pull up, again at a predefined G, into a vertical zoom climb.

The flying skills demanded of this exercise were quite precise. Any wasted energy in terms of excess drag or speed could lead to a failed attempt. G levels of the order of 1.4 were demanded for the pulls, which were a challenge to hold accurately. Also, much time could be won or lost in raising the gear and flaps during the initial accelerations. The best technique appeared to be to set the nozzles, slam to SLW, then, as the ground break occurred, hit the gear button and simultaneously, quickly but smoothly, move the nozzles aft. For me, the exercises were interesting and useful. They proved the computer model, albeit at reduced power and heavy weight, but more importantly they provided practice for the main event.

The next challenge we had to overcome with the Harrier was that of aircraft configuration. The pylons weighed about 1,000 lbs. They would have to be removed for the attempt to stand any chance of success, but the GR5 we used to test the 11-61 had not been cleared nor requested to fly in that fit. There were no blanking plates in this country and those for the RAF-specific outrigger pylons didn't exist. McDonnell Douglas (MCAIR) were brought in on the act to help with parts and advice. British Aerospace (BAe) were already onside as their Dunsfold chief test pilot, Heinz Frick, had been given operational control of the aircraft for the complete trial. In the event, blanking plates were shipped from the States for the wing pylons and the offending pylons were removed.

The next issue was speed limits. The GR5 was cleared to a minimum of 150 knots IAS (indicated air speed) above 10,000 ft and 200 knots above 20,000 ft. The limitation was apparently for engine considerations, but Rolls-Royce denied any interest in that direction. In fact, the AV-8B, the USMC version of the same aircraft, had no such limitations.

Coincident with the aircraft preparations, the administrative side of the record attempt had to be set up. Ray Kingdon of the Royal Aero Club advised us in this respect and officiated on the day. The required licenses for the two crews, Heinz Frick and myself, were applied for and issued. To verify our attempts, we used a MODAS (modular data acquisition system) that was fitted to the aircraft in a modified ex-Hunter drop tank located on the centreline pylon for recording flight test data.

The day arrived, the aircraft and crews were serviceable and the weather perfect for the attempt. We met in the Rolls-Royce Filton flight test briefing room with representatives from BAe Dunsfold and MCAIR in attendance. This is where the fun started; all three companies had brought their own profiles for getting to the various heights in world record time, and all were significantly different. Which, if any, were correct? It was, after all, the same engine/aircraft combination. The problem now was to be sure which profile to use as we had a limited number of flights and the thrust margin over the existing record was thin, to say the least. After heated discussion, it was decided by myself and Heinz that the Rolls-Royce suggested profile be used for the first attempt to 9,000 metres as at least the Rolls-Royce model had been proven in the build-up.

Heinz stepped in for the first attempt. The flight would include handling to prove and clear the configuration, which had never before been flown. Heinz's first flight included clearing the required low speeds at height and it also gave him the opportunity to practise the profile prior to his first record attempt to 9,000 metres (30,000 ft, approx.). After watching his short test flight, we saw Heinz return to the circuit, land, take up position on the starting grid and then, he was off.

We'd consulted with Ray Kingdon prior to the attempt as to what we were allowed to do. Ray had defined a VTO as having 'no appreciable ground roll', so we set 60° nozzle as the best compromise to achieve fast forward acceleration with no ground roll. After the VTO, the plan was to carry out a level acceleration to 0.5 Mach and then make a 2 G pull to the vertical which should be achieved by 14,700 ft at 0.73 Mach. The aircraft would then continue upwards to pass 9,000 metres at 120 knots in a vertical climb.

SLW was used throughout the climb. Theoretically, water flow was not approved above 10,000 ft so we were briefed to: 'Modulate the thrust accordingly in the 1,000 to 2,000 ft band above 10,000 ft in order to respect this limit'. Heinz and I nodded sagely to the engineer, accepting his advice. He was happy and we, of course, carried out his instructions...well, we would have done, had it been practical or possible.

Heinz was now off to 9,000 metres in 'world record' time, or so we thought. We watched him climb, getting smaller and smaller as he disappeared into the blue, then stop, apparently tail-slide, tumble, topple and finally fall into a dive. Shortly after, he broke into the circuit, performed a vertical landing and taxied in to the questioning looks of the team. He didn't look at all happy.

He saved his comments for the debrief. The aircraft had run out of energy in the climb and the flight had topped out at only 27,000 ft. "What went wrong?" he said turning to the engineer who had derived the profile. "Nothing," responded the engineer. "Anyway, 27,000 ft is not that bad, it's within ten per cent."

It was now my turn, but what should we do? We had, by now, discarded the computer models and locked the representatives of such witchcraft out of the briefing room. The decision was left to myself, Heinz and Jon Taylor, the flight test engineer assisting us at the time. In the ensuing discussion Heinz and I agreed that if I held the nose attitude during the pull up to 45° for 3,000 ft and then continue the pull to the vertical, success may arrive. It did, but I fell out of the sky at 30,500 ft. The last 2,000 ft of the climb took an age. I knew I had beaten the record as I sat watching the altimeter and the stopwatch as 30,000 ft slowly drifted by, but it was clear that the profile still wasn't right.

After falling out of the vertical manoeuvre, I collected the aeroplane and looked for home. Filton was nowhere in sight. The ridiculously low figures indicated on the fuel gauge served only to add to the challenge. I had taken off with 1,200 lbs of fuel on board, a figure below which all self-respecting Harrier pilots would not even leave the circuit, let alone set off on a sortie to high altitude. So, now 'lost' and with no fuel to spare, l must admit to a moment's panic. However, common sense prevailed and I rolled inverted to find Filton directly underneath. I had, after all, just carried out an almost vertical climb to 30,000 ft.

A return to the circuit was followed by the now mandatory run in and break to vertical landing. The instrumentation was downloaded and assessed, all under the watchful eye of Ray. It was declared that Heinz had made 6,000 metres (20,000 ft approx) in record time and I had achieved a new record to 9,000 metres.

In the meantime, the aircraft had been refuelled, turned round and re-instrumented while Heinz and I discussed the profile for his 12,000-metre attempt. What he did is known only to him, but again, he achieved the aim.

For my final flight to 3,000 metres, discussions between the three of us centred on maintaining a minimum drag profile. We believed the minimum drag speed for the configuration the aircraft was in to be around 240 kts, and postulated that a pull of around 2 G would maintain that speed. So, the brief was to take off, accelerate to 240 knots and pull about 2 G. If the aircraft accelerated, pull harder – if it decelerated, slacken off. We underestimated significantly.

With the fuel state now down to 1,000 lbs, the take-off performance was stunning. Following take-off and a brisk acceleration to 240 kts, I pulled to 2 G and with the aircraft still accelerating pulled harder, and harder. I hit the vertical with 4 G on the G meter and 300 kts indicated on the ASI (air speed indicator). A few seconds later I noted the ASI reading 320 knots as I passed 10,000 ft. I throttled back and a hard pull brought me onto my back with the horizon in view and a 180° roll re-achieved straight and level flight.

Following the return to Filton and now sitting in the hover with 750 lbs of fuel left, a bit of VSTOL practice in such a light aeroplane was too good to miss. Two press-ups later I was ready to taxi back for the debrief.

Four times to height records were set that day. Both Heinz and I 'lived' for the required time after the attempts and the instrumentation traces submitted were accepted. Overnight, the aircraft was put back into its 'trial' fit but another day was spent on press demonstrations and interviews before we could continue with the 11-61 engine programme. Local, national and international press recognised the achievement and suitable publicity was gained from the event. Whether it was cost effective or not cannot be confirmed, but what it did do was put the 11-61 engine on the map and achieve increased cohesion within what was always a very effective team.

THE DUCK AND OTHER STICKERS

Close inspection of photographs of the aircraft at the time will reveal a fine collection of stickers on the airframe. At times, both the Rolls-Royce and British Aerospace logos appeared above the wing, both together and individually. For one day, when MCAIR chief Harrier test pilot, Jack Jackson, flew the aircraft, the McDonnell Douglas company logo adorned the machine as well, having been 'stuck' on the under fuselage strakes. But perhaps the most bizarre sticker in the collection was 'The Duck'.

At the beginning of the 11-61 trial, one of the engineers in the flight hangar bought a plastic duck in a local charity competition. The idea was to throw the thing into a river with suitable identification and after its hoped-for return, the longest travelled would be declared as winner. This particular entrant persisted in tangling itself in a reed bed, which was not a good thing for a distance floating competition. Its swimming life was duly declared over and a life of aviation substituted. A logbook was created and 'The Duck', as it was affectionately known, became a welcome stowaway on any flight that the owner could get it on. Look closely and you'll see it somewhere in most of the pictures taken of the aircraft at Rolls-Royce at that time. You'll even see it in the cockpit for the air-to-air photos of the 11-61. Accordingly, a duck-shaped yellow sticker appeared on the side of the aircraft one evening during the programme.

In the middle of the trial, another 'duck' appeared. A little larger than the original, but of the same family background. Such was the feeling at the time that one morning the infiltrator was found hanging from the roof of the hangar with the words, 'There is only enough room for one duck around here', tied around its neck. It was never seen again.

'The Duck' rode in the map pocket on each record flight and so assisted in all four world records. Heinz and I achieved two world records each, but 'The Duck' was unofficially accredited with four!

HEINZ FRICK

GR5 ZD402 was built at Dunsfold as a fully operational aircraft, destined for the RAF. It was fitted with the unique, but standard for Harrier aircraft, 21,500-lb vectored thrust Pegasus 105 engine. But Rolls-Royce had always been keen to develop the engine to achieve an increased thrust of 23,500 lbs, particularly at high ambient temperatures, and so the MoD was persuaded to loan ZD402 to Rolls-Royce, who would install their latest version of the engine, developed for the USMC and known as Pegasus 11-61, at their Filton site.

We felt that such a major development of the aircraft deserved a special colour scheme, and as time was critical, I designed the blue colour scheme which was quickly accepted by everyone. For the standard production flight schedule, I flew it in just primer finish. Given that it will have taken hundreds of engineers on both sides of the Atlantic to build the many parts that were finally assembled at Dunsfold, it was always a privilege and a pleasure to be the first to fly an aircraft. For this first flight, the engine was a standard Pegasus 105. The engine handling tests were carried out to determine the base line for future tests. This included shutting the engine down and then relighting it, always a hazardous exercise in a single-engine aircraft, particularly one not known for its gliding performance; the word 'brick' comes to mind.

The record-breaking jet. (BAE Systems)

With the special colour scheme and the 11-61 engine fitted, the stage was set. On 9 June 1989 everything was ready, so, in anticipation and with a little anxiety, I strapped myself into the Martin-Baker ejection seat, the 'just in case' final option, and started up. In the event, that first of the test flights was almost a non-event in that everything went as planned. A further series of intensive flight tests then followed, covering all aspects of engine handling at high altitude and high angles of attack, down to low altitude high G manoeuvres. Relights were again carried out and strain gauges on the engine compressor blades and stators measured the loads within the engine. All these tests proved satisfactory, and it was decided that on 14 August Andy and I would attempt time-to-height records to 3,000, 6,000, 9,000 and 12,000 metres.

The flight profile varied slightly for each attempt, and the theoretical plan quickly changed to a seat of the pants plan. Observers from the FIA were present, and air traffic cleared the airspace above Filton to 45,000 ft.

I flew the first attempt to 12,000 metres. With the nozzles down, I slammed the engine to full power, moved the nozzle lever forward as soon as lift-off occurred, then retracted the undercarriage and raised the flaps. Acceleration was spectacular to 450 kts, and the nose was then raised to 45°. At 17,000 ft, the plan was to climb vertically to establish the record to 12,000 metres (39,360 ft). This profile did not feel quite right, and whilst I beat the record to 6,000 metres, we changed subsequent attempts to a different profile. Andy then flew the aircraft, and broke the 3,000 and 9,000-metre records.

It was my turn again for 12,000 metres and with everyone listening on the radio I proceeded to go. I called out the heights, and with having to control the engine manually to maintain maximum thrust, I had little time to admire the view. I passed 40,000 ft absolutely vertical with the speed rapidly falling through 80 kts. Having recovered the aircraft, I looked down to see the airfield right below me and I spiralled down for a run in and break to a vertical landing. What a fantastic ride! At the end of that busy day we sat down and looked at the figures, which were as follows:

VTO – 3,000 metres	36.38 seconds	Andy Sephton
VTO – 6,000 metres	55.38 seconds	Heinz Frick
VTO – 9,000 metres	81.00 seconds	Andy Sephton
VTO – 12,000 metres	126.63 seconds	Heinz Frick

I have been lucky to have enjoyed a wonderful aviation career, having flown some of the world's best jets, and I have been supported by the most outstanding engineers and friends. The Harrier, I have no doubt, is the most versatile and cost-effective fighter of its era.

CHAPTER 8
GR5 INTRODUCTION

JONATHAN BAYNTON

The end of the Falklands War found me and other 3(F) Squadron pilots living in a tented encampment on Ascension Island, thousands of miles from anywhere, in the middle of the Atlantic Ocean. The plan had been for us to join the Task Force by sailing from Ascension in a commandeered North Sea ferry. The plan had now changed; we waited around for a few more days and then climbed aboard a Hercules C-130 for the most uncomfortable thirteen hours I had ever had in an aeroplane. We had to refuel twice from the Victor refuelling tanker that accompanied us. Each time, in order that our slow C-130 could keep up with the Victor, this took place in a screaming dive, followed by a climb back up to our original altitude. Eventually we reached the Falklands.

I was the 3(F) Squadron qualified flying instructor; the squadron was at the peak of its game and there was nothing we thought we couldn't do. Prior to the Falklands War breaking out the squadron had been preparing for Maple Flag 9, a huge exercise involving air forces from several countries in NATO, which would take place at Cold Lake in Canada. This had involved an ultra low-flying work up in the UK. We spent all our time over the Scottish Highlands 100 ft above the ground at speeds between 420 and 480 knots. We attacked simulated targets whilst being bounced by 'enemy' aircraft. We dropped practice bombs on Tain Range and strafed the targets there. Then in Canada we did more of the same: this time dropping concrete 1,000-lb bombs, firing full pods of HE SNEB rockets and strafing with HE 30-mm cannon.

The exercise was supposed to last for four weeks but the Falklands War intervened. The message came to drop all the weapons and get the aeroplanes back to the UK, oh, and P.S., there would be no tanker support for air-to-air refuelling. Even with the ferry tanks that doubled our fuel capacity we could only fly a thousand miles at a time, so we hopped the aircraft from Cold Lake to Winnipeg; to Bagotville; to Goose Bay. Then north to Sondrestrom (the only time I have ever flown with a point of no return), then to Keflavik, to Lossiemouth and home. The whole trip took four days but we did it and it was a journey to remember. The view after take-off from Sondrestrom up over the snow and ice plateaux of Greenland was spectacular.

That was 1982; the following year my tour was extended and I continued my career very happily as the 3 Squadron QFI, based at Gütersloh. Then, unfortunately, the OCU at Wittering suffered a mid-air collision between a T4 with John Leeming and a student on board, and a GR3 flown by Dave Oakley. Both pilots in the T4 died.

The OCU was now short of QFIs so in August 1983 I left 3 and returned to the UK to join the staff of B Squadron on 233 OCU. A year later I was promoted to squadron leader and took over B Squadron from Bobby Eccles.

By this time the GR3 was growing elderly and the introduction of its replacement, the GR5, started to come into focus. Questions were asked by the MoD as to how the OCU would convert GR3 pilots to the new aircraft. MoD had a budget of around £1.4 million for training devices, and I started trying to work out a training plan. It was soon obvious that flying the new aeroplane would not be difficult for a GR3 pilot. However, getting to grips with the avionics and weapons system would be more of a challenge.

Together with the OCU boss, Wing Commander Steve Jennings, I decided to see what other training units were doing and to investigate new training technology. The GR5 engineering school seemed to be further down the line in these things than the OCU so I managed to piggy back on their visits to industry.

I remember that Steve and I formulated the plan as we drove back from Coningsby one day in his boss' RAF Mini. It would be a stepping stone approach: computer-based training (CBT) with touch screens to teach how to use the up-front controller and multi-function displays then a Harrier avionics system trainer (HAST) to consolidate the CBT work and teach the use of HOTAS (hands on throttle and stick) in conjunction with the angle rate bombing system (ARBS). Simulator training would then follow before touching the aeroplane. No two-seater trainer aircraft would be required, which was a good job because the RAF at the time was not going to buy any.

I must have been in the right place at the right time because shortly after that on

The GR5 HCT. From left: Andy Gollege, Jonathan Baynton, Pete Walmsley and Pete Brockhaus

9 April 1986 the composition of the Harrier GR5 Conversion Team (HCT) was announced. I was to be OC, Pete Walmsley (Wal) and Andy Golledge (Gol) were to be the other two QWI pilots. In addition Squadron Leader Pete Brockhausen (Teach), an educator, was to be part of the team as the training design advisor (TDA). I stayed as OC B Squadron for the time being and the two QWIs continued on A Squadron doing their thing there. The HCT's contact in the MoD was Wing Commander Horace Farquhar-Smith. He suggested that the HCT would benefit from a tour around various training establishments in the States. Thus began the first of three stateside trips for the HCT (though, sadly, Gol wasn't financed to come on the first one).

We flew to Washington then on to LAX and up to Fresno to visit the USN F-18 training unit there. They used CBT for initial training but then missed out the intermediate stage avionics system trainer, putting their pilots instead straight into the simulator. From Fresno we flew to Phoenix to visit the Center for Advanced Airmanship. This was a civilian training unit in the centre of town but they did all the ground training for the T-38 students at the nearby USAF base. This purpose-built establishment was impressive not only in the way the learning was targeted but also the facilities it offered students. All the training records were computerised and it was very easy to track progress and re-visit a particular area a student might be having difficulties with.

From Phoenix we flew to MCAS Cherry Point, the US Marine Corps home of the Harrier. This is a massive base where we saw how they set about training their pilots to fly their new Harrier, the AV-8B. Squadron Leader Chris Moran[3] was the RAF exchange officer at Cherry Point; he was already flying the AV-8B and was instrumental in introducing us to the aeroplane, or rather the simulator. Their sim had no motion, but a fixed cockpit in a large dome with the world projected onto the inside of the dome. We also tried out their procedure trainer which turned out to be a valuable lesson and pointer for the way we wanted to go for ours. In theirs you sat and watched it fly a pre-programmed scenario and you made the switches to match. Wal and I decided there and then that this was not much value and it would be significantly enhanced if one was able to fly it in pitch and roll. When we returned to the UK we were able to get the ability to fly our procedures trainer written into the specification that MoD had already drawn up.

Back on the OCU training GR3 pilots continued. The navy (who were trained in the art of VSTOL by B Squadron) were given the push because the OCU would soon no longer be teaching Harrier Mark 1 type VSTOL. The HCT continued both its day job of GR3 training while liaising with the firms who had been given the contracts to supply the CBT (Rediffusion in Crawley) and

---

[3] Air Chief Marshal Sir Chris Moran died in 2010, competing in a triathlon. He was C-in-C Air Command.

the HAST (Marconi in Edinburgh). We were initially invited to meetings with Singer Link Miles about the sim but were kicked out of a meeting with them and MoD procurement when we asked what we thought were pertinent questions. That was the end of our involvement with the sim[4].

The plan was for the HCT's GR5 conversion to be flown with BAe at Dunsfold in the autumn of '87, having first spent another month at Cherry Point doing the USMC ground school and simulator course. However, in the late summer of '87 there was a tragic accident. BAe test pilot Taylor Scott was flying a production air test on what should have been the HCT's second aeroplane when he was forcibly dragged from the aircraft at 25,000 ft. The manual separation rocket had fired, his seat harness released and his parachute pulled him from the cockpit. The parachute was shredded by the broken canopy and he fell to his death. The aircraft flew on for another couple of hours and crashed into the Atlantic. The GR5 was grounded for six months while the accident was investigated.

In light of this delay the MoD decided the HCT should go back to Cherry Point and complete a ten-hour conversion with the USMC. This we did and I have to say that flying the AV-8B was a delight, though flying the USMC way was not so easy. Some strange (or maybe just different) SOPs, borrowed helmet and flying kit, engine running refuels at the end of a sortie, not to mention the different rules and regulations in the US made it a challenging but great fun ten hours.

The final trip summed up our time there. The three of us were led to the range by a high ranking USMC pilot. After we had dropped our bombs I came off target as number two and looked for the lead where I would have expected to see an RAF pilot… but there was no sign. Where had he gone? Oh well, never mind; Wal and Gol had joined up with me with no difficulty. After a few radio calls I spotted him and led my three-ship to join up with him. In the debrief he did admit that when he saw this tight formation of three AV-8Bs flown by three Brits bearing down on him he wondered if maybe he had missed a vital part of the brief.

The HCT returned to the UK and continued flying the GR3 and T4 whilst preparing for the new aeroplane with more knowledge now that we had actually flown it. The GR5 was still grounded and there were now problems with the OBOGS. These were to do with it having to be modified to allow the RAF to breathe an air/oxygen mixture rather than the 100% O_2 that the USMC breathed. In addition there were problems with the Ferranti inertial platform which was to replace the Litton platform of the AV-8B. In the end this was temporally solved by borrowing Litton platforms for the first couple of years of RAF service. Eventually on 30 March 1988 the GR5 was given a release to service. There were

---

[4] Bob Marston – I was the pilot representative on the USA simulator procurement visits. Flying the AV-8B sim and research back in Bedford convinced us that full motion was needed.

a few restrictions; that the aircraft was not to be flown above 10,000 feet was the main one that affected us. In addition, the engineers had to take the seat out every ten hours for inspection/servicing. However, we could get airborne. The first flight of the GR5 ZD324 took off from Wittering at 1715 hours on 30 March with me at the controls and Wal in the tower to offer support. It lasted 1 hour 15 minutes; the aircraft performed as advertised and was still fully serviceable at the end of it. Wal and Gol flew the aircraft the next day and over the next six weeks the three of us flew the conversion syllabus to ratify it. More aircraft arrived from Dunsfold and the HCT was able to run its first course, consisting of, in the fine traditions of the RAF, the 'wheels' (senior officers).

Around this time the MoD were also getting increasingly anxious about the lack of a simulator. I pointed out that there were indeed a number of simulators in service in the world. There were the ones at Cherry Point and Yuma but nearer to home the Spanish navy had an EAV-8B simulator down at Rota in southern Spain. A quick visit was arranged for me to fly the Spanish sim and assess whether or not it would be viable to use for training and to ratify a GR3/T4 instrument rating for the GR5. It was a fixed-base sim and although it did not fly particularly well it was representative enough to do the job, besides which I saw an opportunity for a spot of R & R for the boys. So it was that each conversion course ended with a week in the sun in Spain with me operating the sim. An HS125 from Northolt would pitch into Wittering first thing on a Monday, fly me and the course down to Rota where we would spend the morning lazing around the pool or playing tennis then go to the sim for the afternoon slot. Then on the Friday the HS125 would fly us home to Wittering. In 1989 I made ten visits to Spain but unfortunately my tennis never got any better. Slim Whitman helped out with the 1 Squadron pilots and when 3(F) Squadron pilots started converting I handed over the mantle of EAV-8B sim instructor to Andy Kirkpatrick, their QFI.

The HCT was a great unit to be on; the three of us converted over sixty GR3 pilots to the GR5 in just over the year. That is a record I'm still very proud of. What is more, there were no major incidents or accidents. We had eight aeroplanes of our own and we were really able to use them as we wanted. On one occasion during the not-above-10,000 ft restriction I took one to Rota, with stops in Bordeaux and Madrid for fuel. ATC could not really understand why I was flying so low.

I was never a fan of being a display pilot in the RAF but as boss of the HCT I thought I should do it and so I ended up doing countless displays both at Wittering and other aerodromes for VIPs from royalty to the head of Chinese armed forces.

British Aerospace wanted to borrow an aeroplane to take to the Dubai 89 air show; the first they had held there. MoD, bless them, said yes but only if an RAF pilot was to fly it. By now there was one jet which was allowed above 10,000 ft, ZD330, so it had to be that one. Chris Moran, who was now back from the

USMC, was picked as my back-up. An AAR probe was fitted and Chris and I flew a couple of sorties practising AAR. Then it was off to the show. Chris flew the leg to Akrotiri and I flew to Dubai the next day. There was a slight concern during the second AAR refuelling: during the bracket over Egypt, the fuel wouldn't flow through either the port or the starboard hose. The hoses were reeled back in and out. The port hose on the VC10 was much easier to use as you only had to fly up the line of the aircraft's fuel dump nozzle and the probe would go straight in. Unfortunately I found myself on the starboard side. However, having missed on my first attempt, I eventually got fuel.

The show committee in Dubai was astonished that I didn't want a practice before going for my display authorisation. Other pilots were taking two or three attempts to get it. The fact was, though, that I had flown the display so many times by now that it was pretty much second nature to me. I flew my display in front of them and the authorisation was granted.

The show lasted five days with the Harrier the second display each day, which gave Chris and me plenty of time to enjoy champagne in the hospitality chalets. I think it was only then that I realised that the public perceived our job as a Harrier pilot to be glamorous. Chris flew one of the displays and then took the aircraft down to Abu Dhabi to do another along the Corniche there. The VC10 stayed there for the week as well, so not a bad deployment for any of us.

In July 1989 I made the decision to leave the RAF and join BA. I had flown 265

Jonathan Baynton and Chris Moran in Dubai. (Jonathan Baynton)

hours on the GR5 in under two years, as well as another 50 odd on the GR3 and T4 in that same period; 2,300 hours in total on all marks of Harrier. Two flying tours as a squadron leader had scuppered my promotion prospects in the RAF. Steve Jennings and I had discussed this before I took the job as boss of the HCT but it was an opportunity that I would never have turned down. I think my views on flying versus that of a career officer stared me in the face when the logbooks of two group captains on the conversion course crossed my desk: despite their much longer RAF service they both had nearly 1,000 fewer flying hours than me.

My career in BA will come to an end in a couple of years after twenty-seven years with the airline. Undoubtedly the best bit of this was being in at the start of the introduction to service of another aeroplane, the Boeing 787 Dreamliner. History repeated itself for me: a new RAF aeroplane then a new airliner. How lucky and privileged I have been.

CHRIS BENN

Between 1988 and the end of 1991, I was a flight commander on 1(F) Squadron, and our role was to bring the GR5 into squadron service. The period was overshadowed by the realisation that the GR5 was in fact going to be short lived, and all the real operational capability was to be vested in its successor variants. At a push, the GR5 could have fired Sidewinders and dropped unguided bombs (BL755 was still the weapon of choice at the time). Otherwise this was a period when other units with other aircraft were to be involved in operations.

Heavily reliant on electrics for a variety of services, the GR5 was one of the first truly electric jets, and was, at least in the early stages, an aircraft that had plenty of unusual electrically induced incidents. The Kapton wiring made pilots wary of electrical incidents that could also be indicative of a fire. This was always in the minds of the aircrew when flying this aircraft and caused a number of incidents that certainly grabbed one's attention at the time. This first tale recalls the only occasion on which I had to seriously contemplate ejecting from a Harrier.

In March 1990, almost exactly a year to the day after I started flying the GR5, 1(F) Squadron deployed to Bardufoss on a routine training exercise for the 'Northern Option'. Bardufoss at that time of year is still snow covered and the runway is ice with a generous sprinkling of small gravel particles to aid adhesion, of which there isn't much. As an aside, one night during this deployment, the SAS MD-81 airliner which routinely landed late at night had performed a 360° skid on the runway during the landing run when one of the thrust reversers failed to deploy properly. In true Norwegian style everyone seemed very relaxed about it, especially as the aircraft was undamaged.

The flying day was very short because of the sun's position. Excess use of power was obviously heavily discouraged as it tended to result in unpredictable skidding from which there was little hope of recovery before hitting the nearest snow bank; taxi speeds were kept under control with judicious use of nozzle and partial closure of the HP cock to reduce idling RPM, while of course watching the JPT as the air flow through the engine reduced. Take-offs and landings were carried out singly.

My wingman on this occasion was Tony 'Nozzer' Norris; I was duly grateful to him at a later stage. Plenty of people taking off from Bardufoss have visited Sweden by forgetting about the proximity of the border a few minutes flying time from the eastern end of the runway; however on this occasion we departed VFR from the 8,000 ft strip and took the second valley on the left to carry out simulated attacks on a couple of dummy targets, and take a look at the blue ice that can be found on some of the 8,000 ft peaks to the north, familiarising ourselves with the wonderful geography of the region. Norway is fabulous flying country when the weather is fine.

The GR5 and its successors had a generous cockpit and very well laid-out controls to the typical McDonnell Douglas/Boeing layout, very similar to the F-18; this was useful on the occasions when, such as this one, pilots wore the full arctic survival dress of immersion suit with the bunny suit underneath. Once in the seat it was easy to forget that you were closely related to Mr Bibendum, the Michelin man. As the sortie progressed it was easy to relax and enjoy the view through the enormous canopy, while monitoring the formation's position on the excellent navigation suite. Nothing could go wrong…

Just as the view of the blue ice was particularly compelling, with the sunlight catching it to make a very fine picture, the peace of the cockpit was shattered by a cacophony of warnings. On looking inside, my initial impression was that just about every warning was on; Jonathan Baynton had once told us there are over ninety possible warnings on the aircraft, most of them on a substantial panel on the right-hand side by the pilot's knee. My thoughts instantly went to the dreaded Kapton wiring and the prospect of an internal fire somewhere, so my first reaction was to tighten the seat straps in case I had to leave the scene. However, some hope was restored when I determined that the FIRE caption was out, the engine was running, the flying controls were operative; however, the upfront controller had taken time out, and the navigation display and HUD were no longer any use.

GR5 cockpit. (BAE Systems)

I carried out some immediate actions including trying to reset the alternator, and starting the auxiliary power unit which had a smaller generator of its own; neither of these were successful, so I made a couple of calls to Nozzer who was about two miles away on the beam in defensive battle formation. Nothing was happening with the radios either, so I tried the secondary radio controls – no response.

I waggled the wings to attract Nozzer's attention and call him towards me, and promptly wished I hadn't as the aircraft was not its usual responsive self. Closer inspection of the still well-illuminated warning panel showed that the SAAHS light was on; this meant that the stability augmentation and attitude holding system was inoperative. A good deal of adverse roll/yaw coupling was evident, and resultant Dutch roll, so I stopped waggling and regained control, finding that plenty of concentration was required to synchronise rudder inputs into the turns and to avoid pilot induced oscillations. Luckily, Nozzer had got the message.

The HEFOE code is a wonderful comfort in these situations – countless lives must have been saved by making simple easy-to-understand hand signals that tell your wingman you have an electrical problem and want to go home, and so we turned for Bardufoss without further delay. I focused on completing all the drills I could find in the flight reference cards that might improve the situation but my recollection is that while the cacophony could be largely silenced, the Blackpool illuminations were still in evidence.

Due to the state of the runway at Bardufoss, the SOP landing procedure was to carry out a 90-knot partially jet-borne landing; touching down at speeds above this would provide something of a stopping challenge, especially as some of the available braking run was going to be consumed by slowing from about 50 knots, the minimum for use of braking stop retardation, the foot brakes being pretty much useless on the ice. Touching down slower than this was assessed to be likely to damage the ice surface of a runway largely used by airliners. Below 50 knots with the nozzles in the braking stop the engine would re-ingest its own jet wake, together with some of the gravel from the runway surface. Given my still evident handling issues with the GR5 'bath tub in a heavy swell', I had to consider carefully what the options were.

The plan was to position for a straight-in approach, decelerate progressively to 90 knots and assess the handling before committing to the final descent. Once committed, touch down on the end of the runway, go to maximum braking stop and kill speed. If the nose-wheel steering wasn't working, stay straight using reaction controls as long as possible (50 knots probably), or if directional control failed, either roll off the runway into the snow, or more dramatically, pull the undercarriage up, stopcock the engine and toboggan. Ejection remained an option throughout[5], except when three hands might be required.

As the speed slowed in response to my lowering the nozzles, it was evident that a further set of forces had entered my flight control world. At first, the reaction controls made coordination more difficult but then as speed reduced towards wing stalling speed, the aerodynamic inputs to the aircraft's flight path were overcome by the reaction controls and life became simpler again. At the point where commitment to the landing was necessary, I initiated a brisk descent. I was later told by an onlooker that there was no doubt it was going to land. I cushioned the landing with a handful of power, touched down well, and closed the throttle, put the nozzles in the braking stop and re-opened the throttle to about 65% in a well-practised movement. Thankfully the nose-wheel steering was operative. The roll-out was uneventful and I managed to get the aircraft off the runway and back to the flight line without further incident.

Undoubtedly this could have been a much more hazardous emergency. Flight in IMC or in formation would likely have proved impossible without SAAHS

---

[5] Bob Marston – In 1971, Steve Jennings found otherwise, upside down in the Norwegian snow. This story is in *Harrier Boys Volume One*.

(has anyone tried it?), and with nowhere else to go, ejection would have moved closer to the top of the option list. However, by sticking to basics, focusing on flying the aircraft and letting Nozzer know what was wrong, the situation was kept in check with plenty of options.

Fast forward to May 1991 and the squadron is at Nellis for the first GR5 Red Flag. Given that the 1(F) team was fully worked up, and that the team of supporting pilots from the OCU were clearly experienced, you could be forgiven for thinking this would be pretty much SOP. There was an underlying glitch however; the only diversion within Harrier range was Indian Springs where the runway was partially out of commission for resurfacing before the arrival of Predators. The briefed procedure for this sortie was to use the out-of-commission secondary runway at Nellis as the crash diversion, relying on Harrier partially jet-borne performance to compensate for lack of runway length, should both the 10,000 ft runways be unavailable. The calculations showed that even if aircraft weight was reduced to a minimum, the aircraft would not hover at airfield altitude that day.

Soon after launching our eight-ship formation, a general recall was announced for weather; the thunderstorms that had been dismissed as unlikely had materialised. Safety dictated that with some aircraft with weapons on, we should all be recalled from any possibility of lightning strikes. The inevitable occurred, and the first two F-16s to land, complete with weapons, overshot the runway and collected the overshoot cables, effectively closing the runway at the critical instant.

On arrival at Nellis it became clear that most of the fleet had been directed to the tankers and diverted to other locations across western and central US; unfortunately we had probe and drogue refuelling gear, not boom receivers, so no tanker option. We all set about dumping fuel in the local area and queued up to land on the old disused runway as briefed (apparently using the remaining parts of the parallel main runways was discounted by the USAF duty pilot, by this time of colonel rank). The first aircraft across the threshold may have been keen to make full use of the space available, but anyway the downwash from the engine, which was considerable given the power settings being used, lifted the ageing tarmac from the concrete base and shredded it across the surrounding desert – each subsequent aircraft doing much the same, until someone made a call about FOD and the need to keep well clear of the man in front.

In an effort to avoid adding to the destruction I tried to avoid the threshold, using power to sustain altitude while decelerating, trying to delay my touchdown for a while longer while carefully watching the aircraft in front; at this stage I felt a restriction in the throttle. I suddenly realised that despite water injection, I was at 'max chat' and there was pretty much nothing left.

Focusing on the HUD, I realised that the power-remaining indicator, a hexagonal symbol which grew to completion as the last vestiges of thrust were

Top left: GR5 head-on, AAR probe extended. (Rick Brewell)
Top right: GR5 firing Sidewinder AAM. (BAE Systems)
Above: Pilot's view before take-off from CVS. (Ben Sargent)
Left: 1(F) Squadron GR5s in winter camouflage. (BAE Systems)

GR5 with trial load of inert BL755 CBU (BAE Systems)

ZD462 being lifted onto deck of HMS *Invincible*. (Author

GR5 mishap at Gütersloh. (RAF Gütersloh)

Top: 3(F) Squadron GR5 taking off from the road at Eberhard. (BAE Systems)
Above: GR5 grass runway trials. (Henry deCourcier)

Opposite top: Sea Harrier FA2 with AMRAAM. (BAE Systems)
Opposite bottom: Pilot in a GR7 cockpit, showing an excellent view. (Ben Sargent)

Top: GR7 with USN Viking tanker. (Mark Zanker)
Bottom: GR7s dispensing flares. (Andrew Suddards)

Top: TIALD pod with fuselage mounting in Gioia del Colle. (Mark Zanker)
Bottom: IV Squadron GR7 and T10. (Rick Brewell)

10 rear seat head-up display. (Andrew Suddards)

Stern view of CVS, as seen by pilot on final approach. (Mark Zanker)

IV(AC) Squadron GR3 and GR7. (BAE Systems)

Left: IV(AC) Squadron GR7 looping. (Geoffrey Lee)
Below: 20(R) Squadron group shot. (20 Squadron)
Bottom: GR7 over the Blue Hole, Belize. (Andrew Suddards)

20(R) SQN
RAF WITTERING 2nd NOVEMBER 200

used, had completed itself and had the 'Billy Whizz' extension which looked like the peak of a cap. It was at this stage that I discovered that by moving the stick forward and hence lowering the nose, the aircraft would stop descending as the airspeed picked up; moving the stick rearwards had the opposite effect and the rate of descent increased again. Well why not? Making use of this newly-discovered technique for a full-power landing, I successfully touched down and after the usual rapid braking stop application arrived under control and taxied back in.

My subsequent discussions with test pilots, usually after a couple of beers, left me in no doubt that venturing into far corners of the flight envelope was not a good idea, most often because the descriptions provided in the aircrew manual are based on the only time the test pilot went into that little corner. Now no-one will ever be able to try it out...

CHAPTER 9

DISPLAYS

Throughout its history, the Harrier has been a show-stopper at flying displays. Its unique abilities have thrilled spectators, who have been drawn away from rival attractions by the unmistakable sound of the mighty Pegasus. It could fly displays from airfields inaccessible to other jets, such as those with short runways or grass strips, and it could put on a display in pretty bad weather, if only in the hover. This popularity soon made the Harrier known to a wide cross section of the public. However, before the Falklands War, it also led to it being dismissed by rival operators as nice entertainment, but not a serious fighting machine.

Over the years, Harrier displays also taught quite a few lessons – sometimes at a high cost. In his displays, John Farley, the manufacturer's test pilot, flew some remarkable manoeuvres, using his deep knowledge of the aircraft's capabilities and limitations. His repertoire included one display in which he flew backwards while leading a formation of helicopters, and another where he yawed through multiple rotations while flying the length of the runway, a manoeuvre which any military pilot would approach with great caution.

He also pioneered the steep climb from the hover, notably against

Farnborough formation.
(BAE Systems)

the dramatic Alpine background in a demonstration in Switzerland, using a technique known as rotating around the nozzles. This technique required simultaneous raising of the aircraft nose as the nozzles were moved from the hover stop to fully aft, starting from the hover and ending with a steep climb away. It was essential to note that at the start of the manoeuvre, reaction controls were being used, while at the end, aerodynamic controls had taken over. The engine air bleed to the reaction controls would be closed shortly after the nozzle angle reduced through 20°, so by that stage, flying speed was needed. Geoff Hulley found this in Cyprus, when his reaction controls stopped before he had elevator authority and the nose of the aircraft rapidly fell to vertically down. He ejected just in time, but landed, injured, in the burning wreckage. Fortunately, a heroic rescuer, an RAF physical training instructor, was on hand to pull him clear.

Another pitfall resulted from a popular means of ending a display from the hover when, as was often the case, the surface was unsuitable for vertical landing. This was achieved by using some braking stop nozzle angle to get the jet flying backwards, then pitching nose down to translate this to forward motion, and descending for a rolling landing. Again, the balance between aerodynamic and reaction controls was the key. The whole manoeuvre was straightforward if only reaction controls were effective, but if the rearward

Geoff Hulley's ejection.
(Unknown)

speed was sufficient to give aerodynamic effect to the tailplane, it would act in reverse, effectively becoming a canard pitch control at the front of the direction of travel. Having started the nose pitching down, the pilot could find that on moving the control column aft, despite the reaction control under the nose trying to raise it, the tailplane would produce a greater force causing the nose to pitch down. Brian Weatherley lost his life at the end of a display when he ejected after the nose of his jet pitched down beyond 90°.

Nick Slater learned about runway surfaces at Bex in Switzerland. It was basically a grass strip, but with a U-shaped piece of tarmac, with threshold markings, where aircraft turned to line up for take-off. Nick did his engine checks on the tarmac, then set off to start his display, not seeing the complete hard surface blown away by the Harrier's jet blast. Nick later died in a Harrier crash when he commanded the SAOEU.

Bex runway. (Author)

The Harrier water injection system held 50 gallons of demineralised water that could be injected, as demanded by the pilot, into the rear section of the engine. This both cooled the engine, allowing higher rpm to be used, and in cooling the air flowing through, made it more dense, so increasing thrust. The water would last for about 90 seconds, so it had to be used only when needed to enhance take-off or landing performance. It could also be the source of some amusement, as in Pete Day's story in Volume One, when his ground crew convinced Guatemalan observers in Belize that the water was being used as fuel.

I inadvertently caused similar amazement at a later demonstration to some sappers in a UK training area. They had built a Harrier site, so I flew a jet in to prove that it worked, and to show them around the aircraft. Another pilot, Glenn Edge, was on the ground with a radio-equipped Land Rover for safety purposes. When the time came to depart, I strapped in and tried to start up, but nothing happened. After trying all the tricks we could think of, we used a phone found tied to a nearby tree (this was before mobile phones) to call base, and were advised that it sounded like the relay that was switched by external power being plugged in, which would prevent the battery feeding the starter. So I climbed in again, pressed the starter button and signalled to Glenn, who kicked the rear fuselage near the external power socket. The engine burst into life, and the sappers were most impressed by the pilot literally kick-starting a Harrier.

Nick Gilchrist was just unlucky when his water pump exploded during his display, wrecking the engine and causing him to eject. As a result, a containment structure was fitted around the pump to avoid such damage in the future. However, this did take time, so I flew a lot of displays without water injection, which limited the available performance.

At Lowestoft in 2002, Tony Cann fell foul of the 'two levers, one left hand' conundrum. A brief movement of the wrong lever caused the aircraft to fall into the sea, with the pilot ejecting safely, but breaking his ankle as he landed on top of his jet. As in Geoff Hulley's Cyprus experience, this again showed that ejection from a hovering aircraft may well leave the pilot close to the crash.

Lowestoft recovery.
(Geoff Lee)

Less dramatically, I learned a lesson about trying too hard to satisfy people with a display at Wittering. The audience was to be the army staff college, who would be watching from the control tower. My station commander was very keen that we should show the army that the RAF could be relied on even in less than perfect weather, so at the appointed time, I taxied out despite a distinct lack of visibility. Still wondering how I would find the runway in the gathering fog, I taxied along the southern taxiway, which passed between the runway and the control tower. Fortunately, the controller called when he saw my lights in front of the tower, so

I stopped there. There being little chance of anyone seeing any flying over the runway, I opted to perform a rolling vertical take-off into a low hover to test what might be possible. In the hover, I yawed through 90° to face the tower and pondered what else could be done. This led to an effect rather like the WW2 FIDO fog-clearing equipment, as the hot air from my jet cleared a bubble of good visibility around me. Foolishly emboldened by this, I banked slightly to move sideways. As I moved slowly one way, my bubble of clear air blew away rather more rapidly in the opposite direction. I settled into the hover once more, yawed through a further 90°, and landed pointing back where I had come from. The army were suitably impressed, but the real lack of visibility became apparent when I found myself accelerating as I taxied downhill. That told me I had reached 1 Squadron, having missed the turn-off for the OCU. Fortunately, I managed to turn round and get back before anyone saw me.

As well as the solo displays, various formation demonstrations showed off the Harrier's excellent suitability for close formation flying. With a small wingspan, high wing loading, abundant thrust and drag, and high control authority, it was a delight to fly in formation. In order to get tactical formations away from and back to airfields expeditiously and in any weather, all pilots were very skilled and current in close formation flying. Two early experiences of Harrier formation displays are related below, from Graham Williams as OC 3(F) Squadron and Jock Heron when on IV(AC) Squadron.

GRAHAM WILLIAMS: THE QUEEN'S BIRTHDAY FLY-PAST

1973 was memorable on account of the Queen's birthday fly-past at Rheindahlen. The plan was for a sixteen-aircraft fly-past of the parade ground at the headquarters of RAF Germany at Rheindahlen. It would be led by four Phantoms, followed by four Buccaneers, then four Lightnings and, finally at the back end, four Harriers. Each section had an airborne spare just in case anyone went unserviceable.

The first couple of rehearsals went pretty well but the final full dress rehearsal was a different story. The weather was appalling and as were going around the racetrack route, the whole formation went into cloud. Almost immediately the leader in the F4s declared 'everyman for himself' and that the fly-past was cancelled. Being down at the back end I could see what was coming and, with my airborne spare, I ducked beneath the cloud. So I headed back towards Wildenrath and, as I did so, I saw Rheindahlen through the mist and rain. I looked at my watch, saw that the timing would be about right, and decided that at least the Harriers would put on a show. So I called in the airborne spare, forgetting that there was a flying order which expressly forbade formations of more than four aircraft (for some unknown reason), and we flew from north to south instead of west to east across the main parade ground about fifteen seconds early on the schedule.

I thought no more about it and returned to Wildenrath. I had to keep the five aircraft airborne for fifty minutes to ensure that we met our monthly flying target again. So I passed the time by giving the airfield the benefit of our formation-flying expertise. And as I turned downwind to land, I got the message that the squadron commander was to report to the station commander as soon as he landed. I realised I had in some way sinned but really could not think what it was that had caused such a violent reaction.

As we walked in from the line, Terry Nash, who had been number three in the formation, thought the station commander might want to congratulate us on achieving the flying target. I said that I did not think so. Ten minutes later, I am standing in front of the station commander and I find out what the problem was. It turned out that the leader of the Phantoms, Derek Bryant, having said that he was cancelling the fly-past, had neglected to say that he was going to carry on with just his four aircraft. So, fifteen seconds after I had flown over the parade from north to south, four Phantoms came across west to east, threading the so-called needle.

Whilst the effect was quite spectacular, it was not quite what was required or expected. I had sinned and George Black left me in no doubt that I had sinned; in fact I had to class it as one of the finest bollockings that I have ever received. George has told me since that when we flew past, his chest swelled with pride that his boys had made it despite the weather. Just for fifteen seconds that was, until the Phantoms came from the other direction. The then group captain ops at Rheindahlen, a certain Laurie Jones, went apoplectic with rage. And thus on the following Monday, after a Phantom from Brüggen had crashed, it was no surprise when I found myself as the president of the Board of Inquiry. But I cannot say that I appreciated the telephone calls from Derek Bryant (aka Doctor Death) who kept cackling down the line at me that he could 'hear the chains rattling'.

JOCK HERON: FOUR'S FOUR

After the 1975 spring deployment I was asked for a squadron contribution towards two major RAF Open Days which were to take the form of air displays at Wildenrath and Gütersloh for the German public and for British service units in the local areas. I offered to lead a formation of four Harriers to demonstrate the aircraft's unique flexibility in conventional and hovering flight. So it was that 'four's four' took to the skies of West Germany for some concentrated close formation practice. We were then tasked to provide the ceremonial fly-past at the nearby NATO headquarters at Brunssum in the Netherlands to mark the official birthday of Her Majesty the Queen in June.

Although all that was required for the ceremony was a straight and level run at about 360 knots there were some difficulties. The headquarters buildings and parade ground were in an old coal-mining area, surrounded by trees and partly hidden in a valley. The event was scheduled to occur precisely as the last notes of the British national anthem faded after the General Salute. The timing was not a specific clock time and, while we knew the schedule for the parade and the duration of the national anthem, the guest of honour was the NATO Central Region commander-in-chief who was an elderly German general with a limp. No one seemed to know how long it would take him to inspect the guard of honour before moving on foot to the dais to take the salute and allow the national anthem to start.

I explained the situation to the parade commander, a British army major, and suggested that I would deploy a radio vehicle with one of our GLOs to a position adjacent to the parade. He could monitor events and would be aware of any delay thus allowing him to brief me by radio on any change to our scheduled time of arrival of 2030 hours. I planned to fly a racetrack pattern at 360 knots about fifteen miles to the east of the parade datum which could be shortened or lengthened at will. Once we were committed to the inbound run at the planned speed our timing options were limited to an increase or decrease in our airspeed, which would make only a small difference in timing, or we could build in a further delay of not less than thirty seconds by flying a tight 360° orbit out of sight of the parade. We had to rely on the radio party on the ground to confirm that the parade was running to time.

Bruce Monk, John Finlayson, Dave Linney,
Jock Heron, Syd Morris and John Thompson.
(Jock Heron)

On the day of the ceremony there was sunshine and very little cloud, which introduced a further complication. The fly-past heading was due west into the setting sun and visibility was poor in haze. However I had taken the sensible precaution earlier in the week to familiarise myself with the route so with reassurance from the radio team that events were running to schedule and confident that the parade commander would do his best under the circumstances, we set off in a diamond formation and duly appeared over the dais just as the last notes of the national anthem were dying away, according to our grateful boss who was in the VIP spectator enclosure with his fingers crossed.

The Wildenrath and Gütersloh open days were due to be held over the Saturday and Sunday of the first weekend in July and we were blessed by a splendid spell of weather. Huge attendances resulted in almost 100,000 people attending at each airfield and the events helped to maintain sound relationships with the German public as well as instilling a sense of pride in our service. I had chosen three good pilots to be my formation members, all of whom were second tourists. Because of the Harrier's small size and the limited manoeuvrability of a formation, the force commander, a very experienced fighter pilot and ex-Black Arrows Hunter display pilot, suggested that I introduce a fifth aircraft to perform a series of coordinated high speed runs to retain spectator interest throughout the conventional display as the formation repositioned. The display involved the five aircraft in tight arrow formation arriving over the runway at 500 plus knots before the main four moved into close formation to perform a series of manoeuvres between about 200 and 450 knots including several formation changes followed by a high speed run in diamond formation before a vertical break into the traffic pattern to come to the hover in line astern over the runway. Despite the high temperatures we had adequate margins and fuel reserves with the Pegasus Mk103, even without water injection, to conduct a prolonged display of the Harrier's performance in the hover and we closed the event with a noisy five-aircraft jet-borne ballet and formation bow to the spectators before conducting rolling vertical landings in line-astern formation.

BOB MARSTON: ALL THE THREES

It wasn't a display; no, really it wasn't, because that would need special authorisation, but I did enjoy the flight that marked my 3,000th hour of Harrier flying. I was OC Harrier Plans at the time, so flew with both Gütersloh squadrons on an opportunity basis. 3(F) Squadron was re-equipping with the GR5, but had a single GR3 remaining.

With the kind collusion of the station commander, Ian Stewart, and the squadron commander, Pete Moules, I flew this GR3, leading eight GR5s, with a T4 as a 'bounce' for a tactical sortie and a formation 'whipper-in'. After the target attack and evasion, we returned to the airfield in a three x three formation, with the GR3 leading. After breaking into the circuit, the GR5s hovered in line along the runway while I flew past in the GR3. Sadly, no good photographs can now be found, but hopefully the stills from a rather misty video give an impression of the occasion.

Similarly, the hovering photo of a IV(AC) Squadron GR3 on the front cover of *Harrier Boys Volume One* is not a display, but a simple demonstration of serendipity and enterprise. As well as running Harrier Plans, part of Ops Wing, I was the

Three's last three. (Kestin)

chairman of the Pegasus Gliding Club. A civilian member of the club was a German in charge of works services at Gütersloh, and the Ops Wg adjutant was Wayne Palmer, who had been an RAF photographer. I noticed that the cherry picker usually used by works services had been temporarily replaced by a larger model during periodic servicing. I also found that a IV(AC) Squadron GR3 needed an air check of its undercarriage function. So it was that the German glider pilot and Wayne with his camera were in the cherry picker basket parked near to a vertical landing pad while I checked out the operation of the jet's undercarriage. Few people noticed what was going on at the time, but the photos soon gained a larger audience. On first viewing the cover photo, the station commander, still Ian Stewart, commented: "That was a good idea, Bob. You won't be having any more good ideas, will you?"

Art Nalls retired from the USMC as a lieutenant colonel, but then went on to become the first, and probably only, private owner/operator of the Harrier. He spotted an opportunity when the UK started the Harrier run-down and bought an ex-development FA2, and managed to get approval to fly it as a private aircraft. Having successfully displayed the Sea Harrier for several years, sharing the flying with retired Major General Joe Anderson, he is now working on an ex-RN T-bird to enable him to check out more pilots, the next two in line being female ex-USMC Harrier operators. Here are his thoughts on the jet.

ART NALLS

Since the beginning of aviation, there have been lots of different airplanes. Some successful, some not so much. But they all contributed to our knowledge and understanding of aerodynamics in some way. Each new model built upon the successes or failures of those that preceded. Good designs endured, bad ones fell by the wayside.

Along the way, there were airplanes that stood head and shoulders above the crowd. They are the icons, the ones we remember, and the ones we aspire to one day fly. The Piper Cub, the Mustang, the Concorde, the SR-71, to name just a brief few that come to mind. There are also the ones we can recall the time and place where we first saw them. That moment etched in memory forever.

The Harrier fits both of these criteria. Love it or hate, it, the Harrier was the first operational vertical/short take-off and landing airplane. The first model successful enough to be put into front-line service. Never mind we hadn't figured out quite how to use all that capability (grass strips, roads, etc) let's get it and figure it out along the way.

It took the Brits and the marines to realise the tremendous potential for such capability, in the art of amphibious, naval, and expeditionary warfare. It was certainly a game-changer. But beyond being just a new type of airplane, it was continuously modified along the way to make it better, more capable, easier to maintain and most important – a better weapons system. While its critics held to the belief it was a little airplane that couldn't, over time it became a powerful and capable weapons system that could and did. Witness the Falklands War of 1982 where Harriers achieved an astonishing twenty-one to nothing air-to-air kill ratio. The Harrier had grown fangs. Equipped with capable state-of-the-art radar, and the latest missiles, V/STOL Harriers proved that lethal power could operate from nearly every surface. All thanks to the visionaries of the British and the marines. Those who knew, from the beginning, this was a capability worth the investment.

The public knew little of this. The public news was always bad. A crash here, and crash there, what were we thinking? The only time anyone ever heard of a Harrier was that it crashed somewhere. The mission given to the Harriers was dangerous in and of itself. Low-level navigation, pop-up bombing, operations from carriers, all carry increased risk compared to cargo haulers. Harrier missions also typically have very short duration, some in just minutes. So the accident statistics 'per flight hour' placed the Harrier at the top of the list. It must be a bad aeroplane. But those who flew and operated it knew differently. This aircraft could do almost anything. It was a capable bomber, an adequate fighter and just what the marines wanted. Not perfect, but adequate to get the job done. We'll gold-plate it later, if it comes to that. Over the forty plus years in service, it changed considerably.

The Harriers are all now being retired from service. One by one, they are sent to the scrap heap, the bone yard, or placed on a stick somewhere. They have passed the legacy onto the F-35B, which by many accounts is a superb weapons system. It too, may have shortfalls in performance, but those, just like those from the Harrier, will be alleviated over time. It too, will grow very powerful fangs to be proven in combat. I only hope they can give credit where credit is due, to those who have gone before. The F-35 didn't just happen overnight.

I have flown over nine different types of VSTOL aircraft, including the Russian YAK-38U. They all bring something to the table. I also continue to fly the world's first and only civilian-owned and flown Harrier at air shows in the USA. I am privileged to be the custodian of this iconic airplane. Hopefully, I can pass it on to the next generation, when I'm ready to hang up the goggles for the last time. Hopefully.

When I fly a show, I often receive the accolades from the crowd. But it's not me. It's the Harrier that deserves them. I'm just the loose nut behind the stick, trying to keep the airplane in the centre of the air. As long as I don't 'tilt the stick' too much, that should be possible.

But beyond those accolades the most common remark I hear at air shows is, "I remember the first time I saw a Harrier!" For the record, so do I. That's the definition of a truly great airplane.

CHAPTER 10

CROSSOVER

MARK ZANKER

I joined the RAF in 1981 and after flying training I was posted to 54(F) Squadron at Coltishall, flying the Jaguar GR1. I loved that first tour as a young, single junior pilot and I assumed that my career path would continue as a Jaguar pilot/instructor and eventually as a flight commander. On 2 November 1987 things took a different trajectory following the death of two friends of mine who were tragically killed in a mid-air collision over Otterburn training range in Northumberland. Lieutenant John Carver was a USN exchange pilot and Flight Lieutenant Dave Sunderland had been with me at Chivenor on the TWU course. These two 3(F) Squadron Harrier GR3 pilots had been flying a simulated low-level attack as part of a six-ship against a mock target in difficult conditions. Crossing undulating terrain, they lost sight of each other during the last part of the attack. Fixated on the task of dropping their practice bombs on the target they actually converged and collided at the point of weapon release. The accident hit me hard as I knew both of these men quite well.

At the same time, I was awaiting my next posting and hoping it would be as a QWI on the Jag. As I hadn't heard anything I gave my posting officer a call to find out if he had any news. "Didn't you know?" he asked. "You're going to be a QFI. You start the CFS course at Scampton in January." I was gutted. This was not what I wanted at all. My boss on 54(F) Squadron was Wing Commander Brian Pegnall, himself an ex-Harrier pilot and an excellent boss, and he was sympathetic to my plight. However, the RAF was committed to recruiting more QFIs from the front line and so the only thing the boss could do was ensure that I went to the aircraft of my choice. For me that had to be the Hawk at Valley. There was no way I was going to swan around the north of England teaching newbies to fly the Jet Provost.

At around the same time there was another Harrier accident at Wittering when a GR3, landing on the double specs strip suffered a brake failure and ran off into the ditch at the airfield boundary. The pilot ejected safely and Peggers was called to be the president of the BoI. During the week he would commute each day from Coltishall to Wittering and so he was rarely seen on the squadron. But one Tuesday afternoon he did show his face and he said that he needed to see me in his office. My heart sank as I desperately tried to recall some misdemeanour that I must surely be guilty of. Whilst working on the BoI at Wittering he had got wind of the fact that the Harrier Force was looking for experienced pilots to replace Dave and John. I was coming to the end of my first tour, I had always expressed a desire to fly the Harrier (who wouldn't?) and being single, I had no domestic 'baggage' to contend with. The conversation went something like this:

Boss – "Would you like to fly the Harrier?"
Me – "Yes"
Boss – "Can you start on Monday?"
Me – "Yes"

And so it was that I came to be a Harrier pilot and in the summer of 1988 I began a posting to Gütersloh to fly the mighty Harrier GR3 on 3(F) Squadron. I didn't know it then but it turned out that my timing was perfect. Had these events occurred two years later I would never have had the chance to fly the GR3 and I would never have experienced flying in West Germany, during the Cold War. The political and military landscape was to change dramatically a few years later with the destruction of the Berlin Wall.

I arrived in Germany just as the squadron was getting ready to deploy to 'the field' for a two-week training exercise. On this occasion our field site was a small wooded copse in Bergen Hohne military range, a couple of miles from the site of Belsen Concentration Camp. I went there by road and the squadron pilots flew the aircraft in later that day. My flight commander was none other than 'No Probs' Bob (Marston). He had earned this title on account of his coolness under pressure and the fact that he seemed to agree to practically anything without the need to consult the boss ("Sir, can I have two weeks leave over Christmas and a week at Easter?" "Yeah, no probs.") I also learnt very quickly on that detachment that when he said that his Land Rover was leaving on a shower run to the local barracks at 1800 hours, what he actually meant was 1755 hours, so be there or be left behind.

The first GR5 was already on the OCU in '88 when I was converting onto the GR3, and the staff were just beginning to build the conversion course that would include 3(F) Squadron in '89. If the GR3 was a bit like a Morgan sports car, the GR5 was a modern-day Aston Martin. It was bigger, could carry more weapons, fly further and was more accurate too. It had internal ECM, a missile-approach warner, better radios and unlike the GR3 the cockpit was roomy and it had a larger head-up display. The Pegasus engine now had a digital engine control system (no more acceleration checks) and more thrust. We couldn't wait to fly it.

When Gulf War One kicked off, the GR5 wasn't deemed ready to go to war. We couldn't hide the fact that we felt a bit left out as we watched the Jaguar Force deploy to the Middle East and the USMC begin sustained operations against Saddam's ground forces in southern Iraq with their AV-8Bs. The Berlin Wall had come down the year before and now our focus had shifted towards the new threat in the Middle East. It was a time of rapid change and it was apparent that the modus operandi of the RAFG Harrier Force would need to change too. The USMC had operated their Harriers from a makeshift strip in Saudi Arabia, close to the front line, generating high sortie rates against Iraqi armour and attacking from medium level and within airspace that was free of any fighter threat. This was an environment that the GR5 ARBS had been designed for, but flying around at medium level was something new to RAF attack pilots who up until then had spent most of their time operating at 250 feet.

In 1990, after flying the GR5 for a year, I was selected to be the RAFG Harrier role demo pilot. The Wittering-based Harrier display pilot flew at the UK air shows during the summer and so my brief was to attend the shows in mainland Europe. A role demo is similar to a full display but for the absence of any inverted aerobatic manoeuvres. For most aircraft this would be quite restrictive but with the Harrier it still meant that I could perform the full range of VSTOL manoeuvres that air show crowds love. Following the tragic crash of the Frecce Tricolori at Ramstein in 1988 there were no flying displays in Germany but there were still some exciting events on the programme in Austria, Belgium, France and Italy. The plan would be to fly to each event on Friday afternoon and return early on Monday. I would take a spare aircraft and the list of volunteers to fly the spare was filling up fast. I would also have a team of five ground engineers to look after the jets, who would travel to the venue by road.

My first show was to be at Seitenstetten in Austria. This was a small grass flying club airstrip nestled in the foothills of the Alps. The Harrier was to be the star of the show, which mostly consisted of gliders, helicopters and light aircraft. My mentor, Steve Fox, flew the spare and we initially landed at Linz Airport, several miles from Seitenstetten. A member of the flying club flew us up to the airfield so that we could get the lie of the land. We were about to park two of the Queen's latest combat aircraft in a field in Austria for the weekend and I was concerned that, a) they didn't sink into the soft earth and, b) they didn't get damaged. Our concerns were quickly laid to rest when we discovered that a convenient strip of concrete in front of the clubhouse was just wide enough for the nose and main wheels to sit on and it seemed that half the Austrian army had been tasked with guarding the jets.

The Harrier was to be last on the flying programme, so Steve and I spent the first part of the afternoon lounging in deck chairs on top of a caravan as we watched the displays. One of these was an impressive demonstration by a Zlin aerobatic aircraft and the pilot really threw the aircraft around as he went through his routine. In his final manoeuvre he pulled up into a stall turn and the aircraft flicked and settled into an inverted rotation. I immediately thought, that doesn't look right and I said something to Steve. As we watched in horror the pilot managed to roll the aircraft upright but it continued to descend until it crashed in a field directly in front of the crowd and right next to an ambulance and fire tender. Miraculously there was no fire and the pilot, although badly injured, had survived the crash. The organisers weren't sure whether to continue the show but I said that I was happy to fly and so they agreed to let me display. I finished my routine that afternoon by hovering in front of the crowd followed by a turn towards the crash site and a bow in recognition of the Zlin pilot.

One of the more interesting shows we were invited to was in Rome. Not near to Rome or on the outskirts of Rome but actually in Rome, at a small airfield called Urbe. Steve Fox flew the spare again using the excuse that I needed more supervision. We based the aircraft at Pratica di Mare Airbase and flew them from there to the show for the day. I have two vivid memories from that event. The first was seeing a Cessna 172 try unsuccessfully to tow a banner into the air, resulting in broken undercarriage, a bent prop and red faces. The second memory was hovering my Harrier over a housing estate in Rome and worrying just how noisy it must have been for those poor people down below. So after attending two air shows I had witnessed two crashes. This display flying lark was a dangerous business.

The Harrier generates a lot of thrust in order to keep it in the hover and as Harrier pilots would often say, 'Lift is a gift but thrust is a must'. At one air display I got to demonstrate just how much thrust the Harrier does have, and not in a good way. The show was at Yverdon-les-Bains in Switzerland and the event was the World Aerobatic Championships. At that time Yverdon only had a grass runway and it was a busy weekend with lots of light aircraft parked around the airfield. It was a hot, dry summer's day and consequently very dusty. The Harrier can only land vertically onto a hard surface that is clear of dirt and debris. To land on a grass strip we would carry out a rolling vertical landing, touching down with 50 knots of ground speed to ensure that any debris or foreign objects would not be sucked into the intake on touchdown. This would not have been a problem at Yverdon except for the fact that all the shiny competition aircraft were parked wingtip to wingtip along both sides of the strip. I stressed my concerns to the organisers about the amount of dust I would kick up during the take-off and landing but they assured me that all would be OK. I guess they were chuffed to bits to have a Harrier at their event and realised that it would draw more crowds. So off I went and performed my twenty-minute routine. I decided that I would hover over a field at the end of the runway, well clear of the parked aircraft. The temperature was 30°C and the airfield was at an altitude of 1,500 feet, so I had very little hover performance. I tried to do a 360° turn in the hover. Moving the rudder pedals to yaw the aircraft around opened the reaction control shutter in the tail, taking thrust from the combustion chamber to push the aircraft around. That caused a reduction in the thrust going to the nozzles which led to the aircraft starting to descend. I already had the throttle pinned as far forward as it would go and so with no excess thrust available I had to stop after 180° of turn. The aircraft stopped descending and I had just enough power to climb back to the correct hover height of 150 feet before commencing a very gentle turn back towards the crowd. Taxiing back to parking at the end of the show I waved happily to the crowd. The assembled aerobatic pilots glared back at me and that is when I saw that their once highly polished machines were now covered in a thick layer of reddish-brown dust. I was not very popular that day and spent the rest of the weekend keeping a low profile.

In 1991 RAFG received a request from the Czechoslovakian air force for the Harrier to display at one of its air shows that summer. The Berlin Wall had only just been torn down and the ex-Soviet Bloc countries east of the now defunct Iron Curtain still remained a bit of a mystery. I was now the RAFG Harrier display pilot; I got wind of this request and was quite determined to do it. But there was a problem. The Czechs had no budget. They couldn't pay for hotels let alone fuel and so it looked like we wouldn't be able to attend. I started to lobby the boss and the station commander and impressed upon them that this was a rare chance to wave the flag and establish ties with the Czechs. Commander-in-Chief RAFG was keen that we do it and a plan started to come together that involved getting my ground crew team to position in on a 748 transport plane ahead of the two Harriers.

The air show itself was to be at a small grass airfield called Roudnice but we were to base ourselves from Zatec airfield, home to a couple of MiG 29 squadrons. You have to remember that in 1991 the only MiG 29s I had ever seen were in grainy black and white photographs which were flashed up during our regular squadron recce tests. The chance to visit an actual MiG 29 squadron was incredibly exciting. Our contact in Czechoslovakia was the RAF air attaché in Prague. I managed to call him to get some details about the weekend. Apart from our low-flying topographical charts we had no airway maps for Czech airspace, no air traffic control frequencies or any detailed information about their airfields. Unfortunately, and quite surprisingly, the air attaché couldn't provide me with much either. I had to make do with a faxed, hand-drawn sketch map of Zatec airfield and a couple of ATC frequencies we were to call on crossing the Czech border. We had a planned arrival time on the Saturday morning and a rendezvous with a MiG 29 escort that would lead us to Zatec. What could possibly go wrong?

RAFG were going to foot the bill but in order to keep the costs down it was agreed that the Czechs would accommodate us on base and take care of transport to and from the venue. As this was such a high profile event the Gütersloh station commander, Group Captain Gavin Mackay, decided that he would fly as my number two in the spare jet. He could certainly sniff a jolly from a mile away. The adventure began on a sunny summer's afternoon as we launched off eastwards, climbing to medium level under the control of German ATC. Approaching the Czech border, we were handed across to Prague control and we checked in with them. We were at around 25,000 ft in wide battle formation, about a mile-and-a-half apart, line abreast. There was no cloud and we could practically see our destination from the border. My radar warning receiver indicated that we were being looked at by an air intercept radar and soon after that we were told that two MiG 29s were approaching from the east. We quickly picked them up visually as they flew down our right-hand side. At this point the controller told us to begin our descent and so down we went, still in battle. The MiG 29s were obviously turning in behind us and I strained to look over my shoulder and pick them up but I couldn't see them. Were we going too fast for them? Not likely. My wingman couldn't see them either so we pressed on regardless, following our nav kit towards Zatec and contacting the tower controller on the radio. We descended to 2,000 ft, lined up with the runway at 5 miles and set ourselves up for a run-in and break over the airfield, a standard military fast-jet arrival. Well it may have been a standard procedure west of the Iron Curtain but it seemed that no one had told the Czechs that. As we arrived low over the runway threshold at 450 knots we narrowly missed a Czech air force L39 trainer that was joining the circuit at 90° to us. I extended upwind to get clear of the traffic and broke left downwind. As we both landed the MiGs arrived into the circuit. We subsequently discovered that by descending we had dropped off their radar screens and they had not been able to re-acquire us. So much for Soviet radar systems.

The Czechs were as excited by our arrival as we were and the welcome we received was tremendous. Like fighter pilots the world over they wanted to show us their aircraft and I quickly found myself in the hangar sitting inside a MiG 29. Their command of the English language was excellent and after looking around the squadron we showed them around the Harrier. The air attaché had arranged for us to fly across to Roudnice by helicopter for a quick recce. We jumped into a VIP version of the Mi8 and lifted off for the short flight. After years of training against all manner of Soviet ground and air weapon systems I suddenly found myself peering out of the cockpit of a Russian transport helicopter as we flew low across the countryside, skimming over Russian-built SAM sites and radar installations, finally coming in to land next to a Hind helicopter gunship and a Sukhoi Frogfoot attack aircraft. Roudnice airfield had been built as a wartime dispersal for military aircraft and as such it was actually a concrete runway with a camouflage covering of grass. You could have landed a 747 on it.

Back at Zatec that evening the Czech pilots were keen to entertain us and we were taken, with our ground crew, to a grassy area behind the squadron building where they had a pig roast and a large quantity of Czech beer. One of the MiG 29 pilots was also the Czech air force display pilot and so we chatted about display flying. At that time I was flying on average a flight every day, sometimes two. In contrast he was working as a staff officer in Prague and only flying a handful of times each month. Blimey, that would be challenging to just keep current on the jet, let alone fly a full display in it. The beer was flowing and Gavin had brought a few bottles of Scotch for the Czechs to tuck into. It would be a busy weekend and I was pacing myself with the beer. It was getting late and I asked our hosts if I could be taken to the accommodation. One of the Czech pilots suggested that I come with him to his home for a night cap. Thanking him for his hospitality I declined the offer but he insisted. It really was late and I needed to get some sleep. He pressed me again but I declined as politely as I could and he agreed to take me to the barrack block. I jumped into his car and off we raced down the taxiway. I expected him to turn left towards the domestic site but suddenly he swerved to the right and headed at high speed across the runway towards the HAS shelters that loomed out of the darkness. I guess we aren't going to the barrack block then? We shot past a HAS, left the taxiway and bounced onto the grass headed for the tree line. What the f***? As the car bounced through the trees I realised that my host was headed for the perimeter fence. Well he would have been if there had been one, but there was no fence as the Czechs didn't have the budget to maintain one. After his demonstration of off-road driving we made it to the highway and within ten minutes we were in Zatec town and pulling up outside a grey apartment block. Out of the lift and he was banging loudly on the door of his apartment. His wife opened the door and there followed a brief conversation which I interpreted as, 'this is a distinguished British pilot who needs some food and drink, so get cooking woman'. All I could do was accept their wonderful hospitality and we drank and ate into the early hours.

The next morning Gavin wasn't looking too good and it was obvious that he had eaten something the night before that had disagreed with him. I came up with a new plan to leave the spare at Zatec and fly back by helicopter if we needed it. The station commander endorsed the plan. The display went well and there was a huge crowd at the show. We met lots of lovely people that day but the highlight was when we got to shake hands with a Czech Spitfire pilot who had flown with the RAF during the Battle of Britain, who proudly turned out that day in his RAF number one dress uniform complete with all of his medals. We returned to Zatec to discover that the spare GR5 had been 'decorated' by the Czech ground crew during our absence. To some of them the GR5 looked a bit like a mouse so they had decided to draw a pair of ears and some whiskers on the nose together with some additional graffiti. At least they had only used chalk. On the flight home we joined up with two MiG 29s for some formation flying and a photo opportunity and this time they didn't need to use their radar.

In 1992 I was posted to 233 OCU at Wittering to be a QWI on A Squadron. Pete Day was the boss and Nick Gilchrist (Gil) was my flight commander. Gil had a robust work ethic that revolved around always getting the best deal and

Czech decoration. (Mark Zanker)

ensuring that he and his pilots had the most fun, whatever we were doing. The Harrier display pilot was an OCU instructor and Gil, himself an ex-display pilot, had negotiated a deal with a car hire firm for the supply of a number of cars for squadron use. I remember having some fun in a Cosworth-powered saloon car of some sorts. In 1993 the annual Gibraltar air show was going to be the last one as the RAF station there was due to close and Gil stated that it was his mission to get some Harriers there and to put on a display. He told us that in previous years the Jaguar Force had always put on a good show there and that we needed to do a better one, especially as this would be the last at the Rock.

On Friday we launched from Wittering with a five-ship which consisted of two GR5s, two GR7s and a T4 with the SEngO in the back. Gibraltar is a spectacular sight from the air as the huge rock juts out from the Spanish mainland. Space is at a premium and the runway has been built out into the bay and parallel to the border with Spain. The small RAF station was between the runway and the border and the public road ran straight across the runway, traffic being controlled by traffic lights. We all arrived at Gibraltar in good shape after a fuel stop in Portugal and after putting the jets to bed we headed for the mess. We were told that for accommodation we would be sharing a couple of old married quarters which were close to the mess. There was a perception in the RAF that the Harrier boys were comfortable slumming it. After all we did seem to spend most of our time living in tents so surely a married quarter would seem like the Ritz to us. Before we had time to complain that one bathroom without a shower, between four of us was not acceptable, Gil had made the decision to go 'off base'. After a short recce down town we checked into a very nice hotel on the hillside with large en-suite rooms and a splendid swimming pool which we agreed would be a nice place to meet. We settled ourselves by the pool and Gil struck up a conversation with a gentleman from Norway who worked for a shipping company. It seemed he had flown to Gibraltar to meet with the captain of one of their ships, which he pointed to, anchored in the bay below and just too large to get into the harbour. After a while Gil managed to get us an invitation onto the ship the following afternoon.

But before that, we had a display to do and Gil had a great plan that would see us as the finale to the show and a fitting end to the RAF presence at Gibraltar. The display consisted of the four GRs, led by Gil. We would get airborne, form into a neat box four and fly around the Rock and over the runway doing various manoeuvres and being sure to keep well out of the adjacent Spanish airspace. Then we would drop back into fighting wing, swoop fast and low down the runway before pulling up, in a break to downwind but high over the peak of the Rock and in full view of the crowd. Gil would extend out to sea whilst the remaining three of us would make our approach to the runway decelerating to the hover at 200 ft so that we were spaced evenly down the runway. Gil then timed it so that as the last aircraft settled in the hover he would appear from crowd left and fly down the runway, flat out at 100 ft and slightly to the side of the runway. The effect was to appear as if he was actually flying underneath the hovering Harriers, which of course he wasn't. He would then pull straight up into the vertical and the three hovering Harriers would RVL onto the runway and get clear ready for Gil to do a final hover, bow and land. The weather was perfect and the display went without a hitch. I distinctly remember hovering next to a super yacht moored in the marina by the runway.

We climbed out of the jets feeling like bloody heroes and made our way to the officers' mess for a well-earned beer and the traditional post-air show party. Imagine our surprise and frustration when, on arriving at the mess reception we were told that we wouldn't be allowed to attend the party in flying suits. It didn't matter how much we argued our case, the PMC was having none of it. We would have to go back to the hotel and change into a jacket and tie. It was at this point that we came up with a plan B. If we had to go back to the hotel, then why not stop off at the marina and bask in the glory of our recently completed display. I reasoned that if we showed up in our flying suits we would be hailed as bally heroes and treated accordingly, so off we headed towards the marina in search of a cold beer. A few minutes later we were casually strolling along the dock when we came upon a very large yacht, the owners of which were relaxing with a drink on deck and enjoying the sunset. They had obviously witnessed our feats of derring-do, and of course they were honoured to have us in their presence aboard their humble yacht, drinking their lovely beer and wine. It would have been rude not to accept and after the third drink all thoughts of the air show party disappeared.

The next day we were ferried out to the large LPG tanker in the bay and welcomed aboard by the captain and his crew. Like many sailors, they had spent a long period of time at sea and even though they were anchored off Gib they still couldn't get ashore easily and so our presence was warmly welcomed. It did help that we had flown our display right above their ship the day before. After a tour of the vessel we were treated to a terrific buffet in their wardroom and at the end of the day we promised to give them a bit of a fly-past on our flight home. I think they got a pretty good view of the jets the following day as we departed. It had been a great weekend and I like to think that we provided a fitting display to mark the end of RAF Gibraltar.

CHAPTER 11
IN WITH THE NEW

SIMON TURNER

With a combination of good fortune and a natural ability to avoid promotion above the rank of squadron leader, I managed to achieve a career full of variety and some fabulously operational flying with an unbroken fourteen years on the jet of choice. My career straddled GR3 to GR7 and included most of the GR3 highlights, like Belize, Norway, OLF, Option Zulu, the Field, Deci for APC and ACMI. Thereafter, it was the transition to GR5, with all its frustrations, teething problems and operational limitations, into an exchange tour flying the AV-8B with the USMC at Yuma before the GR7 at Wittering with 1(F) and 20(R) Squadrons. I was lucky enough to gain extensive exposure to all of these Harrier types, with good continuity whilst in positions of operational significance to either my squadron or the force.

GR3 ops can be summarised as being extensively about Cold War tactics, essentially two dimensional with everything happening at low level. Weapons were relatively imprecise and employed the shotgun principle using multiple warheads to hit the target, mostly in the forward edge of the battle area. Most weapons were employed at relatively close range to the target, thus reducing the time of flight of the weapon and therefore minimising the miss distance associated with aiming errors. The results achieved during GR3 weapons training were mostly good, despite the limited capabilities of the aiming system and weapons in use. But there was no doubting that the operation was very dynamic and intense in nature. For example, my first tour of 4½ years with IV(AC) Squadron yielded 991 flight hours (excluding OCU flying) and 1,243 flights. Pilots could expect to be well qualified by the end of their first tour, unlike the later Harrier days. For me it was FRI, ACI, QWI, Zulu Leader and a whole bunch of routine quals like fours lead, aggressor, ACL etc.

The trademarks of GR3 ops were field operations and multi-aircraft formations like Option Zulu. I flew twenty-six flights in five days on my second field deployment. With this kind of continuity the aircraft becomes another limb, everything is at your fingertips and the cockpit feels like home, comfortable and familiar. Flying the max of six flights per day left the aircraft available for another three waves thereafter, the jets were reliable, the engineering extremely efficient and the responsibility was as huge as the rewards. Field peculiarities included no radio transmissions so no ATC, always a plus. The threat from Soviet jamming equipment was such that they could locate and jam a frequency after a two-second transmission. So we checked out to every operational frequency to avoid being jammed until we had at least managed to make urgent operational calls, such as missile breaks, before checking out or auto chopping to the next frequency. The net result was that we flew most of our missions from the field without making a single radio transmission. This included large multi-aircraft formations, which made the formation rendezvous interesting when we consider that formation members may have launched from different sites having received a briefing, second hand via secure telephone and telebrief. We avoided becoming too wrapped up in the complexity and dynamism of field ops to the detriment of real operational capability. The job of attacking targets, either with a camera or a weapon, was always the primary focus. I saw examples where a complex operation associated with the take-off and landing phase would lead the operation to become focused on that part of the mission at the expense of the main task.

The USN was a classic example; whilst on exchange in the US I thought they often became so concerned about their performance on and around the ship that they spent too little time analysing and honing their operational skills in the target area. I once had to debrief a team of F-14 pilots on why it was inappropriate to plan and execute CAS using 500,000:1 scale maps that simply don't provide enough detail to plot targets and friendlies that might be as close as 200 metres apart. F-14s doing CAS – what do you expect? With the HF it was all about the target and whether or not you survived any pre-target engagements to see if the tasking had been satisfied, and post-target engagements to see if you lived to fight another day. Notwithstanding the GR3 limitation of post-flight video being around ninety seconds long, this scrutiny fostered enormous attention to detail in all aspects of the mission and was a very effective learning process. I saw a contrast in the USMC's approach; a debrief was far less detailed and analytical of the finesse of an attack, perhaps down to the mindset of operating in a permissive environment with the expectation of air supremacy and the availability of truly enormous amounts of firepower. I witnessed this on a firepower demo at the 29 Palms desert ranges when tasked to lead an eight-ship to a target, with wall-to-wall firebombs. It promised to be a good show but we were only a small part, as I found later. We were to follow a ten-minute barrage of M270 multiple launch rocket system (MLRS) that was due to end one minute before our TOT. Running in at low level, this barrage looked impressive and quite scary, with nothing but dust and explosions in front of us. We had given ourselves a line feature that marked our escape point if rockets had not ceased impacting the target area. The last rockets landed what seemed like a nano-second before the line so we pressed on. There was nothing left of the target other than dust, scattered tyres and scorched holes. We dropped on time but on this random array of mythical targets and our ninety-second fire storm seemed utterly insignificant when compared with the MLRS barrage.

The recce role was mastered on IV(AC) Squadron with its own RIC and recce pods in abundance. Each day started with a met brief and recce training with an 'around the room' test of your ability to recognise some seriously well camouflaged, very distant and often poor quality imagery of friend or foe military equipment. These were often tense moments. The last thing you wanted was the embarrassment of misidentifying friend for foe or simply getting the wrong answer in front of the massed squadron pilots. This serious approach prevailed but the occasional slide would enter the test as a set up to catch someone off their guard. OC IV was once framed by the FRI with his turn to identify the distant vehicle in a tree line. The boss had a brave guess, it was wrong and the next pilot got it right. We moved on, and so this continued with the boss failing to get any right during that session. It was eventually revealed that the boss had been looking at slides of empty fields with no military equipment in shot.

To RAFG Harrier pilots, Option Zulu was a significant event. It would define day one of a central european conflict and meant that Soviet forces had crossed the Inner German border and WWIII had begun. The mission entailed the massed ranks of RAFG Harriers launching from either field sites or Gütersloh to attack the first rank of Soviet tanks in the geographic choke points of the border area. Once again, not a single radio call would be made throughout the whole mission. I recall the then Flight Lieutenant (later Air Marshal) Dave Walker issuing a massive bollocking to some poor 3 Squadron JP for breaking radio silence, perhaps for some trivial matter such as a bird strike, such was the intensity of the mindset of the day. There could be few sights as pleasing as a sky full of Harriers following you to a target area as each pair crested the Bielefeld ridge en route to the Zulu target area; it brings a smile to my face just writing about it.

Most training was of similarly high intensity and focused on the anticipated task within the operational theatre. It was often difficult to differentiate between air combat and low-level evasion, other than the extra dimension, use of the vertical. Evasion could be very dynamic and was seldom limited to the manoeuvres defined by the letter of the law. On an early combat-ready work-up flight my four-ship was bounced on recovery to base. Whilst talking to approach control and joining up, this jet popped out of the weeds doing 480 kts just north-west of the field and started turning and burning with us. It was Martin 'Cliffy' Cliff setting the scene for the years to come.

During a squadron exchange to Colmar we were tasked to fly eight Harriers with six Mirage III and V aircraft mud-moving against a four-ship CAP of Mirage 2000, which was a very advanced threat for its day. We had little or no information of its capabilities but knew it had an all-aspect and BVR capability when we only had stern hemisphere heat-seeking missiles. The French CO was leading the mission and Tim Ellison and I were JPs with few qualifications; we were certainly not aggressor qualified nor ACLs. During the brief the French CO picked Tim and me to run a sweep five minutes ahead of the main package of mud movers, to find and harass the Mirage 2000s. As OCU course mates and good friends, we shared a glance which said 'this won't happen' expecting our boss, Pete Harris, to step in and nominate a better qualified pair. He didn't and we flew the brief and had a hoot. With an early tally on a pair of Mirage 2000s, we managed to evade their radar and jumped them unsighted. Just as we were calling the first two shots we gained a tally on the second pair closing into our eight o'clock; despite thinking we were about to be shot if not already hit, we continued manoeuvring, switched and gained advantage to get two guns kills on them. It was only at the debrief that we learned that the Mirage 2000 crews had not claimed a single shot against any Harrier all day. For the first time in my life I felt ten foot tall and so proud to be a Harrier pilot.

There were many moments like this with the Harrier, and especially the least capable of all marks, the GR3, when we managed to achieve better operational results than the aircraft should have been capable of. Fighting F-15s in Deci, we should never have got close to any shots against them but we did, and many times. We used the mythology of Harrier peculiarities such as VIFF. We warned any adversary fighter in training to take great care when closing from behind as VIFF could generate enormous closure rates without plan-form change; this was always over exaggerated to gain a psychological advantage when in reality VIFF was pretty much a last-ditch option due to the enormous loss of speed that followed, a big disadvantage in an air combat environment where 'speed is life'. The best of these exaggerations for effect came from Paul Warren-Wilson (Wibs) who surprised us all in a dissimilar air combat brief with our F-15 adversaries in Deci by warning them to take care when looking towards a Harrier as we might be using the laser to assess range and obviously this could be very hazardous to their vision. They bought it, and he was so convincing that some of us were left wondering if we were missing a trick.

Flying the GR3 in RAFG was a great place to learn the mud-moving trade and consolidate all aspects of VSTOL, navigation and situational awareness, skills that were to become second nature and superb tools for flying the next generation Harrier. It was an uncanny coincidence that the GR5 entered RAF service as the 'Wall' came down and things began hotting up in Iraq. Around this time I returned from Germany and joined 1(F) Squadron for a relatively short tour. Although we continued to train at low level for the worst-case scenario of UK-only operations or bad weather, partly because that's all we knew and partly because, as a nation, we could not rely on our conflicts always being within a NATO coalition, another Falklands for example. When Gulf War 1 kicked off the GR5 was deemed non-operational due its lack of weapons clearances, despite the fact that the USMC had a very extensive inventory of weapons that they used to great effect in the 'kill zones' over Kuwait and Iraq. So effective were their attacks that Major Gen

Norman Schwarzkopf named the Harrier in his top ten weapons systems of the war, one of only two aircraft to make the list. A later USAF statistic revealed that 83% of all of its aircraft shot down from the Korean War to the end of Gulf War 1 were lost to small-arms fire. So they operated above this threat and invested in equipment to neutralise the SAM threats present when operating at altitude. High-level attacks also suited the Harrier II's kit, with its angle rate bombing system (ARBS) and its dual mode tracker (DMT). This suite enabled the USMC pilots (and DAK) to loiter covertly at altitude, with no noise or visual signature on the ground, waiting to identify targets, using the DMT to give a six-times magnified image, then contrast or laser track the target before commanding an automatic weapon release. Most Iraqi tanks were in sandy bunds to protect from attack by coalition tanks with their longer range guns and higher speed capability. From the air, this set-up provided good contrast with shadows and easy acquisition from above. The DMT would lock every time and accurate aiming could be easily achieved; the system could deliver 6mR accuracy in this type of attack – more accurate than the F-18 conducting a radar attack from the same profile.

I missed some of the frustrations of the RAF changeover when on my exchange tour with the USMC at Yuma flying the AV-8B, a similar beast to the GR7, but some having the big engine with an extra 1,500-lb of thrust, an enormous inventory of weapons, 100% LERX and a fully-developed night-attack capability. There were also many subtle differences between this aircraft and the GR7, mainly the avionics, a completely different range of ancillary equipment, better performance due to the lighter airframe (the additional bird-strike protection of the GR5 was not fitted and nor were the outrigger pylons or the ZEUS EW suite). I learned a great deal in just over two years with two different USMC squadrons flying a mix of day and night-attack missions. I dropped easily 100 times more weapons than I had dropped in my whole RAF career and flew to and from a variety of USN ships. The tour had proved to be a great way to prepare for my return to the new GR7 force and participating in ops in the northern Iraq no-fly zone.

On return from the US, I briefly joined 1(F) Squadron again and had a great time gaining CR status, flying in the northern Iraq no-fly zone and gaining night-attack (EO) CR before moving to the job of my career, that of OC A Flight on the Harrier OCU (20 Squadron). As a QWI, this was the best tour I could have hoped for. With its QWI STANEVAL post within my terms of reference, I inherited interesting responsibilities at a time when the HF was reaching maturity with night attack and a variety of weapons clearances coming our way. The RAF had changed the way weapons clearances were issued and the OEU had become a tool to streamline and speed up the process of improving operational capability. Towards the end of the GR5, all later converted to GR7, we had clearances for recce with a variety of high or low-level recce pods, and we could extend the range and endurance of the aircraft with the approval of a four-tank fit and an AAR capability. AAR was far easier to perform on the GR5/7 due to the retractable probe, which presented reduced drag and far fewer handling issues than the GR3 when fitted with a probe. Most GR3 pilots had flown with recce pods and were very competent with recce procedures, but the GR5 with its variety of pods presented slightly different challenges when operated from medium altitudes. Unlike the low-level recce pod with its array of five cameras providing horizon-to-horizon coverage, the field of view of the LOROP pod, with its single long-range oblique camera, was more limited. It required very accurate flight parameters, especially with the track and angle of bank of the aircraft, to ensure the target appeared within the camera's field of view (FOV) when operated from typical slant ranges of up to 20,000 ft or more. A few degrees of bank angle could change the swathe of coverage over the ground and create a target miss.

I was once tasked to lead eight GR7s to gather imagery of Mosul airfield in northern Iraq. Most of the aircraft had LOROPs and all had centreline recce pods as back-up options, despite these being of limited use from medium altitude. The ROE limited ops to above 5,000 ft in some areas within the AOR due to the small-arms threat, which was ever present. I had briefed the attack with routing west to east running south of Mosul with LOROP pods looking north to the airfield. We all had different tracks in order to gather differing views of the target area. However, on arriving in the AOR it was obvious that a thunderstorm, the only storm around, had inconveniently positioned itself on our track, preventing a medium altitude line of sight to the target. Using our frequency agile radios, and exercising Harrier Force flexibility, we re-briefed the attack to make the same run at low level using our low-level pod, running all five cameras. We mitigated the small-arms threat by running in a wall of eight jets, line abreast with about 4,000 ft lateral spacing between aircraft. This helped ensure that lead elements didn't alert ground threats to the presence of followers, with all aircraft ingressing and egressing the target area simultaneously. I called buster, meaning we all set full power to run as fast as possible, and began running the cameras at the airfield boundary. We were in and out of the target area within fifteen seconds and pulled out of low level when clear of the storm. The procedure after landing was to give a verbal MISREP, a mission report, before heading to the RIC to run through individual films with the PI (photographic interpreter). Entering the RIC it was quickly apparent that something exciting had happened. My first thought was that we were in trouble for operating at low level in this area. Fortunately, it was the imagery that created excitement. Our pictures, taken from quite low level, had revealed items of vital intelligence within one of the hangars on the airfield. The hangar doors were open and a nice oblique view from a typical operational low level revealed the contents of the hangar as being two rows of FROG 7 transporter erector launchers. These were tactical ballistic missiles and capable of delivering nuclear, biological or chemical warheads; surely this was evidence of WMD. The excitement in the RIC was tangible and the pictures were allegedly beamed to the Pentagon within 30 minutes. Fortunately, nobody seemed to care about our deviation to low level after this.

By now medium-level tactics were maturing, although some of our attacks were executed using the 'force', a mystical sixth sense that came with experience, maturity and luck – or simply bravado. We benefited from our USMC exchange experiences and input from other sources such as the OEU before we achieved a fully mature set of medium-level procedures. It was a few years after the GR7 introduction before we perfected the art, whereby we could achieve release solutions at a required height and dive angle without too much difficulty. We were able to run formations through such dynamic three-dimensional attacks without losing each other and to maintain mutual support. In the good old GR3 days mud-moving packages went alone and unafraid with no supporting air assets. With GR5/7/9 operations in the various theatres there were numerous supporting assets from escort and sweep fighters, CAPs and SEAD assets, AWACs etc. Air pictures were passed in various ways, giving the God's eye view of the battle space. We were very much choreographed into the air order of battle to extend mutual support beyond the wingman and into the big picture with other assets all synchronised to support our efforts. Comms were much more complex and a well developed set of coalition SOPs provided code words for critical events to achieve the mission objective whilst preventing blue on blue (fratricide).

The basic GR3 skills that still prevailed within the HF differentiated us from other air forces. For example when a pair from 4 Squadron operating in Bosnia were targeted by a SAM launch, the missile was sighted by the wingman and the missile break was called over the radio; the targeted jet manoeuvred and simultaneously deployed IR flares and defeated the missile. The pair continued with their mission; another day at the office. The wingman that called the break was an excellent USMC exchange pilot, who admitted that the reality and intensity of our training had prepared him for operations.

I recall my first mission in the Iraq no-fly zone with another eight-ship. We were required to conduct a simulated attack, but carrying live bombs, against a SA-6 site NW of Mosul. We planned a 30° dive attack with all aircraft deploying flares in the pull off target. Within the formation three of us were on our first mission in theatre and the adrenalin was flowing. The more junior of the first timers was at the rear of the formation and required to rendezvous with the number seven off target. A relatively simple process at low level, but at medium level following a dynamic attack with significant vertical manoeuvring, especially in a very bright blue Iraqi sky, it proved too much for him. He was split from the formation for the next ten minutes, he lost situational awareness and mutual support in the excitement of facing a real live SA-6 threat at close quarters. The debrief took a while.

With the force-wide commitment to becoming night EO capable, the HF became the stuff of legend. It was exciting and motivating to do the routine things we did in the Harrier, but to then take these disciplines, skills and capabilities into the darkness and perform with equal success was simply incredible. Night attack brought a very advanced capability to the HF, one that no other force had, at that stage, perfected to the same high standard. Operating at low level using FLIR and NVG imagery was empowering. Entering the night low-flying system we were allowed to turn off all external lights and become totally invisible, while any potential adversary on CAP could be seen easily through the NVGs. We made a habit of sneaking up on such CAPs and dispensing with the threat before heading to our target. Of course there were difficulties and many hazards associated with flying on artificial imagery produced by these sensors, but these could be mitigated with training and robust procedures.

There were a few scares, such as one wingman losing sight of his leader from a fighting wing position at low level; by the time visual contact had been regained the wingman had somehow overtaken the leader and crossed to the other side. Neither pilot saw the other until the new positions had been established. We learned from such events and created procedures to prevent recurrences so accidents from similar situations were avoided. We even introduced night EO operations into the OCU syllabus for ab initio students. There is no doubt though, by this stage the HF had become quite a safe place to fly. With the GR5/7 the accident rate had fallen significantly when compared with the days of the GR3. In my view, the main reasons for this were the improvements made to the handling qualities of the AV-8B variants, the reduced dynamism of the operation after the demise of the Soviet Union but also the introduction of probably the best training tool available to the force. With the GR5 and beyond came video capable of providing good quality HUD imagery[6] for all or most of the mission. This allowed for a great deal more scrutiny of a pilot's performance and certainly improved capabilities across the force. It became the norm for a very high degree of scrutiny of HUD video to follow each flight. This became glaringly obvious during our first combined QWI course Op Phase with the Tornado OCU. By comparison, the Tornado QWIs would spend far less time scrutinising their HUD video post-flight than we did. Our way may have been seen as oppressive to outsiders, but the whole emphasis was to improve and learn, and as a force we embraced this ethos.

For me, it was great to see fewer accidents and retain my friends and fellow GR5/7 pilots. The GR3 days were very exciting and perhaps more dynamic in some respects but there was a mindset that an accident is inevitable and you wondered who would be next. I saw this clearly on 4 Squadron where all of our

---

[6] The multiplexed recording also showed FLIR imagery with superimposed HUD symbology for night operations, and recorded radio and cockpit audio.

new GR3 pilots were invited to become members of an insurance consortium. The aim was to ensure that any deceased pilot would have others to pay for and organise the wake, pay for the funeral and cater for the family's immediate well-being if the worst should happen. Sinister perhaps, but none of us seemed perturbed by this possibility and we all signed up. Although I recall a tangible sense of relief, some surprise and enormous celebration when my good friend and course mate, Marc 'Rambo' Frith, landed and climbed out of his GR3 for the last time. "I survived," he exclaimed in a manner that clearly indicated his expectation had been that he would not. Some, like me, got lucky in the Harrier.

From 1985 to 1998 I flew GR3, 5 and 7 and various marks of AV-8B for fourteen fantastic years. I had two scares, one when a Tornado missed me by about 20 ft when operating in a prohibited area in Germany; I was tasked to be there and he wasn't. During a busy phase of my low-level attack, whilst talking to a FAC and lining up on the target, the proverbial hairs on the back of my neck stood up. I looked up to see a Tornado head-on at close range at the same height. Our closing speed was 900 kts, I pushed to avoid, it went darker momentarily and I heard a very loud whooshing, as it passed close above me. I made contact with him on the emergency frequency, and despite my junior rank, gave him some choice words. We spoke later on the phone and I repeated my angry rant before realising that he was a squadron leader. Thankfully, he took it and apologised. During one of my early GR5 flights, a 1v1v1 air-combat flight, in the midst of turning and burning, my engine failed to respond to the throttle position and stuck at idle power. Lots of audio and visual warnings illuminated; I was above complete cloud cover heading east away from Wittering. After steering myself away from the other aircraft around me I realised I needed to select the manual fuel system as the digital engine control (DECS) had failed and with idle power I couldn't get back to base. The trouble was where was this switch in the GR5? My motor skills had been honed in the GR3 with the switch being in front of the throttle, whereas now in the GR5 it was behind the throttle. With the throttle at idle the switch was hidden, there was a lot going on outside, I'd just entered cloud and had a wingman carrying out a visual inspection whilst trying to contact Wittering and turn homewards and issue a Mayday. Having recently crossed from GR3 to GR5 without any simulator flying, I was struggling to find the switch I needed so elected to shut down and relight the engine to reset the DECS. Fortunately it worked, and I landed safely. During my first tour on the GR3 there were seven fatalities; I for one am very thankful that this trend didn't continue in the HF beyond the GR3.

To be a Harrier pilot, for me, began as a dream, became a realistic possibility and by the time it happened it was engrained in my DNA. There is no cliché, sound bite or catchphrase that accurately conveys the significance of being a Harrier pilot. The old saying, 'How do you know if there's a pilot in the room? – He'll tell you'. It's not an ego thing – it's raw enthusiasm, a desire to share the love of the profession, a need to complete the perfect mission and survive in the ridiculously dynamic battle space. The tools of the trade can be as complex as the most advanced fighter with state of the art technology, a multitude of man/machine interface protocols and numerous sub-systems, all with varying degrees of importance when employed in the time critical context of the operational theatre. Yet we could never ignore the operational advantages gained through effective employment of the 'back to basics' tactics that were as relevant in the first aerial battles as they are now; using the sun, terrain, weather and remaining unpredictable with a knowledge of how the enemy will fight are all critical to our success. We must have a mind's-eye view of the dynamic aerial battle in three dimensions, keeping pace with the positional changes that occur in ultra-quick time of not only our aircraft, but our supporting elements and especially our adversaries. Today's airman has no spare time to ponder options, but makes numerous crucial decisions on each mission. The many advantages offered by the effective use of airpower can be achieved largely by selecting the right individuals to be your airmen and training them in the right way, then providing the right aircraft and equipment. Airmen measure their worth in terms of mission success and operational effectiveness, achieving aims and objectives and getting the job done. There is no point in 'making holes in the sky' for no tactical gain. Being a Harrier pilot was a state of mind, a bond to other Harrier pilots, a professional identity of monumental significance and, for me, was quite simply my greatest professional achievement.

CHAPTER 12

NIGHT ATTACK – PROOF OF CONCEPT

MIKE HARWOOD
TWENTY-FOUR-HOUR AIR POWER – THE REALITIES OF CONFLICT DEMAND NOTHING LESS

I still dream in green. I see that small circle of colour before my eyes, cutting a hole in the darkness ahead, making it possible to fly my combat aircraft down a twisting valley. In my peripheral vision, there is nothing but the blackness of the night, and yet I am fully aware of the wall of granite that lurks therein, brooding, waiting its chance to catch the unwary. Briefly I glance up at the aurora borealis, even more spectacular as my night-vision goggles expose a billion diamonds in the sky. But then there is nothing...

Dense cloud hides the heavens and the moon. I am straining to find any recognisable feature ahead as I approach an area of black-out I know should have a landing pad. Fuel ... low enough to hover ... just ... the sound and vibration of the mighty Pegasus engine, as the nozzles are tweaked a few degrees down, allowing that thrust-dependent deceleration to start. Scanning all indicators at lightning pace; denied the normal comfort of all-round vision so taken for granted in the daylight; watching the engine temperature, close to the limits; angle of attack; wind; distance-to-go. Then nozzles to the hover position, slowing rapidly, that free gift of wing-lift gone, utter reliance on thrust to hold several tons of machine. Moving my head, front to side, side to front, trying to stabilise in the right place in the dark is a miracle.

I wake. I reassure myself. This is no miracle. This is repeatable, built on years of hard work and occasional flashes of genius from people who have influenced my life. This is possible for normal mortals. And this chapter opens up a window on our early days of night development. Be in no doubt, these insights are no more than a goggle-eyed view of the whole: a cut-out as I saw it but I know all too well there is more to tell.

Darkness. The middle of the night. Cold War Germany, 1987. The door-flap to our tent opened and a cheerful yet business-like voice said, "Good morning gentlemen, this is the NATO Taceval team." Rudely awoken, my mind instantly turned to thoughts of proving to strangers that our field-deployed Harrier squadron was fit-for-purpose. Martin Cliff's lightning reactions from deep within his sleeping bag mirrored his talent in the air, "This is a day recce/attack unit; come back in three hours." His precise words were different and perhaps not suitable for polite society but his aimed and aptly-named flying boot added further weight to his philosophical perspective on our capability.

However, the inquisitive part of my brain was sparked at that moment: warfare has no respect for the time of day. Surely we must evolve or suffer the consequences of creeping mediocrity and even irrelevance.

What an evolution from the 1960s and 1970s… I recall exceptional innovators like John Farley, making jaws drop as he flew backwards in an early-model Harrier at the head of a flight of army helicopters during a display. Then there was Tom Lecky-Thompson, taking off vertically from St Pancras in London and landing vertically in New York a little over six hours later[7]. For me, there was something equally mystical about this potential new era of night flying. Helmet-mounted tubular goggles magnified light levels not normally visible to the naked eye, as long as it wasn't too dark. Their sheer weight soon led to an extra inch of muscle in my neck. A forward-looking infra-red sensor showed the scene ahead on a tiny TV screen, or more crudely in the head-up display, not affected by darkness but most certainly affected by classically wet British weather. Perhaps I relished it all because there were so many unanswered questions. Or perhaps it was my natural competitor's love for anything that created asymmetry – namely, an edge that the other side does not have or cannot master to the same standard. It made me feel as alive (and hyper-attentive) as those pioneering aviators who challenged received wisdom on the laws of flight. Life with a capital 'L'.

There were many obstacles before we could harness technology and establish procedures for radically changing our approach to the night but, as Marshal Ferdinand Foch declared decades before, "The most powerful weapon is the human soul on fire." And I was on fire. World-class individuals like Bernie Scott and Les Evans[8] put me through an embryonic 'night electro-optic' conversion in January and February 1989. Their ever-present humour and downright skill not only taught me the basics but, crucially, prepared me for those moments when I would encounter the unknown. There was much we did not know. And my scientific colleagues at Farnborough were equally on fire; Pete Tanner and Andy Probyn worked their magic with the science behind everything we were doing, in close co-operation with defence industries who themselves were going out on a limb.

I had been posted to the Strike Attack Operational Evaluation Unit (SAOEU)

---

[7] Six hours and 11 minutes tower to tower, rather less flight time, see *Harrier Boys Volume One*.

[8] Bob Marston: later a BA Concorde pilot.

in late 1987, to join a small team of Tornado, Jaguar and Harrier flying and engineering specialists. Our remit? To make those aircraft not just fit-to-fly but fit-to-fight. As a lodger unit at Boscombe Down, we were separate from and often in an uneasy relationship with the Aeroplane and Armament Experimental Establishment. Air Commodore John Lumsden and his Central Trials and Tactics Organisation took local responsibility for our work, a commander who had the ability to pay close attention yet resist the temptation to delve into the details of tactical activities that were not exactly risk-free. He also helped keep the disbelievers in their place.

It was obvious we had to train hard with those night technologies available at the time. Work was not restricted to the aircraft itself. Whilst safely on the ground, our study of painstakingly-constructed terrain models using our goggles, varying the illumination provided by a simulated moon and streetlights, helped reinforce a range of lessons such as how difficult it was to see wires between pylons. We had a long way to go before front-line maturity was attained.

The more fundamental requirement was to educate our minds, to ensure we could keep adapting and innovating, creating scope for improvements in five or ten years' time. Hence I chose to immerse myself in the culture of those who had operated at the cutting edge of Air Power potential over the years, and specifically those who had done so whilst facing menacing enemies in the hours of darkness. Their acts of courage. Their stubbornness. Their resolve. Their willingness to experiment. I still knew we had to find our own way. 'The old boys' were not going to provide the answers but they certainly implanted a few extra nerves of steel for those inevitable dark moments.

Michael Allen DFC** was one such inspiration. Much later, in 1999, he wrote *Pursuit Through Darkened Skies*, about his flying experiences in World War II. He assuaged my suspicion of poetry, introducing me to words which reminded me that magic is for the movies; magic will not create a night-capable Harrier:

> *'The heights by great men reached and kept*
> *Were not attained by sudden flight,*
> *But they, while their companions slept,*
> *Were toiling upward in the night.'*

> Henry Longfellow
> *The Ladder of St. Augustine*, 1850

I felt it deep in my heart: unless we mastered the night, we would find our manoeuvre space threatened by our adversaries. Second place can be impressive and even honourable in many walks of life but it is fatal in war. The title of Group Captain Tom Sawyer's World War II memoir *Only Owls and Bloody Fools Fly at Night* provided a humbling reminder of something that might be an eternal truth and yet in Brigadier General William Mitchell's unmissable *Memoirs of*

World War I, that controversial prophet of air power provided a host of examples of why envelopes need to be expanded and what is expected of leaders: 'The great captains were those who thought out new methods and then put them into execution.'

Going beyond that vital reflection brought about by constant reading of insightful books, the psychological and human aspects of night operations truly started to hit home in the company of legendary survivors of Bomber Command and the Mosquito Aircrew Association. Veterans of 604 (County of Middlesex) Squadron added further backbone – even being in the same room as John 'Cat's Eyes' Cunningham was enough to up my game in terms of professionalism and hard-nosed analysis, let alone the daily process of overcoming fear of both the known and unknown.

There was the night when Dave Mackay[9] and I were flying the experimental Harrier T4 Nightbird (later renamed Nightrider by an MoD-based admirer of the 1980s TV series **Knight Rider**). I had just simulated an attack on an aircraft hangar on a coastal airfield. The approach to the target had been dead flat and I was flying at our minimum height of 250 ft above the ground. The instruments in this trials aircraft were somewhat rudimentary. Its head-up display gave erroneous attitude indications far too often, the result of the inertial navigation system insidiously starting to fail. The good thing was that this left us always flying with the greatest of suspicion: check, double-check, trust nothing unless verified. I flew a hard turn through 100°, leaving the comforting coast and looking closely at the waves below us through my NVGs. I rolled wings-level under the moonless sky. The goggles picked up the white water, foaming on the waves, pretty well. However, a lack of depth perception – the result of NVGs showing a flat image rather than the three dimensions we see with our normal eyesight – made it difficult to judge height and distance. I checked the digital altimeter and couldn't make out why there were only two figures as opposed to the expected three. In a split second, I went from thinking the read-out was corrupted to a realisation of what happens when below 100 ft. "Ahh" I said, almost calmly. "Ahh" said Dave in the back seat as I eased the stick back and brought the aircraft up the 200 feet or so lost in that turn ... The cruel sea ... A salutary lesson in the need to scan cockpit instruments and visual cues at a far higher rate when denied the all-aspect peripheral vision of conventional flying. And the equal need not to overreact to this event.

Unquestionably, that two-seat platform provided stark lessons for us aviators as well as evidence on equipment requirements for those fighting balance-of-investment battles in the Ministry of Defence. As but one example, we night flyers recognised the absolute importance of precision navigation systems at night. They

---

[9] Bob Marston: later chief pilot of Virgin Galactic.

did not exist at that time. And the brick walls of bureaucracy and intransigence faced would have been all too familiar to a legendary advocate of precision, Air Vice-Marshal D.C.T. Bennett CB, CBE, DSO. His 1958 book, *Pathfinder*, was a sobering yet inspirational reminder that as many adversaries would be found wearing our own uniform as those of traditional foes, but it taught me resilience. And to listen to trustworthy engineers, from corporals to chief technicians, who understood how all the little black boxes were meant to work and who kept me safe by exposing limitations and finding timely workarounds.

I also gained immeasurably by flying with both our modern-day Hercules night specialists (47 Squadron) as well as those aircrew operating the Chinook helicopter. For some in my fast-jet world, the relevance of a slow transport aircraft or an even slower rotary machine was hard to fathom. How wrong they were. Rotary expert Sean Reynolds was one of the first to impart words of wisdom. Just as mirages befuddle in the desert, so the night has its illusions; his advice hit home. Seeing the extraordinary workarounds our under-resourced C-130 crews used also helped me appreciate the relative excellence of the purpose-built night-compatible cockpit of the GR7. And I recognised too how many thanks were due to the work of my old friends in the United States Marine Corps. This warrior organisation thinks long and hard about combat. It has always turned mere aeroplanes into agile weapon systems that give genuine battle-winning options. Sharing experiences with them out in Yuma was immensely helpful. An RAF fighter controller, Mike Greatorex, was on exchange there with Marine Aviation Weapons and Tactics Squadron 1. He found us ideas and opportunities and opened doors in the finest traditions of those who gain the trust of our most important ally.

In those early pre-GR7 days of 1988-1990 though, I really didn't know if Harrier Force traditional low-flying tactics could be repeated in our single-seat aircraft at night. Let us not forget we were not equipped with the radar and auto-pilot terrain-following system so successfully employed on the Tornado. I was certain of one thing however: the rationale used by our naysayers was the result of prejudice and culture. When faced by a steep mountain, it is easy to feel overawed, doubt even, and hence the traditional approach is 'just to take one step at a time'. But time was not on our side. The answer was to take small steps quickly, flying at night and writing-up in the day, and to conduct trials that examined the most challenging scenarios. This was only possible because our small team of aircrew and engineers knew each other so well and trusted expertise rather than rank. Two SAOEU trials proved decisive to my thinking.

The first was Trial Pugnacity, with me flying hybrid Harrier T4 XW269 on the first official night low-flying trials' flight on 31 October 1989. Dave Mackay occupied the rear seat, as he did on several sorties thereafter, providing those essential pithy comments, soaked with meaning but which needed no further clarification at the time – "Speed", "Height", "Happy", "I have control", "Brilliant". My SAOEU partner-in-crime was Ken McCann[10] – calm under pressure and blessed with ego-free judgement when it comes to those moments when retreat is sensible. Better to live another day and try another angle, than die ignobly in some premature act of what history might call bravado.

With Keith Grumbley as our boss, bringing years of cunning and raw can-do to our business, the scene was set to take a few giant steps. Specifically, this was the phase of Pugnacity that saw us set up a classic Harrier field site in the corner of RAF Hullavington. Deliberately flying on nights with no moon to enhance our goggles' grainy image, we flew 'typical' night combat profiles and then returned to land vertically on our traditional MEXE pad far from the comforts of a normal airfield. Our ground crew also worked without conventional lights, with monocular goggles fitted to their Kevlar helmets. It was the ultimate test: copying everything we did during the day, at night. It worked. There could be no turning back.

The second trial that convinced me we were not insane as we looked forward to the potential for the night-capable GR7 was Trial Vowed. During March 1990, Ken McCann and I flew several night missions in aggressive attack formations in the company of fellow SAOEU Tornado and Jaguar aircrew. Taxiing out for one such sortie is memorable. We were soon to leave Boscombe Down to land at West Freugh in Scotland, intending to fly low en route and being ready to 'fight off' Tornado air-to-air fighters who were themselves developing night tactics and using the older Generation 2 NVGs – they joked that we 'had it easy' with our 'Gen 3' devices. My old friend Dave Mackay was back with his test pilot world and, at that moment, was going through the meticulous testing of whether it was safe even to taxi at night. Looking back, it was necessary rigour to ensure there would be no surprises in the future; at the time, the lengthy process was immensely frustrating. Our aircraft passed each other in the darkness and we waved. Our respective operating authorities were light years apart; our personal friendship would be forever.

With low cloud and thick mist shrouding parts of Scotland, I flew tactics I had rehearsed in more benign conditions in the weeks prior: moving into close formation on a Tornado's wing and then letting his radar guide us safely over the cloud-shrouded terrain. Only sitting behind a refuelling tanker buffeted by strong winds way out over the Atlantic, needing to 'plug' first time, have I felt as alive, with every sense in my body, including my sixth, working at maximum capacity. Those ensuing nights at West Freugh, flying with and talking to experienced aircrew who flew the Tornado and Jaguar, proved to me that our particular aircraft was on the right path. And when Dave Keenan took command of the SAOEU we once again were fortunate not only to have an exceptional aviator

---

[10] Bob Marston: later the penultimate Harrier Force commander.

at the helm but also someone who knew how 'the system' (MoD and industry) actually works – he could make our ideas resonate where it mattered.

In terms of a Harrier night capability, we were by no means there yet but we knew how to progress. It started by sorting in our own heads our fundamental purpose: offer combat and recce air power twenty-four hours per day, no excuses. NVGs and infra-red did not turn night into day but 'night flying' had been revolutionised. Every aspect of our standard operating procedures and rules had to be addressed: close formation flying, those wider-spaced 'battle formations', air-to-air refuelling, low and high-altitude tactics, weapons profiles (including the effect of forward-firing weapons on goggles), and how to avoid one of the most pressing risks, mid-air collisions. The simulator was used extensively to rehearse cockpit drills remorselessly – everything had to be committed to memory, with instant, fault-free recall. We also demanded brutally honest communication between all the participants, whether flyers or ground crew or air traffic controllers, striving for perfection, banning complacency and arrogance, never forgetting Bernie Scott's little book of 'I'll never do that again', even though we occasionally needed to add to its contents.

I flew my first night electro-optic sortie in a single-seat Harrier GR7 on 13 December 1990, a huge relief after years of necessary proof-of-concept work in that hybrid T4. I begrudged day flying; the night was my home. By August 1992, the time arrived to take our trials' experience and convert the oldest squadron in the world to night attack. Its motto of '*In omnibus princeps*' – 'First in everything' – was perfect. My journal entry for 30 September 1992 stated: '0300. Can't sleep. Too many things to do'. However, thanks to OC 1(F) Squadron, Chris Burwell, team-enhancing characters like Gerry Humphreys, high-quality flight commanders, and sheer all-round talents like Rob Adlam and Chris Norton, we walked that thin line between success and failure – that's a great story in its own right.

By January 1995, in the middle of the third official 'night season' of 1(Fighter) Squadron's experience with the latest night-vision technologies, the then Wing Commander David Walker wrote in its official history: 'The Harrier has truly come of age'. Pilots who fought in their Harriers during the 1982 Falklands conflict might have something to say about that. Rightly, they would suggest that their demonstration of operational relevance would have challenged those who once shook their heads disdainfully at the sight of Rolls-Royce's ground-breaking 'flying bedstead'.

Those of us who grew up under their wing, witnesses to their compelling and passionate recollections of the realities of war, knew that records must continue to be broken. That is the real arms race, one for which the Harrier Force family was more than ready: one of mind and spirit as well as equipment.

In 2008, I was deployed as the UK's air component commander in an area stretching from Afghanistan to Iraq and to the Horn of Africa. Having served for thirty years by that point, I still loved these real-world 'operations'. Not only did they bring out the very best in people deployed but all the practice and all the exercising was now over: the truth revealed. I oversaw and loved what we could do with all the fixed-wing aircraft and remotely-piloted air systems under my command. However, despite 'insider knowledge', I was still stunned by the capability I saw on display from RAF and RN Harrier pilots across the entirety of Afghanistan. I could rely on them to operate by day or night, at low or high level, in all weathers. In close proximity to our own troops, they were protecting, informing and reassuring. Even closer to our adversaries, they were deterring, warning, and, when necessary, using precise and lethal force. Twenty-four hours per day, seven days a week, always there when needed.

When the Harrier GR9 said its final farewells in 2010, every version along the way of this iconic aircraft had been significant and many take their rightful place in museums designed to educate and excite. Those men and women, of all ranks and trades, who have Harrier 'DNA', and especially night 'DNA', will not rest in a museum just yet; for them, the innovation and can-do spirit simply continue, such attributes are a way of life.

Harrier pilot with NVGs. (BAE Systems)

CHAPTER 13

NIGHT ATTACK – REALISATION

CHRIS BURWELL
THE INTRODUCTION OF NIGHT OPERATIONS TO THE HARRIER FRONT LINE

I took over command of 1(Fighter) Squadron in April 1991. The squadron had recently converted to the Harrier GR5 and was planned to commence night operations in autumn of that year, on a two-winter front-line night trial, re-equipped with the eagerly anticipated night-capable GR7 variant. With three tours on the Harrier behind me, I was only too well aware of the demands of daylight single-seat offensive support operations – and now we were being asked to do this at night! Up until this time, Harriers and night flying had been very rare bedfellows. I recalled a time in the Falkland Islands early in 1983 when 'normality' began to return to RAF Stanley and OC Supply Squadron put out a station order to the effect that stores exchanges and issues would only be available between the hours of 0900 and 1600. As Harrier flight commander I promptly put out an order saying that with immediate effect the Harrier Detachment would only be available for the air defence of the Falkland Islands between 0900 and 1600 hours and that outside these times the Phantom Detachment should be contacted for assistance. This was not far from the truth, of course, since our role in that theatre was limited to daylight hours only. But now the Harrier Force was going operational in the dark.

Although by this stage in my RAF career I had about 130 hours night flying, quite a lot for a Harrier pilot but much of it gained as a flying instructor, the rest of the squadron had much less night experience than me. In addition, from a personal perspective, I had now been away from flying for over five years on staff tours. So one concern was whether I would have the flying currency to lead the squadron into this task and another was whether we all had the experience and background to undertake the new role. But what did the task entail? And what experience and background did we need? My own first-hand experience was confined to one night trip in a Harrier T4 with Keith Grumbley when he was boss of the SAOEU; he had NVGs, I didn't, and it was frankly pretty scary. But there was no doubt that the ground-breaking work undertaken by the SAOEU, much of it on the very demanding Nightrider, had provided a sound experiential basis for us to introduce night operations to the front line and a firm belief that a Harrier day-combat-ready pilot should be able to cope with the demands of this new role.

In the event, due to delays with the introduction of the GR7, the night programme was delayed for a year and it was not until September 1992 that the squadron undertook the first night sorties. Even then, although the NVG-compatible cockpit lighting was ready, the goggle ejection system[11] was not, and we commenced night operations without the benefit of NVGs. By this time I had acquired an OC Night – Mike Harwood – from the SAOEU, who was experienced in NVG/FLIR operations and who would be key to converting the squadron to night operations over the coming two night seasons. Since none of us apart from Mike had any experience of NVG/FLIR, it was incumbent on me as the squadron commander to be at the forefront of whatever we were doing. Whilst Mike had devised a night-combat-ready work-up syllabus, I would have to ensure that I was happy with what we were asking the pilots to do and put a stop to anything I was uncertain about. I chose Rob Adlam, my squadron QWI, an experienced and very capable Harrier operator, as the man to join me in stepping out into dark and unknown territory and to help me decide what was safe. Without the NVG clearance, Mike's view was that we would benefit from flying without the goggles (using the naked eye and FLIR only) as this would help build our confidence. The early sorties achieved this although, at times, they could be somewhat exciting. Rob and I did quite a lot of night close formation and although the exterior night formation panels on the aircraft were excellent, without NVGs it was very difficult to assess how close you were to the other aircraft. I remember one night Rob calmly asking me to ease out as I had settled in too close to his aircraft without realising it – he could feel me interfering with the airflow over his aircraft. Trust was certainly required. 150 ft night bombing at Tain, rejoins into close formation and night tanking all had their moments as well. We quickly realised that we were all learning things by experience and, at times, making mistakes that we might not want to own up to. So we introduced a 'lessons learnt'/honesty book in which all pilots could put down anything that they thought might be of use to the rest of the team; entries were unattributable and hugely valuable.

It was a great source of comfort to me that I had one pilot who had a good amount of experience of EO operations; I also knew that Mike had an excellent reputation from his time with the SAOEU. However, this did not assuage my concern that, as squadron commander, I was responsible for the two-year trial and that no-one above me in the command chain had any appreciation of what

---

[11] A system to blow the NVGs off the pilot's helmet in the event of an ejection. Otherwise, the weight distribution with the goggles still attached to the helmet might result in the pilot's neck being broken on ejection.

we would be doing. It was a privileged position to be in and I was very grateful for the trust placed in me by the AOC 1 Group, his staff and both my station commanders over this period; they allowed us to get on with the job without any undue interference. I remember Group Captain Syd Morris saying that he always knew when we were getting towards the end of a night-training period because I would start getting tetchy. It wasn't a complaint; just a statement of fact that I, and the rest of the squadron pilots, would get noticeably tired after two-three weeks of continuous night operations.

In November 1992 we got the NVG clearance and began the night work-up properly. By this time it had become apparent that the aircraft modification programme for the blow-off system was going to be protracted which would limit the pilot conversion rate; this presented a new challenge since all the pilots were desperate to be at the cutting edge of bringing night operations into front-line service. Reluctantly, Mike and myself agreed that we would have to split the squadron into three groups of pilots: the A team who would get priority for night assets this first winter; the B team who would convert at a slower rate; and the non-combat-ready pilots who would not commence night operations until they were day combat ready, when they would join the B team. The exec, Ashley Stevenson, took over leadership of the B team. Unfortunately, but quite understandably, the B team always felt like second-class citizens. I was acutely aware of this and had trouble addressing it to their satisfaction. However, it says much for the commitment and engagement of the pilots on the squadron that this was how they felt. With the squadron operating a day team and a night team during our two or three-week night phases, just carrying out routine but important tasks like execs' meetings could prove difficult. At one point, it had become so difficult to get the flight commanders and SEngO together that I said we would have to meet after night flying one night; and this we did, starting a meeting at 0030 hours in the boss's office with a beer. In addition, with a pilot complement of just sixteen, all the execs (including the boss) took their turn as duty authorising officer, doubling up as duty pilot in the tower once the last night wave had been despatched.

Late in 1992 we were fully into night operations with Mike selecting the weeks we flew nights depending on the phases of the moon i.e. the light available, initially flying on well-lit nights but later on choosing nights with no moon at all so that we were using 2 millilux[12] from the stars at best to find our way around at 250 ft. During night-flying weeks, the squadron and the station had to adjust to us starting flying in the early afternoon and continuing through until around 2300 hours when the night low-level flying system closed. I was very fortunate

---

[12] In comparison, a full moon might provide 90 millilux or more. In such conditions, in dry air, the performance of the goggles was outstanding although never anywhere near daylight visibility.

to have those understanding and supportive station commanders throughout this period. Besides reorganising the station's support to meet our requirements, they also agreed to keep the bar open late for us so we could unwind after flying. It was not unusual for pilots to find it difficult to sleep after night operations because of the level of adrenalin in the body; unsurprisingly perhaps, we found that a beer or two with the other night fliers was a good way to wind down.

We had some visitors to the squadron to see what we were doing. I took a film crew from ITV to the ATC tower to 'watch' a pair of aircraft departing on a night sortie. They were somewhat surprised as we drove to the tower when I explained that I had twelve £14m Harrier GR7s on my squadron, 130 personnel and the task of introducing night operations to the Harrier Force yet my squadron commander's car, which they were travelling in, was so unroadworthy that it was not allowed off-base. In the tower we could hear the engines start and listened to the leader call for taxi clearance. We then went out onto the balcony to look across a completely black airfield (no light from the squadron apron either as the ground crew had, as always, despatched the aircraft in black-out conditions) and saw just two red wing lights accelerate rapidly across the unlit airfield, lift off and depart at low level towards the west; and that was it. We also had a visit from a very senior RAF officer from the MoD who came to find out what we were doing. Unfortunately he impressed by interrupting the two ex-Tornado Gulf War pilots, who were debriefing their mission for his benefit, to complain that they were not wearing the aircrew watches which he had fought a major battle in the MoD to acquire. My pilots wrapped up the debrief very quickly after that somewhat misplaced interjection.

Whilst the focus of what was happening on the squadron was decidedly on the air operations, it should also be remembered that the advent of night operations meant a huge change for the ground crew as well. Over the preceding year, the squadron had been busy relearning off-base deployment skills, culminating in a two-week deployed Maxeval[13] to a woodland site on the north side of the (at the time) disused airfield at Kemble. The two training exercises in Vigo Wood at Wittering and the deployment to Kemble had enabled the squadron to come together as a team and this stood us in good stead as we moved into a new phase in the squadron's development. In between night seasons, the squadron also deployed to Incirlik, Turkey, on Op Warden carrying out reconnaissance missions into northern Iraq in the aftermath of the First Gulf War. With Peter Coyle, followed by Peter Ewen as SEngO, and 'Charlie' Chaplin as squadron warrant officer, everything that we asked of the ground crew was done without

---

[13] A tactical evaluation carried out by HQ Strike Command. On this deployment, the single field site numbered well in excess of 300 personnel with support from RAF Wittering, other RAF units and the Royal Engineers, almost certainly the largest single Harrier field site ever deployed.

a quibble. Despatching the aircraft from a fully dark apron became routine and this continued whenever possible on deployed operations as well. It was probably just as well that the Health & Safety at Work representative tended not to come out at night.

Towards the end of the first night season, we deployed to Leuchars in February 1993 to carry out night operations in the Highlands including dropping 1,000-lb high explosive bombs on Garvie Island off Cape Wrath. Late one afternoon, some Tornado F3 crews came into the planning room and asked if we were planning our low level for the next day but thought we were joking when we said we were going to fly the route that night in the dark. I recall one particular mission on that detachment when I was flying as number two to Chris 'Snorts' Norton, one of the most capable first tourists in the Harrier Force at the time. Encountering some decidedly poor weather, I eventually gave up the struggle to keep with him in fighting wing[14] as we went through rain and snow showers in some demanding terrain and I pulled up above cloud. A quick exchange on the radio and we had agreed a rendezvous en route/on time with Snorts taking the north side of a valley whilst I let down through gaps in 5 octas[15] of cloud cover on the south side of the valley. The GPS/INS[16], navigational display, software and NVG/FLIR combination in the GR7 made such a task reasonably straightforward. At the debrief I asked Snorts how he had managed to remain at low level when I had pulled out? His answer was that as the NVG performance reduced, you could get more texture from (i.e. visibility of) the terrain by flying lower. I could appreciate that he was technically correct, but we all had to decide where our own personal levels of ability, comfort and safety lay.

A couple of months later the squadron deployed to the USMC base at Yuma to undertake night operations in the desert (very low or nil cultural lighting/poor NVG – dry air/excellent FLIR) and at the end of the second night season, we carried out night operations out of Bardufoss in northern Norway in March (some good cultural lighting with the Northern Lights and white snow-covered ground – moist air/limited FLIR). It was during this exercise that Gerry Humphreys and I undertook some of the first night close air support profiles as a pair, inputting the FAC brief direct into the GR7 through the upfront controller as writing the brief down in the cockpit at night was a non-starter! Towards the end of the Bardufoss detachment we were hosting a cocktail party for our Norwegian hosts which I required all officers to attend. Mike Harwood insisted that that night

---

[14] A 'swept' position on the leader with the range being adjusted as required depending on the weather, terrain and manoeuvre.

[15] Cloud cover is measured in 'octas' or eighths of cover.

[16] An integrated Global Positioning System/Inertial Navigation System. This provided a very accurate GPS position which ensured that the moving map display in the cockpit was always reliable.

was the last opportunity in the season for Ian MacDonald, the next OC Night, to get night-combat ready. I agreed that they could fly the mission provided they overflew the officers' mess at exactly 2000 hours at 250 ft as part of Ian's combat-ready check. I started my words of thanks to our hosts at 1957 and at 1959:30, after a timing nod from Gerry Humphreys, made our apologies for the two missing officers – "oh, here they come now!" – right on cue. The head-up display video was impressive and Ian passed his combat-ready check. In Norway we flew our first night three-ship and on return to Wittering, the last night trip of the season, and my last ever Harrier flight, was the first night four-ship. The next day I handed over command of the squadron to David Walker who would shortly lead the squadron into night operations for real in Bosnia.

Looking back, those two-night seasons were amazing – an exciting, challenging yet hugely rewarding eighteen-month period. We had progressed from a bunch of novices that knew nothing about offensive night operations to a team that could fly tactically at night with up to four aircraft, in different EO conditions, evade an aggressive air threat, locate a target and deliver weapons with a high level of precision. But what of the risks? I believe that by acknowledging from the outset that what we were about to undertake was inherently risky, we had already gone a long way to reducing the risk. In addition, by being open and honest when we could, using the honesty book when we couldn't, and carrying out extended debriefs in the bar into the small hours of the morning when necessary, we shared our experiences for the benefit of all. We had a huge respect for the role we were trying to get to grips with and this, as much as anything else, helped keep us safe. Tragically, we did lose a squadron pilot during this period, but not at night. We had asked for the USMC exchange post to be transferred from IV(AC) Squadron for a tour so that we could have an experienced AV-8B night operator and benefit from the USMC's night experience. Very sadly, Captain Brenden Hearney was killed when he flew into the ground on a low-level training exercise whilst he was attached to 233 OCU in January 1994.

There will not be a pilot who flew with the squadron over the two-night seasons that did not have 'moments' and, in truth, we were fortunate that none of them became more than that. I will end by sharing two of mine, which typify the pitfalls and risks:

- Rejoining the circuit at Yuma, as leader with my number two in fighting wing. The airfield is fully lit so we have removed our NVGs[17] and my number two is now following my tail light and using air-to-air TACAN to maintain separation from me. I decide that I am too close to the airfield so I turn left by about 40° to give us some

---

[17] The 'cultural lighting' from runway lights is so bright that it would cause the goggles to be swamped out by an excess of light and become unusable.

more separation from the runway before starting a turn back towards
the airfield. Shortly after rolling out of the turn there is an incredibly
loud roar as my number two flies right over the top of my aircraft,
missing me by a matter of feet. He had not detected my turn and
we were only saved from a mid-air collision by his religiously sticking
to always flying higher than his leader in fighting wing when close
to the ground.

- A singleton low-level night-navigation exercise. I coast out from the
  Lake District heading west over a very dark sea climbing to 1,500
  ft. There is virtually no goggle performance and little on the FLIR.
  I start my turn back to coast in again and begin a gentle descent
  on instruments so that I will be around 500 ft crossing the coast.
  The trip has gone well and I am feeling on top of things, so when
  I realise I have to do something in the cockpit I start to do it. A small
  voice in the back of my mind is telling me that this is not a good
  time but I assure myself it will only take a moment. Before I know
  it, the radio altimeter low-altitude warner is going (225 ft) and I am
  rolling wings level, pulling hard back on the stick and seeing 180
  ft on the altimeter. A salutary reminder – and I sadly needed one –
  that there is no room for complacency or over-confidence in single-
  seat, night, low-level operations.

We shared an amazing experience on 1(Fighter) Squadron over that eighteen-
month period. The most gratifying part was that the squadron's two-season
night trial, built upon the excellent work of the SAOEU, provided a sound basis
for night operations to be adopted by the other squadrons; and that night EO
operations were used in anger in a number of operational theatres by the Harrier
Force, from 1994 until the demise of the UK Harrier in 2010.

CHAPTER 14

HARRIER II BECOMES OPERATIONAL

STUART ATHA
HARRIER GR7 ARRIVES
Academics continue to argue over the factors that led to the collapse of the Berlin Wall in 1989. Although perhaps guilty of bias, Harrier fans would offer the view it was not mere coincidence the Soviets capitulated at a time when the Harrier Force, fielded in Germany, received an aircraft that signalled the most significant step increase ever in Harrier capability: the GR7. By the turn of the decade the GR3 was past its sell-by date, was less relevant to the needs of contemporary operations, and was desperately in need of an upgrade. The GR5 had served as a warm-up act for a couple of years but it provided only the faintest sense, the merest glimpse, of the quantum leap in capability the GR7 would deliver. The arrival of carbon fibre composite material and a large increase in wing area meant there was a vast improvement in range and payload; but even more impressive was the introduction of a glass cockpit and an array of modern avionics and sensors (notably forward-looking infra-red) that ensured the GR7 would be operated with equal ease and effectiveness by day and night, at tree-top and stratospheric heights (more to follow on this particular challenge), ashore and afloat, precisely delivering weapons of variable explosive yield regardless of the weather.

Some have argued the continuation of the name Harrier obscured the revolution in capability heralded by the GR7, but this would be to overly focus on the technology and to underestimate the critical importance of the Harrier Force ethos, in the air and on the ground. As has been demonstrated in earlier chapters, the pilots, engineers and support staff of the Harrier Force had rinsed out every ounce of capability from the GR3 through professionalism, dedication, innovation and good old-fashioned teamwork. Equip the force with an aircraft boasting cutting-edge technology, match it to a force of this calibre, and the RAF had a capability second to none.

THE WORLD CHANGES
The arrival of the Harrier GR7 coincided with a seismic shift in geo-politics as the Soviet Union crumbled, large states fractured into smaller ones, and suppressed

ambitions and ideologies flourished. The spectre of a NATO-Soviet conflict, which had dominated Harrier Force basing, equipment and tactics had gone, to be replaced by a myriad of hotspots ignited by the shifting new world order. Whilst the Falklands conflict stands as an exception to the orthodox narrative, the events that followed the fall of the Berlin Wall were to drive the RAF from a static deterrent posture, which if unsuccessful would herald Armageddon, to an expeditionary force which politicians could choose, and did so regularly, where and when to employ. The flexibility and ubiquity of air power meant that, in quirky concert with Olympic and World Cup periodicity, the RAF would conduct significant operations on a four-yearly basis – 1991, 1995, 1999, 2003. Although conceived for a different era, the GR7 ensured that the Harrier Force would play a central role in areas as diverse as Iraq, the Balkans, Africa and Afghanistan. But this proud record of service was not to include a part in the first post-Cold War test, the Gulf War of 1991.

THE WALLFLOWERS

Following its prominent role in the Falklands War, it was something of a blow in 1991 for the Harrier Force to sit on the side-lines of the most significant UK military operation for decades, Op Granby. Whilst the sheer professionalism and bravery of the Tornado and Jaguar aircrew in the skies over Iraq was beyond doubt, it was frustrating for both Harrier pilots and ground crew that the GR5/7 capability was insufficiently mature to play a part. Although little compensation, it should be noted, however, that it was an RAF Harrier pilot (Flight Lieutenant Andy Dakin) flying AV-8B Harriers on exchange with the USMC, who delivered more weapons than any other member of the Royal Air Force during the 1991 operation. Moreover, the US Harrier flew more sorties (over 3,000) than any other coalition aircraft type and it was only surpassed by the B-52 in terms of ordnance dropped. The RAF Harrier Force 'head' understood that the absence of the RAF's 'AV-8B', the GR7, was simply an unfortunate issue of timing – but the 'heart' realised that Harrier Force bragging rights had been seriously undermined, for the time being.

OPERATION WARDEN

Directly following the end of formal combat on Op Granby, a US-led operation – Provide Comfort – delivered humanitarian relief to the Kurds in the north 'to create places and conditions in which refugees can feel secure' (Foreign Secretary, Parliamentary Statement, 15 April 1991). Almost all the 400,000 Kurdish refugees who had fled into the mountains on the Iraq-Turkey border region returned to their homes or to the camps constructed for them by coalition forces and on 24 July 1991 a United Nations protection zone was established for the Kurds. Under the banner of Op Warden, RAF Jaguars policed the associated no-fly zone north of the 36th parallel to prevent Saddam from attacking the Kurds.

A similar no-fly zone was established in southern Iraq in August 1992 after Saddam's persecution of the Shia Marsh Arabs. Op Jural was the UK element of that operation and was supported by RAF Tornado squadrons. In the following years two Iraqi fighter aircraft were shot down and the Iraqi ground-based air defence system proved to be an enduring irritation to coalition crews flying in the north and south of Iraq. By 1993, the Harrier Force was ready for its first operational outing with its latest mount. Much more GR7 potential had yet to be unlocked, but it had sufficient capability for the Harrier Force to replace the hard-pressed Jaguar squadrons operating in Turkey. Therefore, in April 1993, IV(AC) Squadron spearheaded a Harrier Force deployment to Incirlik air base in Turkey – marking the first operational employment of the GR7.

CLIMBING OUT OF THE WEEDS

Fortunately, given its immaturity, the Harrier GR7 would be employed on relatively simple armed-reconnaissance missions that needed a fraction of its capability. Operations were conducted by day and were restricted to above 5,000 ft – unless operating in the Kurdish area. The GR3 could have been employed on the operation, with shortfalls in range being overcome through the employment of VC10 and TriStar tanker aircraft. However, the greatest challenge for the GR3 would have been that posed by operating at medium level in an aircraft designed for flying in the weeds of Germany. The losses suffered by the courageous Tornado crews during the First Gulf War drove a paradigm shift in RAF tactics and risk appetite. The sacrifices expected in the war of survival NATO was prepared to wage, were not acceptable in the wars of choice. The 'mud-moving' club, of which the Harrier Force was a fully paid-up member, needed to adapt and the force needed to embrace the third dimension and join the 'cloud dancing' community that was previously the preserve of the 'air defenders'. GR7 pilots and engineers needed to work out quickly how the Harrier steed could be equally effective at all altitudes.

The 'big wing' of the GR7 was exploited with the standard load for Op Warden including two external fuel tanks, two Sidewinder Aim-9L missiles, a reconnaissance pod, a PHIMAT chaff pod and a couple of US CBU-87 cluster bombs. The integral electronic warfare systems (appropriately named, perhaps, Zeus – god of the sky) was rapidly tested and proven against the likely Iraqi SAM systems, although its tendency to provide spurious warnings prompted by other aircraft or even the Iraqi telephone network was to prove particularly annoying. More seriously and belatedly, pilots became aware that Zeus was another system optimised for low level and therefore designed to look ahead, to the side and behind but not below. This meant there was a black hole of ignorance beneath the Harrier that became bigger the higher you flew. In this void, the enemy radars could find and target the GR7 without any warning from Zeus. The only way to fill the gap was to regularly weave as a pair of aircraft, constantly checking each other's 'six-o'clock' below as well as behind. The threat posed by the wall of advanced Soviet RF SAMs had driven the RAF to hide at low level. The US, however, followed another philosophy that relied on using other aircraft to jam and effectively blind the Soviet radars. Whilst Zeus was capable of this to a degree, it was not powerful enough to allow the RAF to operate at the same altitudes as the USAF or the USMC. Consequently the RAF had a weapon inventory designed for low-level delivery – in contrast to the US which had procured weapons that could be delivered from much higher altitudes. The Harrier staple diet of BL755 cluster bombs needed to expand. Fortunately, given that the RAF and USMC operated a common platform, there was the ability to clear USMC weapons on RAF Harriers. Sadly this did not extend to the software that included the important US weapon ballistic performance (i.e. how far forward a weapon would travel at a particular height and speed). As a result, Heath Robinson (if ever there was a man who should be made an honorary member of the Harrier Force) was yet again called into action to allow the GR7 to be armed with the US CBU 87 cluster bomb. The QWIs pulled out their calculators and trigonometric tables and quickly came up with a series of tables and delivery profiles that acted as a bridge between UK and US weapon performance.

WAR PAINT

The Harrier GR5 and GR7 aircraft had arrived in a livery of drab olive, a lichen green that NATO had adopted to allow low-flying aircraft to hide in the verdant countryside of Europe. Change environments to the blue skies of Iraq and spotting Harriers would become a popular and undemanding sport for the Iraqi army. The answer was to paint the aircraft a light grey colour. Although the shade of grey would evolve over time, the deployment of the GR7 to Iraq marked the start of the transition away from the familiar green camouflage scheme for good. Another permanent change to Harrier GR7 external marking that was driven by the operation involved the emotive issue of tail letters. The history of Harrier tail letters is long and complex but immediately prior to the operation, 1(F) Squadron had numbers, 3(F) Squadron and IV(AC) Squadron had two letters, the first of which was A and C respectively. The requirement to pool aircraft to meet the operational demand meant that all aircraft nominated for Warden had two letters, the first of which was a W. In time the fleet would transition to a logic-rich, history-poor, solution involving fleet numbers.

BACK TO THE RECCE ROLE

Despite the GR7's inbuilt dual-mode tracker TV system and the addition of stand-off reconnaissance pods (VINTEN long-range optical reconnaissance pod and the VICON 18 Series pod), the limited GR7 reconnaissance capability meant that old GR3 recce pods were dusted off and rushed back into service on the GR7. The GR3 pods were optimised for low-level flying and had five cameras of varying focal lengths that provided 'horizon-to-horizon' coverage. At the heights being flown it was only the outer cameras pointing just below the wing tips that could provide photographs of useable resolution[18]. Yet again innovation was required. With a 20° field of view and the need to reduce slant range, pilots had to conduct a knife-edge manoeuvre past targets (guided by lines drawn using chinagraph pencils on the aircraft canopy) to have any hope of producing photographs of sufficient quality to allow the highly talented imagery analysts eagerly awaiting back at Incirlik to exploit the photographs for scraps of intelligence about the Iraqi army. Frustrations were further compounded by ever-present oil smears on the camera lenses (oil leaks sadly were an enduring challenge for the Harrier, regardless of mark). Somehow, despite the abundance of challenges, some outstanding photographs were produced using the GR3 pod, including images of Iraqi barracks and the Roland SAM sites around the town and dam of Mosul. It is not known whether the best images were produced by pilots flying on a knife edge at 5,000 ft or those rumoured to have resorted to conducting 1980-style ultra-low-level recce runs. Flying at low level was permitted behind the 'Green Line' that defined the Kurdish safe areas to the north. However, as OC 1(F) Squadron – Wing Commander David Walker – was to discover on 2 February 1995, this did not necessarily mean it was safe for Harrier pilots. But before then, in November 1993, the Harrier Force was to lose its first GR7 on operations.

THE FIRST LOSS

On 23 November 1993, six IV(AC) Squadron GR7s launched from Incirlik. Their mission was a standard reconnaissance sortie into northern Iraq. As usual, the six launched as three pairs for the 50-minute transit through southern Turkey and into northern Iraq where they would rendezvous with a VC10 tanker aircraft of 101 Squadron. The weather for the medium-level mission was marginal with extensive cloud cover between 10,000 and 25,000 ft. The refuelling element of the sortie was carefully choreographed to ensure aircraft left the tanker with the maximum amount of fuel. Flying just above the cloud tops, the pilot of ZD432, Squadron Leader Jim Fernie (Fer)[19], was about to finish topping up with fuel when the aircraft engine surged. Despite descending into cloud, in the mountainous area of northern Iraq, Fer made several attempts to relight his engine, none of which were successful. With options and height running out, Fer ejected at 8,000 ft, just 1,500 ft above the mountain tops.

Shortly after Fer had disappeared into the cloud, the other pilot in his pair, Squadron Leader Steve Forward (Fad), decided to follow Fer into the murk

---

[18] In the GR3, the fixed camera in the nose usually had a lens with 3-in focal length. In the pod, the outer cameras had 6 in, the inner obliques 4 in, and the vertical camera 1.5-in focal length.

[19] For sortie programming convenience, all RAF pilots are commonly identified by a trigraph.

below, very aware of the mountains puncturing the cloud base below. Thanks to a mixture of courage and skill, Fad emerged into an Iraqi valley and hauled his GR7 through gaps between the ground and the clouds, desperate for any sign of Fer. Above the cloud, the remaining four Harrier pilots maintained a silent presence alongside the tanker aircraft, uttering not a word, listening to the emergency radio frequency on which they hoped that Fer would call, using the emergency radio attached to his combat vest.

Fortunately, despite landing heavily in the mountains to the north of Sirsenk, Fer suffered only a twisted knee. Aware of the potential for Iraqi forces to be in the area, and hearing some activity in the distance, he quickly hid behind the nearest large boulder. Whilst trying to compose himself, he heard a loud thud from behind him. Slowly, he turned around to see a fearsome-looking Peshmerga fighter armed with an AK47 assault rifle and wrapped in belts of ammunition. Fearing the worst Fer raised his arms in surrender. At this the Kurd raced towards him and delivered what Fer described as the biggest and most welcome hug he had ever received.

Mohammed Abdullah, as we now know, and his cousin – curiously named Abdullah Mohammed – helped Fer to safety, handing him over to US Special Forces who recovered Fer back to Incirlik in their Blackhawk helicopters. Within hours of his ejection a relieved Fer joined Fad and the equally relieved members of his formation for a very welcome steak in a rather well provisioned Incirlik officers' club restaurant.

The subsequent securing and recovery of the crashed aircraft presented many challenges. The IV(AC) Squadron armourer who 'volunteered' to support this effort was not sure what posed the greatest threat – the bullet fired through the floor of his Blackhawk helicopter by angry natives below or the vertiginous Iraqi slopes, across which ZD432 and its weapons were strewn. Thankfully, the Kurds of northern Iraq could not have been more helpful. Peshmerga fighters volunteered to guard the crash site and facilitated the slow recovery of the Harrier pieces back to the UK. This included the ejection seat, which after much searching was eventually discovered in a village, where one of the elders used it as a rather uncomfortable throne in his hut.

The aircraft accident investigation failed to conclusively prove the cause of the engine surge or provide a technical explanation for the failure of the engine to relight. However, it is clear that it was thanks to the US and the Kurdish community we recovered Fer quickly and safely. Members of the USAF 305th Rescue Squadron, an air force reserve unit, were subsequently honoured for the role they played in Fer's rescue. In recognition of the exceptional levels of support provided by Mohammed Abdullah, his cousin and the rest of the Kurdish community, the British government presented the local village elders with forty pregnant goats and a water-damming facility. For their part, the members of IV(AC) Squadron presented Mohammed Abdullah with the ubiquitous signed squadron print of a Harrier GR7.

Some ten years after the event, the Home Office approached RAF Cottesmore seeking confirmation that northern Iraqi Kurds had helped recover an RAF pilot in 1993. Apparently, a Kurd going by the name of Mohammed Abdullah was in London seeking asylum and had the signed picture of an aircraft to prove the crucial role he played saving a Harrier pilot. Needless to say, his asylum application was supported by the Harrier Force.

A CLOSE SHAVE

Whilst the Harrier Force deployed to protect Kurdish safe havens, it may well have been a stray Kurdish bullet that nearly downed OC 1(F) Squadron on 2 February 1995. Rather unusually, the mission that day for a four-ship of 1(F) Squadron GR7s was to conduct an area search of large parts of the Kurdish area for heavy weapons (such as Soviet D-20 and D-30 artillery pieces). The search area was a large rectangle behind the Green Line in the vicinity of Erbil, which meant that the sortie could be conducted at low level. The mission involved Flight Lieutenants Atha (Hat) and Ingle (Nig) in the lead pair and Wing Commander Walker (Wak) and Flight Lieutenant Wharmby (baby[20] Wam) following behind. The weather was beautiful with no clouds to interfere with the transit or refuelling element of the sortie. The four aircraft split into two pairs. During the first sweep through the area a D-20 was spotted and photographed by Hat/Nig. During the second sweep, near the south-western edge of the area, a bullet hit the left-hand side of Wak's canopy arch, smashing the acrylic canopy into thousands of jagged shards. Despite injuries to the left of his face, Wak managed to climb his now open-top Harrier away from the ground and into the relative sanctuary of higher altitudes, carefully shepherded by his wingman Wam.

As always, the crew of the 101 Squadron VC10 tanker aircraft provided the Harrier Force with exceptional support, relaying updates back to base at Incirlik and providing a reassuring presence overhead. Having completed all their immediate tasks, the ever helpful VC10 crew asked if there was any more they could provide. The response from Wak that a jumper would be welcome met with stony silence. Never wishing to pass up a photo opportunity, Wam used his reconnaissance pod to take photos of a windswept and bloodied Wak crouched forward in the cockpit as they limped back to the nearest Turkish airfield across the border. Wam elected to land with his squadron boss at the isolated and desolate base, a selfless decision he was to regret when Wak ordered Wam to remain with the Harrier cabriolet whilst he jumped in Wam's serviceable aircraft and flew back to join the squadron at Incirlik. Yet again the officers' club was the venue for the debrief. Leaning against the bar in his bloodied flying suit, with the skin on his face and neck looking like it had been assaulted by a blunt

---

[20] His brother was Wam. Both ejected from GR7s.

razor, Wak regaled his coterie of junior pilots (absent the unfortunate Wam) with his tales of derring-do. The notorious unreliability of the HUD recording system was a contributory factor in the failure to determine whether Wak's Harrier had been targeted by the Iraqi army, an irate farmer or that he had flown too close to feuding Kurds or a wedding celebration.

FIELD CONDITIONS

In a force that prided itself in the ability to operate in the most austere of environments, from San Carlos to Sennelager, Incirlik air base provided unaccustomed luxury. The USAF had invested heavily in the base since the 1950s and allowed the Harrier Force to take full advantage of the facilities. With a golf course, cinema, supermarket, gymnasium and the aforementioned officers' club, deployments to Incirlik were not a hardship. Whilst the officers lived in comfortable hotel-like accommodation, the airmen lived in a tented city. But even the tents were a far cry from the usual leaking 12x12 canvas tents erected in German field sites. With wooden floors and air conditioning, life was comfortable. And being Harrier Force engineers, life was made even more comfortable with the opening of the Hover Inn, a social facility as popular with US colleagues as it was with the whole Harrier Force. The 'special relationship' was further deepened by reciprocal visits to similar US social facilities, preferably those with hot tubs, such as Prime Beef, Twin Tails, The Outback Bar and Raven's Roost. The sense of a coalition team was forged during many social occasions and provided an important opportunity to build both personal and professional relationships with US and French colleagues.

BLACKHAWK DOWN

The strength of the international relationship was tested on 14 April 1994 when two F-15 aircraft, operating under the control of a USAF AWACS aircraft, misidentified two United States army UH-60 Black Hawk helicopters as Iraqi Mil Mi-24 'Hind' helicopters. The F-15 pilots fired on and destroyed both helicopters, killing all twenty-six military personnel aboard, along with civilians from the United States, United Kingdom, France, Turkey, and the Kurdish community. Whilst the Harrier Force was not directly involved in this tragic incident, 1(F) Squadron pilots played a supporting role in the aftermath, including through the provision of airborne imagery of the crash site.

THE HARRIER FORCE RETURNS HOME READY FOR THE NEXT OPERATION

During the Harrier Force deployment on Op Warden, the situation stabilised and the immediate threat to the Kurdish community reduced. In return for the protective air umbrella provided by coalition forces, the Kurds supported the RAF when needed, as demonstrated on 23 November 1993. Memories of the genocidal gas attack at Halabja in 1988 remained seared in the minds of the

Kurds and underlined the enduring threat posed by Saddam and his regime. Whilst the Harrier Force was proud of its contribution, this was tempered by the knowledge that the same Kurdish villagers they protected from the Iraqis were being caught in the cross-fire between the PKK and the Turkish armed forces. The sound of Harriers overhead could equally be warning of an imminent attack by the Turkish air force. It would be some eight years before the Harrier Force returned to the skies over northern Iraq during the Second Gulf War and some twenty years later the RAF would yet again be supporting the Kurds and the Peshmerga fighters, this time in their battle against the extreme terrorism of Islamic State of Iraq and the Levant.

But back in the winter of 1994/95, the focus of the Harrier Force was beginning to shift from Iraq to an even more complicated situation in the Balkans, where events were spiralling out of control. Whilst the deployments to Incirlik had allowed the Harrier Force to re-establish its operational credibility, the challenge posed in the Balkans was significantly greater. After two years of rotational deployments between the three front-line Harrier squadrons, 1(F) Squadron, 3(F) Squadron and IV(AC) Squadron, the Op Warden commitment was handed over to Tornado squadrons, which for the first time were responsible for policing both the northern and the southern no-fly zones. The deepening instability in the Balkans increased concerns over the risks of genocide and the direct threat posed to British army units deployed throughout Bosnia. Every combat indicator suggested that the time might be coming for the Harrier Force to employ the GR7 in the night-attack role for which it was ideally suited.

CHAPTER 15

COMBAT OPERATIONS COMMENCE – THE BALKANS

After a short tour in Operational Requirements in the MoD, where getting clearances for the GR7 was my priority, I was a little surprised to find myself flying the Jaguar as a wing commander. There were several areas of read-across between the two single-seat attack forces, not least in the introduction of TIALD. In OR, I was frustrated by the slow integration process for GR7, but I was then able to see the Jaguar proof-of-concept demonstrator, which had been used to show how a pilot could, unassisted, operate the system, become, through a UOR that bypassed the original design authority, a real capability, albeit on the Jaguar first. My final Jaguar mission over Bosnia was on 22 May 1995, flying at medium level with a LOROP pod, on a cloudy day, to photograph suspected SAM sites. Having spent time flying around over Bosnia looking at the desolation below, there was an inevitability in my next posting, in 1995, to command the UN AOCC in Sarajevo, where I resumed, remotely, my connection with the Harrier Force.

STUART ATHA
1(F) AND 3(F) SQUADRONS PREPARE

Whilst the Harrier Force had performed with customary professionalism over northern Iraq, the operation (day, medium-level, recce) only tapped a fraction of the force's capability. But the brewing troubles in the Balkans and the increasing likelihood that the situation in Bosnia would soon implode, drove the development of a highly-classified British army extraction plan that required intimate night-time close air support – a task ideally suited to the Harrier GR7.

Who better to prepare the force for such a task than the 'Prince of Darkness' (POD) himself, Mike Harwood. Building on the experience gained in previous night seasons, POD orchestrated an intensive 1(F) Squadron training programme in 1994/95, preparing the squadron to support the emergency evacuation of British soldiers from the Gorazde enclave. The contingent operation required the squadron to play an integral part in a highly-sensitive night-time heliborne extraction plan. Key to success would be the intimate synchronisation of Harriers, helicopters and Special Forces. In preparation, a series of rehearsals were conducted covertly in both Wales and Scotland through 1994 and early

1995. Pilots familiarised themselves with every nook and cranny of Gorazde, helped by the creation of a classified room at Wittering which had 3D images of the town and surrounding terrain pinned to the walls.

The sensitivity of the mission, combined with the need to preserve the confidence of the Special Forces, was such that the circle of those involved was kept tight. This inevitably added tension to relationships within the Harrier Force and between the squadron commanders, particularly with those outside the circle, that is OC 3(F) and OC IV(AC) Squadron. The threat posed to the rescue mission by the Bosnian Serbs' air defence system drove layers of sophistication into the plan, including necessary attack missions against radar sites. The evolving mission required more night-qualified pilots than 1(F) Squadron could provide – enter OC 3(F) Squadron and his cement heads. They were quickly read into the plan and tasked with the less challenging but just as important air interdiction missions that would require precision attacks against radars using Paveway bombs guided by Special Forces, which would blind the Serbian air defence system to the incoming extraction force.

In the event, the trigger for action, and the bloodying of the Harrier GR7 in combat, was a mortar attack on a Sarajevo market in August 1995. Rather surprisingly, less dramatically, and disappointingly for those involved in the derivation and evolution of the complex Gorazde extraction, the Welch Fusiliers simply drove out. Whilst the two Harrier squadrons involved in the classified extraction plan proudly boast that 'The Third Shall be First' or that they are 'First in All Things', it was the 'big noses' of IV(AC) Squadron, led by the only squadron commander not read into the sensitive Gorazde extraction plan, OC IV(AC) Squadron, who were first to employ the GR7 in anger, and the first RAF squadron to lead a NATO combat mission.

IV(AC) SQUADRON EXECUTES

The Balkans imploded in the summer of 1995. In July the town of Srebrenica was ethnically cleansed and many thousands of Muslims were slaughtered; the UN peacekeeping mission was failing and UN peacekeepers were becoming hostages; over 100,000 Croat soldiers attacked the Serbs in Krajina; and then many innocents were killed in the mortar attack on Sarajevo. The patience of the international community had exhausted and NATO responded on 30 August 1995 with the launch of Operation Deliberate Force.

IV(AC) Squadron, on behalf of the Harrier Force, had replaced the Jaguar Force in the last week of July 1995 and had done little more than read the orders and conducted familiarisation sorties when operations commenced, much to the surprise of all, not least the commanding officer of IV(AC) Squadron, Wing Commander Chris 'Boggy' Moran, who was still back at Laarbruch. The mission required laser-guided bombs to be delivered, which was rather inconvenient as the GR7 was not yet equipped with the targeting pod necessary to fire the laser that would guide bombs to their targets. This led to the recall of two Jaguars and pilots (Squadron Leader Alex Muskett and Flight Lieutenant Simon Blake) back to theatre.

Whilst much banter was exchanged about the relative merits of 'carrying' bombs versus 'guiding' them, it is to the credit of all that the team, Jaguar and Harrier, operated as one. The first mission on 30 August was led by Squadron Leader Andy Suddards, although to the chagrin of the QWI fraternity it was a QFI combo (Flight Lieutenants Linney [Dins] and Blake) who released and designated the first attack using a laser-guided bomb. The final mission of the first day was the first NATO formation (Strike Package Delta) to be led by the RAF, with Squadron Leader Stuart Atha (Hat) at the helm, ably assisted by his wingman Major Mike Hile (Zieg – USMC exchange officer) and Squadron Leader Alex Muskett in his Jaguar.

STRIKE PACKAGE DELTA 30 AUGUST 1995

Strike Package Delta involved twenty-four British, French and American aircraft tasked with attacking targets surrounding Pale, a Bosnian-Serb stronghold. The sortie had not started well with both Zieg then Hat's aircraft developing faults, which delayed mission launch. Although this involved swapping precision bombs for dumb bombs, it was decided that Muskett would continue to support the mission by using the Jaguar laser to help the Harrier pilots locate and attack their targets. Despite the delayed launch, the mission proceeded because the attack plan included enough time over target to allow any late comers from Strike Package Delta to flow in at the end of the bracket. This meant that the RAF formation would be the 'tail-end Charlies' of the mission, never the safest place to be in any attack. The new order of arrival over the target was therefore, Americans, French then the British. The weather over Bosnia was not great with a general cloud base of around 12,000 ft which dropped even lower where there were showers. To identify targets, aircraft were forced to fly within the range of Serbian missile and gun systems below.

After a challenging descent through cloud, the RAF aircraft transited across Bosnia, passed Sarajevo and joined the tail of Strike Package Delta. As they approached the target area near the Serbian stronghold of Pale, the scene was reminiscent of World War II footage with plumes of smoke billowing into the air and many of the ammunition storage buildings and factories surrounding the town already ablaze with flames leaping high into the sky. Musky fired his laser at the designated target, helping Hat lock on the Harrier GR7's dual-mode tracking system to the ammunition storage shed. With seconds to go, Hat's thumb was hovering above the control column ready to press the bright red circular bomb release button, when Zieg spotted the launch of two missiles from a spot high up on the side of Mount Igman, north and west of the target area. Responding to Zieg's warning call, Hat aggressively manoeuvred his aircraft and dispensed flares, the ingrained response drilled into all Harrier pilots. As Hat threw his aircraft round the sky he looked over his shoulder to see, disappointingly, the upwards expanding smoke trail of two surface-to-air missiles continuing to arc towards him. Readying himself for the well-practised Harrier end-game manoeuvre, which involves the pilot conducting a violent barrel roll around the missile to generate sufficient miss distance to survive, both missiles, rather disconcertingly, disappeared. The end of the smoke trail marked the end of the rocket-assisted boost phase of the launch but not the end of the missile's flight. This had not been mentioned in the tactics manual – how do you fight a missile you cannot see? After a tense couple of seconds, the missiles reappeared, thankfully as they automatically detonated some 2,000 ft from the aircraft.

Despite the shock of the missile launch and the descent to low altitude over Mount Igman during the manoeuvres to defeat the missiles, Hat and Zieg reformed formation and re-attacked the target from a different direction. In the mayhem during the missile launch, Muskett had very sensibly continued to fly his Jaguar south of the target and the time remaining prevented him rejoining the formation. The re-attack had mixed success with Zieg successfully destroying his target; Hat, however, could not release his bombs because of a wiring problem in the aircraft pylon, which had a whiff of irony given Hat could have jettisoned his bombs during the manoeuvres to defeat the Serbian missiles.

Unlucky as this might be, the French crew of a Mirage 2000 aircraft in Strike Package Delta were much less fortunate. Flying ahead of the Harriers, they had not spotted the Serbian missile fired at them as they attacked the target (video of shoot-down available on YouTube). Both aircrew, Captains Chiffot and Souvignet, survived the shoot-down and the potshots taken at them as they floated down in their parachutes. But they were taken prisoner and endured an extended period of incarceration by the Serbs until they were released four months later. Hat and Captain Chiffot met again some fifteen years later in Paris and discovered that they had both been attacked by missiles fired from the same location on Mount Igman. Chiffot revealed that the Frenchmen had broken legs on landing and had been subject to brutal physical and psychological torture through their period in captivity[21]. The RAF Harrier Force has benefited much from its links with its cousin in the USMC. On this occasion, it was thanks to the eagle-eyed look out of the USMC pilot, Major Mike 'Zieg' Hile, that Hat had not joined Captain

[21] Bob Marston: After the bombing, there were attempts to normalise relations. One day, a party of Serb local politicians crossed the front line to talk with their Bosnian counterparts. As usual, a couple of British troops stayed at the crossing point to see it remained safe. It soon became apparent that they had disappeared. Our commander in Sarajevo quickly pointed out to the Serb army that the politicians would remain as our guests until our two men returned. They reappeared 24 hours later, apparently unperturbed by the light torture they had endured.

Chiffot as a prisoner of war, or worse. *Semper Fi.*

OPERATION TIMBER

After this incident a friendly rivalry grew between the French and British squadrons. This was best exemplified by the 'race' to be first to destroy an important and particularly large communications mast north of Tuzla, a mission that became known as Operation Timber. Both nations had made a number of attempts but had been thwarted by the weather. However on 7 September 1995 the weather had turned fair and it was the Harrier Force's turn to attack the mast. To maximise the chances of success four aircraft armed with a mixture of slick and laser-guided bombs were tasked against the mast and on the day were joined by a fifth Harrier, which was re-tasked in the air to join the formation.

Unfortunately it was rather late in the afternoon, and with the sun setting, there was time for only one attack by the formation against this prestigious target. Therefore all five aircraft dropped their bombs simultaneously. Unsurprisingly, the mast was successfully downed. As the Harriers also carried reconnaissance pods, a photograph of the mast lying on the ground was taken and subsequently sent to the French detachment declaring Operation Timber complete. 7 September 1995 will not only be remembered as the day we got one over on the French, but was also the first and only day in the history of the squadron that every combat-ready member of IV(AC) Squadron successfully dropped a bomb on combat operations.

Over the three weeks of Op Deliberate Force, NATO's strategy was more 'talk and act' than 'shock and awe'. The flexibility of air power was highlighted through its ability to be integrated with diplomatic activity. Diplomacy offered the carrot, whilst NATO's air forces wielded the stick. Together, the Harrier and Jaguar Force flew 144 sorties and delivered forty-eight laser-guided bombs and thirty-two freefall bombs against a range of targets, including ammunition dumps, communications sites[22] and radar sites. The culmination of military action was diplomatic success; NATO bombing alone did not bring peace to Bosnia, but it was the catalyst to the negotiations that followed, which in turn led to the signing of the Dayton Peace Accords and the years of relative peace that have ensued.

Whilst peace persisted in Bosnia, this was not the case with Serbia. Less than four years later the Harrier Force would embark yet again on offensive operations in the Balkans, this time under the banner of Op Allied Force. It would be 1(F) Squadron's turn to lead the Harrier Force into war.

---

[22] Bob Marston: When the American-led NATO AOCC (a brigadier general + 100) took over in Sarajevo from me and my ten men, they were initially frustrated by the lack of cell phone connection, forgetting that NATO had destroyed much of the network.

CHAPTER 16

OPERATION ALLIED FORCE

MARK ZANKER

In January 1999 I was a QWI with 1(F) Squadron and we were detached to Nellis AFB, Las Vegas, to participate in Exercise Red Flag. The exercise consisted of day and night low-level attack sorties, dropping live 1,000-lb bombs on targets in the desert ranges of Nevada. At that time there were frequent news bulletins about the tension that was building between Serbia and the southern province of Kosovo. Since the Balkan civil war in the mid-1990s there had been an RAF presence at Gioia del Colle air base in southern Italy and it was 1(F) Squadron's turn to take over there in February. We watched the news with interest.

On return from the US, and whilst peace negotiations took place in France, we began training in the UK in preparation for our deployment to Italy. Our main concern was that we had little training with precision-guided munitions. We would be potentially going to war with the Paveway II LGB and the TIALD designation pod and the squadron needed more training in their use. There were only three TIALD pods available for squadron use. As one of those was being used to train the engineers and one was usually being repaired, it only left one for the pilots to fly with. To make matters worse we had no air weapon range on land in the UK that was big enough for us to safely drop a Paveway II from medium level. The TIALD pod also needed further work to get it fully integrated and working as it should on the GR7. Seeking some experience of designating a target with TIALD and dropping Paveway II from medium level we took a formation to Aberporth range in Cardigan Bay, off the Welsh coast. A barge was anchored as a target and we flew a number of runs with one Harrier designating the barge and another dropping the weapon. We needed clear air from target acquisition to weapon impact and not surprisingly the UK winter weather was proving to be challenging. Another problem was that the target was just too damn small. It was extremely difficult to acquire it in the first place and once it was acquired the TIALD pod refused to track it. This was to be an ongoing problem for the months ahead. The pilots were struggling to keep the laser steady on the target. In the end there just didn't seem to be enough reflected laser energy for the bomb to guide on and it missed. It was bloody frustrating and we were running out of time.

Ten days later 1(F) Squadron took over at Gioia and we began flying recce sorties over Bosnia as part of Op Deliberate Force. More acts of aggression were taking place on the ground and it was looking more and more likely that NATO would be taking action. We tried to do some more TIALD training against simulated targets on a range in Bosnia but again we were having trouble with acquisition. The plans for the first missions against Serb targets were being finalised, involving combined night attacks against military facilities. On 23 March I spent the morning working on the final plans for what would be the first sortie of Operation Allied Force. We were led to believe that the opening shots would not be for a few days and in the afternoon we were stood down and returned to the Hotel Svevo. I hadn't been in my room for long before I received a frantic phone call from ops. It was on, tonight, and I was to get back to the squadron asap. So with a deadly serious expression on my face I drove back to the squadron operations building. Imagine my surprise when I arrived in the car park to the sight of all 9 Red Arrows pilots chatting away merrily. They had decided to stop off for fuel at Gioia and say hi to their mates on their way to winter training in Cyprus. Their timing was lousy.

Well so much for being fully rested. The plan was for a six-ship, led by the boss, Wing Commander Andy Golledge, to drop LGBs on storage buildings in a military compound south of Pristina in the early hours of the 24th. I would fly as number two. It was a combined operation with, amongst others, USAF F-16s also attacking the same area ahead of us. Once airborne from Gioia we would RV with a tanker over the Adriatic before routing inland to the target. Shortly before we walked for the mission the boss received a phone call from the prime minister. He wished us luck but he also stated that if we were in any doubt about the target then we shouldn't drop. He didn't want any collateral damage. The bus ride through the darkness out to the aircraft was a quiet one with a definite lack of the usual banter being exchanged between pilots. The weather was kind to us that night and we managed to RV successfully with the VC10 tanker. Tanking was done lights out, using NVGs, and in radio silence and I distinctly remember thinking that the other formations looked dangerously close when viewed through the goggles, as they took fuel from their respective tankers in adjacent areas. On the way in to the target we heard a Dutch F-16 ahead of us request permission to engage a fast-moving target coming south from Belgrade. The AWACS controller made him wait for what seemed like an age and the Dutchman was getting more and more agitated, concerned that his target would elude him. He finally received permission to fire and I believe it was probably the only enemy aircraft to get shot down during the entire campaign.

As well as the fighter cover ahead of us there were also a number of SEAD assets, who would fly in above us and launch anti-radiation missiles into the target area. These things looked spectacular when viewed through NVGs. The rocket motor burned brightly as the missile accelerated out in front of the launch aircraft and then it would pitch up into a steep climb. The motor would burn out soon after but one could still see the glow through the NVGs as it arced out ahead. We never saw them land but the Serbs soon got the idea that it was foolish to turn on any threat radars because these things were deadly. There was also quite a bit of communications jamming on some of the strike frequencies. The Serbs would play music or recordings of previous radio transmissions; the latter being quite distracting but nothing that we couldn't cope with.

As we ran in towards the target area we began to see bomb flashes from other elements of the package ahead. There was some broken cloud cover too and together with the drifting smoke from the detonating bombs it became more and more difficult to positively identify our targets. The message before we left had been loud and clear, if in doubt do not drop, and so we all returned from the first mission without releasing a single weapon. It was a disappointing start to the campaign but we all knew it had been the right decision.

The following night I was assigned to fly the spare aircraft for a similar mission against a weapon storage facility. As an insurance policy against any possible technical failure by one of the formation we would launch a spare aircraft to go as far as the tanker. All six aircraft were fully serviceable that night and so after a short flight over the Adriatic I returned to Gioia. This time the attacks were successful and all bombs struck the target.

For the first ten days of Operation Allied Force the weather over the Balkans was bloody awful, with layers of medium-level cloud and thunderstorms. Our rules of engagement were clear, in that we needed to be able to see our targets in order to attack them, and so with cloud obscuring the target area we experienced several mission aborts. The tasking cell decided that we needed to have a back-up or dump target for each mission, in case the first was obscured by weather. For us the rules of engagement remained the same but hopefully we would now have a better chance of hitting something. After the first couple of days of the campaign the Serbian air and ground forces had been effectively suppressed. They couldn't turn their targeting radars on for fear of a HARM attack and there was so much allied fighter cover over Kosovo that their fighter aircraft stayed on the ground. In early April we switched to day sorties and as well as attacking fixed military installations we also began to get tasked with close air support.

One of the most critical elements of the allied air campaign was the logistics of getting a large package of over fifty aircraft assembled and coordinated and the only way to do that was with the use of air-to-air refuelling. Some aircraft were taking off from other European countries and flying significant distances to reach Kosovo and they had to have in-flight refuelling in order to extend their range. The tanker plan was critical. But for 1(F) Squadron at Gioia, we were about as close as one could get to Kosovo and it became obvious to us that we really didn't need to tank at the beginning of each mission. The AAR planners were overjoyed and by now the squadron pilots had had all the in-flight refuelling practice they needed.

The GR7 has a dedicated air-to-air missile launcher pylon just ahead of the outrigger fairing on each wing and so from the start of the conflict we carried two Sidewinder AIM-9Ls for self-defence. Whilst it initially felt great to carry them it became pretty obvious after the first week, that we were highly unlikely to be engaged by any airborne threats. Carrying them also meant that we had to strictly adhere to a set procedure for arming them in a safe direction every time we went flying. The procedure for disarming them on our return was also cumbersome for both the pilots and the armourers and so it was decided not to fly with them.

It is no secret that the Serb ground forces were doing a pretty effective job of staying hidden by day. This was no conventional war and there was a great deal of frustration in the allied camp at the lack of juicy targets. After the first month most of the fixed military targets such as barracks, storage facilities and airfields had been struck. The Serbs had deployed their forces into the towns and villages and were proving very hard to find. In an effort to catch them in the open we began to get tasked for CAS. In this scenario we would launch as a pair, armed with RBL755 cluster bombs or 1,000-lb freefall bombs. Each pair would be tasked with holding, either over Albania or Macedonia, whilst awaiting target information. Targeting was being done by USAF A-10s, who were also based at Gioia, and were tasked as the airborne forward air controllers (AFACs). Their job was to look for possible targets and pass the information to us through an airborne command post. The Serb ground forces were not using their radar-guided anti-aircraft weapons but they still had a lot of AAA and portable IR missiles. The A-10 pilots would occasionally venture down below 10,000 ft in order to get a better look at a possible target and when they did they would often be met by a barrage of AAA. On one occasion an A-10 diverted to Skopje with an unexploded missile lodged in one of its engines.

On 14 April I was tasked to lead a pair on a CAS sortie. The weather was good and we set up a hold over Albania to await a target. The Albanian terrain is quite hilly and the land rises into a ridge of mountains which form a natural barrier along the border with Kosovo. These mountains rise to a height of around 10,000 ft and in March and early April the higher peaks were still snow-capped. Most of western Kosovo appears to sit in a bowl with a few rolling hills, lakes and forests. It's a beautiful country and from 25,000 ft it was hard to imagine the horrors that were being perpetrated below. By now we had adopted a number of new procedures and one of those was to have the wingman listen out on the strike frequency using the second radio[23], that way we would get a 'heads up'

---

[23] In Harrier II, the pilot could listen to two selected frequencies on the two radios, and to the guard frequency. The transmission button was a rocker switch; pressing the top transmitted on box one, the bottom on box two, and the centre both together.

Top: GR7 landing on deck in front of a FA2. (Geoffrey Lee)
Above: ZD402 with Heinz Frick at the controls. (BAE Systems)

Top: GR7s with Tristar tanker over Macedonia. (Mark Zanker)
Bottom: GR9A refuelling over Afghanistan. (Crown copyright)

Above: GR9s of 1(F) Squadron, IV(R) Squadron and Naval Strike Wing. (Jamie Hunter)
Right: AV-8B Plus over St Louis. (McDonnell Douglas)

Top: IV Squadron group shot. (IV Squadron)
Bottom: 3(F) Squadron in Kandahar, Afghanistan. (Ben Sargent)

Above: GR7 with Maverick missiles. (Geoffrey Lee)
Left: A full deck on HMS *Invincible*. (Mark Zanker)

SAOEU GR7 in trials fit.
(BAE Systems)

GR7s with VC10 tanker.
(Geoffrey Lee)

GR9 with a mixed-weapon
load. (Ben Sargent)

Top: The Harrier bow. (Tim Croton)
Bottom: Lead aircraft of the final UK fly-past in a special colour scheme marking Harrier history, flown by Harrier Force commander Gary Waterfall. (Jamie Hunter)

Top: GR7 flying low. (Tim Cro...
Left: Naval Strike Wing GR9 f...
final fly-past. (Jamie Hunter)

of any possible action. After a while my wingman called that there was a lot of chatter on frequency about a Serb convoy that had been spotted out in the open. That certainly seemed strange to me because the Serbs were not in the habit of parking military vehicles on a road in broad daylight. Sure enough, after a few more orbits over Albania, we were told to switch to the strike frequency and await tasking.

The 'target' was on a main road south of a town in western Kosovo. We entered the target coordinates into the nav kit and flew towards it. Entering the target coordinates into the computer gave us steering information in the HUD and a position on the digital moving-map screen. It also allowed us to accurately point the TIALD pod at the target so that we could view it with a normal TV camera and an IR camera, which was useful for seeing hotspots such as vehicles. We were also issued with image-stabilised binoculars and once overhead the target I put the aircraft into an orbit, engaged the autopilot height hold and had a scan with the binos. Below us was a formation of USAF F-16s who had found the target earlier. There was also another pair of 1(F) Squadron Harriers led by Rob Cockerell, our USAF exchange pilot, who had arrived earlier.

I could see a straight road that came south from the town for a mile or so before crossing a large river. Between the town and the river was a long column of vehicles, parked by the side of the road. Through the binos I could just make out a few military APCs at each end of the convoy but most vehicles were tractors connected to trailers. Some of the tractors were red and the fields adjacent to the road were full of people. We four Harrier pilots discussed the target on our own in-house frequency and quickly came to the conclusion that this was a convoy of refugees that were being herded by Serb soldiers. We didn't know why they had stopped but I was pretty sure that they could hear us and had moved into the fields away from their vehicles in case of an air strike. The F-16 formation leader was effectively the on-scene commander and we persuaded him to bring in an A-10 for target verification. After about 10 minutes an A-10 arrived and after being directed to the target he dropped down to about 5,000 ft for a 'better look', at which point a barrage of AAA came up from somewhere down below. The F-16 formation were disappointed when the A-10 pilot confirmed that the convoy was civilian and shortly after that we were all told to RTB. After we landed we were summoned by the boss into one of the briefing rooms. He came straight to the point. Had we dropped any weapons, he asked. No we hadn't, was the reply. He looked very relieved and it was then that we discovered that a similar refugee convoy had mistakenly been bombed earlier in the day (not by Harriers) and it was all over CNN and Sky News.

On 19 April I led a pair against a SAM servicing facility near Pristina Airport. This was the first daytime Paveway II attack against a fixed target. I would self-designate the target with my TIALD pod and drop two LGBs. My wingman would give cover in case of any SAM launches and then drop 1,000-lb freefall bombs into the compound. As we ran in, there was some cumulus cloud at around 10,000 ft but I reckoned the area would be clear enough to hit the target. I brought the TIALD seeker out of its parked position and it immediately slewed to the target location. I could see the compound and buildings on the cockpit screen. As it wasn't exactly on the planned target I manually slewed the crosshairs with my left hand, using the thumb ball on top of the throttle, and pressed down on the controller, which commanded the seeker to track the target. Everything looked good for the drop and so I pressed the other button on the throttle to fire the TIALD laser. With the weapon aiming set to drop the bombs automatically I held the button down until the computer released them with a double clunk and I heard the high pitch tone in the headset that indicated bombs gone. At the same time the low height warning tone sounded momentarily as the radalt pinged off the falling bombs beneath the aircraft.

After about five seconds a fluffy white cloud appeared in the top of the screen and moved down towards the crosshairs. At this point the TIALD should have gone into a memory mode to keep it roughly pointing at the target, but it didn't. Instead it decided to track the ever-changing edge of the fluffy white cloud and off it went. With a mind of its own the seeker then shot off, somewhere I didn't know and was clearly looking nowhere near the target that the two bombs were now dropping towards. I pressed a button to command the seeker back to the GPS-designated target position and what then appeared on the screen was a field which I reckoned was probably right underneath the aircraft. I parked the seeker head and then un-parked it, which would hopefully cause it to go back to the target (a bit like CTRL + ALT + DEL). With only a few seconds left I managed to rapidly re-acquire the building, get the crosshairs back onto the centre of the roof and fire the laser. Miraculously the free-falling LGBs both managed to re-lock to the reflected laser light and had enough energy to steer themselves right into the centre of the building with a huge flash. After landing I spent quite a bit of time debriefing the TIALD problem with the engineers but there was no easy fix and after that I decided not to use the auto-track function again. Many years later I was surprised to see the TIALD video of that event being shown as part of a Discovery Channel documentary about the campaign. The producers were using the video to demonstrate just how difficult it was to find targets in Kosovo, which was not quite true.

Not all of our targets were in Kosovo. On 30 April I led a six-ship against a road viaduct on the main Serbia to Montenegro road. Bridges are notoriously difficult to destroy, being built with reinforced materials to carry significant loads. To drop a bridge, the attackers need to know what sort of bridge it is and what it's made out of. I received the target coordinates and plotted it on a map but that just showed me that it was a two-lane road bridge over a river.

Today I could go onto Google Earth and see satellite images and photos of the bridge but in 1999 there was no such information readily to hand and it seemed that the intelligence cell had no information either. We didn't know how many spans it was, if it was a suspension bridge or not or exactly what material it was made out of. I took a guess and had the armourers set an appropriate fuse delay on the LGBs. We would attack in three pairs, with the leader of each pair designating the target and the number twos dropping the bombs. As we ran in towards the target there was a layer of stratus cloud above us which could make us easier to see from the ground and there was rising ground below as the bridge was in the hills. It wasn't ideal but we pressed on.

Getting closer to the release point I could also see through the TIALD that there was more cumulus cloud between us and the target. I looked up from the screen and scanned ahead to the target area. It looked clear. With only a few seconds to go to bomb release I still couldn't see the target in the crosshairs but I was confident that there would be enough tracking time to get a hit. My number two released his bombs and after about five seconds the cloud cleared and I saw the bridge. This time I dispensed with the auto-track function and zoomed in to the bridge. I could now see that it was a three-arch viaduct and so I manually slewed the crosshairs to the centre of a span. The laser fired and every now and again I would nudge the crosshairs back to the target if they started to drift off. The bombs seemed to take an age to reach the bridge but when they hit the explosion was spectacular. The other two pairs successfully struck the bridge and

in the subsequent video debrief we could see that a very large hole had been created in the centre of the road. We had luckily managed to hit one of the arches but without accurate information at the planning stage we were never likely to be able to destroy it completely.

Paveway II on bridge. (Mark Zanker)

As mentioned before the Serb army was not making it easy for us and there was a lack of juicy targets. What I haven't yet mentioned is that we still had our recce pods in theatre, with their vertical-facing wide-format camera. This was still the days of wet film and we had a RIC on site at Gioia to process and interpret the images. When the tasking switched from night to day sorties we decided to fit the recce pod on the centreline of a few of the jets with the idea that we would just run the camera continuously once we crossed the border into Kosovo on whatever mission we were tasked on. This gave the photo-reconnaissance interpreters something to do instead of just playing cards and drinking espresso. As soon as we landed the film would be removed from the pod, processed and viewed within about thirty minutes. The interpreters were fantastic at spotting anything of interest and they quickly began to find military kit that was being concealed. Vehicle tracks would often give away the location of military vehicles and in one shot I remember seeing the barrel of a towed artillery piece sticking out of a barn. These were the things we could never hope to see from the kind of altitudes that we were flying, even with a TIALD pod. For a while the RIC would compile a montage of possible targets, together with their coordinates and take them to the A-10 boys across the street. I'm not sure how many targets were hit in this way but I think it was quite effective. The trouble is that the CAOC soon got wind of our in-house tasking and rapidly put a stop to it.

By the end of May, it was obvious that the war was coming to an end. Military and political pressure seemed to be working and the allies were preparing ground forces to cross the border after a negotiated surrender. The British army were preparing to come up from the south but they were aware that Russian forces would be coming down from the north in a race to get to Pristina. There was also some doubt as to how secure any ceasefire would be. The British commander wanted 24-hour air support for any land action and the only unit that could provide 24-hour CAS was 1(F) Squadron with the Harrier. We might be called upon to get below the weather and attack at low level but none of us had flown any night-attack low-level sorties since Red Flag in January and we needed some practice. The boss quickly came up with a plan to get us back to the UK for one day low-flying sortie followed by a night sortie around the same route.

On 7 June I flew my last combat sortie over Kosovo with Johnny Earl as my number two. It was a CAS sortie and after a short hold over Albania we were tasked to contact the AFAC, which just happened to be a USN F-14. The target was an area of artillery and mortar pits and he lased the target, which made it quite easy for us to find and attack with our 1,000-lb airburst bombs. It was late afternoon and after we landed I conducted a quick debrief before jumping into an RAF HS125 to be flown back to Wittering in readiness for the following day's low flying sorties. By 6pm I was at home with my wife, eating dinner and trying to come to terms with the day's activities in what seemed like a world away from rural England.

The rest of June dragged by as we loyally held standby at Gioia for the land war that thankfully never happened. As proud as we were to be capable of supporting our troops 24/7 the reality was that we would spend hours and hours sitting around on standby both day and night. We managed to keep current by flying a few AAR sorties over the Adriatic but at the end of June the squadron was relieved at Gioia by another Harrier squadron and we all returned to Wittering. In the two-and-a-half months of Operation Allied Force I had flown forty combat sorties.

CHAPTER 17

BOYS?

With the world, the RAF and the Harrier Force subject to so many changes, you might think that a simple declaration of gender equality would suffice to comply with the aspirations of the 21st century. But it was not quite so. There were various technical problems to be overcome. These became apparent to me from my later viewpoint in the flying training system. At the very start, during the selection process, fewer females than males, proportionally, met the anthropometric criteria. A general difficulty was that military aircraft had been built to a specification that they could be flown by the range of 5-95 percentile men. But this 90% of the male population overlap in size with about 20% of females. Even within that overall limitation, there are still more details to overcome, such as the tendency for female arms to be shorter relative to overall height, making functional reach, a critical factor in some emergencies, a potential deficiency.

There are even detailed skeletal differences to consider. When I tried to get a talented female student pilot streamed to fast-jet training, it was apparent that her light weight put her outside limits. Having been told that the ejection seat was the stumbling block, I enquired of Martin-Baker why this was so, only to get the standard 9-95 percentile response. In particular, the gun-only Tucano seat, a necessary training step, was the extreme case. Asked to extrapolate, Martin-Baker thought that the light weight might be acceptable, but then the female pelvic structure came into consideration. Remember that Kate Saunders had broken her pelvis when she ejected from Ashley Stevenson's Harrier T4, as related in Volume One. So in that case, the answer was no. When night operations became more common, another unforeseen problem became apparent. NVGs add weight to the front of the flying helmet, tending to make it rotate forwards. In the standard RAF helmet, there is a strap across the back of the head that can be tightened to impinge on the occipital protrusion of the male skull, while this does not generally work for the female skull. Despite all of this, and some residual chauvinist attitudes, women pilots did prove themselves up to the challenges of Harrier flying, as described here.

MITCH WEBB

Of course the Harrier Force was not just 'boys'. There were a large number of excellent female engineers, intelligence officers and operations personnel helping to keep the jets in the air. There were also three female pilots in the short span between the RAF and RN accepting female fast-jet pilots and the sad decommissioning of the Harrier.

Until I reached RAF Valley, I wasn't sure what aircraft I wanted to fly, I was just trying to do my best and move on to the next course. It didn't, however, escape my notice that the Harrier had a fearsome reputation as a difficult aircraft to fly and, until that point, there had been no women chosen to fly her. So whilst waiting to start at Valley on the Hawk, I volunteered for a six-month holding job at Wittering as the manager for the Harrier display team. During this time I had a couple of flights in the T10 and got to know some of the characters on the force; many air shows and tequila slammers later I decided that I was going to be the first female Harrier pilot.

I came top of my fast-jet conversion course at Valley and I had always made it known that I wanted to fly Harriers and nothing else; yet there was no place for me on the Harrier OCU. At the time I didn't think anything of it and my squadron boss and flight commander engineered it that I was posted to 100 Squadron to fly the Hawk until a slot came up on a Harrier course. I had to wait fifteen months until I was given my place on the Harrier OCU, which seemed odd at the time as I was supposed to be waiting for the very next course. I subsequently found out that the Harrier member on the Role Disposal Board (the committee that decides where each group of graduating fast-jet pilots should go) was set against the prospect of a female Harrier pilot. Hence over a year had to pass by before he was posted out of the job and replaced by someone more in tune with the modern RAF and less bigoted. I have the quick thinking of my course commander at Valley to thank that I was given a job on 100 Squadron and didn't end up flying the Jaguar or worse.

As the only woman flying Harriers it was impossible to get away with anything, as people could clearly recognise my voice over the radio. That said, the IV(AC) Squadron boss, who had quite a high pitched voice, was 'cleared to land ma'am' by Goose Bay ATC, who knew there was a female pilot on the detachment!

Transatlantic flights posed a problem for women in fast jets. The boys had their pee bags and after much searching the safety equipment catalogues Daz, from 3(F) Squadron safety equipment section, delighted in telling me that there were nappies available for female fast-jet pilots; would I like him to order some for me? I declined the offer and instead prepared for transatlantic flights by dehydrating myself with a beer the night before and no liquids within two hours of a flight. I think the boys on the squadron were quite taken by the idea of nappies for themselves as they found the pee bags quite tricky, but no-one could face the ridicule so the nappies were relegated to the catalogue.

On one transatlantic flight, we were routing through the Azores en route to the east coast of the USA and having spent a jovial night downtown we were all dehydrated and ready to get going. The Junta had put together crosswords and quizzes to amuse themselves en route and the tanker crew had 'Who Wants to Be a Millionaire' ready to play over the airwaves. The only other enjoyment on the 8-hour transit would be refuelling, inevitably in or near a thunderstorm to ensure maximum turbulence, and the packed lunch. Imagine our dismay, strapped in to our Harriers waiting to taxi out, finding places around the cockpit to stow the lunch items, when we unpacked pot noodles and grated cheese sandwiches. Some joker on the Azores had probably heard that the Harrier carried water and didn't stop to think it might not be boiling or accessible from the cockpit. Also grated cheese in a confined space – nightmare.

Most Harrier pilots have had a near miss or two in their career; mine came during my night combat-ready check ride over Otterburn in Northumberland. The sortie was a typical Harrier trip, in that we tried to squeeze as much as possible into the 2½ hours. As a two-ship we dropped inert 1,000-lb bombs at Holbeach range, met a tanker over the North Sea, and attacked two targets in Northumberland before going to Otterburn range to carry out close air support with the army. We then planned to return to Wittering and carry out stream night vertical landings. The night was as black as ink; no moon and overcast so there was no star light and humidity was high. For those who have not been to Otterburn there is no cultural lighting either so the NVGs and FLIR were both pretty worthless. Needless to say we tried our best and coming off the first target everything was going well, until I looked behind me to try to catch a glimpse of my number two's strobes. Why I did this I can't say, it was unnecessary and not something that you would need to do at night. Anyhow I looked back without noticing that I was flying towards rising ground and as I was banking fairly steeply the radalt unlocked so I had no warning of the impending danger. I was lucky. As I rolled out the radalt locked back on and I saw 120 ft in the HUD (our minimum operating height at night was 250 ft); I pulled the aircraft sharply upwards to climb away from the ground. Reviewing the video back at base, later that night, the lowest height recorded was actually 70 ft[24] during my pull away from the ground. It took a while to settle back in to night flying after that.

One of the most important things for me during my career was to work hard and earn the respect of my peers. I avoided the newspapers and publicity that would probably have swamped me when I qualified on the Harrier and I was extremely fortunate that my bosses all respected my privacy and protected

---

[24] If in a 5° descent, just one second from impact.

me from all unwanted publicity or press. I felt sorry for the previous female fast-jet pilots, whose fantastic achievements were tarnished because they had been treated as media pawns. I imagine that, like me, they wanted to get on with their careers and just be one of the boys on the squadron. I was subject to one amusing media incident though. I was on maternity leave with my six-week-old second child when two reporters knocked at the door looking for my husband. They wanted him to comment on a newspaper article that had appeared in *The Sun* that morning, claiming that his wife was flirting with Prince Harry over the radio from her Harrier cockpit in Afghanistan. I asked to look at the article, and accompanying photo, as not being a regular subscriber to *The Sun* I hadn't seen it yet. When I pointed out to the reporters that I was the woman in the picture and that it was extremely unlikely that I could be in Afghanistan flirting with anyone whilst nursing a six-week-old baby, they left empty-handed. So the whole article had been fabricated by a reporter in Afghanistan, desperate to send something back to his editor and not caring whose lives he affected with his lies. I was very cross at the time, as this was exactly the kind of media rubbish I had been seeking to avoid throughout my career; it did cause my parents and extended family some amusement though and I received a few congratulations on the birth of your baby cards with Prince Harry's face pasted onto the front. You can't believe anything you read in the papers.

Landing on the aircraft carrier for the first time was terrifying; we'd practised it in the simulator but you know that it's not real and that your pink body isn't really on the line. My first ever landing was not great, the aircraft's nose was turned in towards the superstructure and the touchdown was on the firm side. When I got out my legs were shaking and I was quite pale. My second landing was not much better and the nose of the Harrier kept turning in towards the deck, despite my best efforts at trimming the rudder in the opposite direction. I thought that perhaps the aircraft turning was caused by wind bouncing off the superstructure and the aircraft trying to weather cock into the wind; again my right leg was shaking badly. The light didn't dawn until a shrewd QFI (if those words can be used together), having reviewed my video, suggested that perhaps I was bracing my right leg against the right rudder pedal whilst trimming the aircraft to the left against my leg power. Hence the aircraft cocked to the right, my shaking right leg, and full opposite trim. Clearly I had subconsciously been trying to brake. This was solved by wiggling my toes as I came in to land so I could no longer lock out my quads. I'm pleased to say that with this problem cured my landings were much improved thereafter.

The Harrier Force was always regarded as a male bastion, with over-inflated egos and an unnecessary amount of testosterone. This was not my experience of the force. I found that the squadrons operated as well-oiled units with a great sense of camaraderie between engineers, pilots and support staff with everyone trying to achieve the best for their squadrons. Outwardly this would have made the force appear insular and perhaps hostile to outsiders, but the truth was that we were all working very hard to squeeze as much from the detachment, or flying day or sortie, as possible.

CHAPTER 18

THE SEA HARRIER

Before the Falklands conflict, there was a plan to sell one of the UK CVS carriers to Australia, but the efficacy of the Harriers in that fight put an end to this idea. When the Royal Australian Navy retired its Skyhawks from operational service, several of their pilots moved to the northern hemisphere to become Sea Harrier pilots. Bringing their carrier experience and antipodean humour with them, they fitted in well. One who enjoyed notable success, commanded a Sea Harrier squadron, and saw the transition from FRS1 to FA2, was Dave Baddams. Here, he describes some memorable periods of his RN service. After that, Brian Johnstone gives an insight into the challenges faced by those who looked after the maintenance of the Sea Harriers while embarked. Both Dave and Brian were awarded an MBE for their Harrier service.

DAVE BADDAMS
This story begins when I took over as senior pilot 800 NAS aboard HMS *Invincible* in Hong Kong during the fleet deployment cruise Orient '92. My CO on 800 NAS was the very famous and senior Lieutenant Commander David Braithwaite, known as 'Brave' since his early days as a naval aviator because it is said he landed a burning Sea Vixen back on board ship rather than risk losing his observer due to an apparently dodgy seat/hatch interconnect on the ejection seat mechanism. He was an avuncular and supportive boss who allowed me much leeway in keeping his squadron on the right path.

My predecessor in post was my guide and mentor for many years. Lieutenant Commander Simon Hargreaves had been my air warfare instructor during my initial Sea Harrier training, and had remained a key figure in my development as an operational fighter pilot in the ensuing years. Both Brave and Simon were incredibly capable fighter pilots and fine leaders, and they provided much inspiration to me in developing my own leadership style.

Orient '92 was a training cruise, and the opportunity was taken to display British military prowess east of Suez for the first time in many years. We trained and operated with elements of the USN 7th Fleet, Republic of Singapore Air Force, Royal Australian Air Force, Royal New Zealand Air Force, Royal Malaysian Air Force, and while I was on board we visited Singapore, Malaysia, UAE and Israel. After arriving home in December 1992 things started to move quickly.

In January 1993, HMS *Ark Royal* and 801 NAS (Lieutenant Commander Tim Mannion) were scrambled for operations in the Adriatic. NATO had taken on a role to police the skies overhead Bosnia/Herzegovina, and to provide support to UN ground forces, should they deploy. Two 800 NAS aircraft were transferred to 801 NAS as reinforcements, along with myself and Lieutenant Bob Nadin.

Due to political constraints, after a very rapid force generation and deployment, the build up to operations screeched to a halt. We were all ready for action, but the authorities were not sure how to apply force in an effort to curtail the brutal civil war on the ground without picking sides…where no side really appeared to be blameless in the competition for brutality. With this delay to action in mind, the reinforcement of 801 NAS was only in place from 11 January – 19 February 1993. There was a clear NATO requirement for fighter cover to provide airspace denial, close air support and reconnaissance, and to that end, *Ark* was deployed. These were all skills SHAR pilots were trained for, but with the politics in mind, the rate of progress did not enable any notable operations to take place for the entire first deployment of HMS *Ark Royal*. As soon as the likely delays became apparent to me, as senior pilot of 800 NAS, I fed back to my squadron what areas and techniques needed to be honed, and arranged for my return to the UK in order to participate in the preparations for the deployment of HMS *Invincible* and 800 NAS planned for July 1993 as a relief for *Ark*.

There is no doubt that 800 NAS was in a much higher state of preparedness for operations over Bosnia when they sailed in July 1993. Within a few days of arriving on station in the Adriatic, 800 NAS commanded by Lieutenant Commander Chris Neave commenced the first RN fixed-wing operational missions over land since the Falklands War. It was my honour to lead the first mission, an armed reconnaissance sortie, with Lieutenant Jon 'Chips' Lawler as my wingman. We flew up to Bihac in the north-western corner of Bosnia where we photographed artillery positions on the road to the south east.

From August 1993 until the end of January 1994, 800 NAS was committed to the NATO mission over Bosnia. 492 operational sorties were planned in that period, and the squadron achieved a 100% sortie success rate. The missions 800 NAS was tasked for were armed reconnaissance, operational close air support, exercise close air support (training of FACs on the ground in theatre) and offensive counter air. The aircraft configuration was varied for each role as appropriate; every mission flying overland was armed and ready to participate should the need arise. As is the nature of modern offensive operations, the political process remained slow. Ground operations were hectic and if they could not be called open warfare between the various factions, it was most certainly bloody conflict involving armed criminality. Throughout *Invincible*'s initial deployment to the theatre, there was an increasing level of tension calling for air support. The skies were swept clear of most activity although rules of engagement were never relaxed enough to curtail suspect helicopter activity. Everyone knew helicopters were being used for hostile purposes, but it was impossible to differentiate peaceful helicopters supplying aid and emergency services from those carrying arms and soldiers into battle. The answer, despite multiple intercepts and engagements, even at night and high altitude for a helicopter, was to leave them alone.

It was apparent from the increasing tempo of operations that live military activity was very close as *Invincible* turned for home whilst *Ark Royal* picked up the baton on behalf of the Royal Navy. 800 NAS had laid the operational leadership and ground work, and placed the whole SHAR force in a thorough state of readiness for what was to come; three further years of watch on stop on carrier deployments in support of NATO during the conflict in Bosnia/Herzegovina.

When the squadron returned to the UK in March 1994 I was appointed to the Naval Flying Standards Flight (Fixed Wing) for a two-year tour. During this time I was able to fly every fixed wing type available to the Fleet Air Arm, and my relationship with the Royal Naval Historic Flight commenced. Major milestones on the way were: monitoring and assisting the RAF Strike Attack OEU on board HMS *Illustrious* in preparing the Harrier GR7 for embarked duties; providing instructional services and standards oversight to 899 NAS, the Royal Navy's Sea Harrier training unit; converting to the new Sea Harrier FA2; and as an aside I was lucky enough to fly the venerable and much loved RNHF Swordfish for two display seasons at the same time as re-introducing the beautiful Hawker Sea Hawk jet fighter back into the RNHF for the first time since the mid 1980s.

My next appointment commencing January 1996 was to be my last in the navy, and I felt most honoured to be selected as the senior pilot 899 NAS (Lieutenant Commander Mark Boast). With my background in flying instruction reinforced by the two years at NFSF (FW), it felt like the very best way to spend my final appointment prior to retirement. By 1996 the FA2 was in serious front-line service actively participating in the NATO Orbat, and being on 899 bringing on the next generation of young Sea Harrier pilots was particularly thrilling. The most important aspect of my time at 899 was much more personal though. In January 1997 the naval officers' appointer approached me, and offered me a continuance of my commission if I accepted an appointment in command of a fighter squadron. To reach this point in my career, and not accept such an offer felt like it would be reading a book without finishing the last chapter. My decision was quick and easy. I agreed to a command and asked which squadron I could have. The appointer said, and I paraphrase, "You say which one you want and I'll tell you when you start. Then all you'll need to agree to is at least 2 years in command." In January 1997, I told the appointer I would like 800 NAS aboard HMS *Invincible* as my command, and he told me my appointment would commence 26 August 1997.

Joining 800 NAS in command at such a point made it feel like I had personally selected each and every member. Squadron morale was high and team spirit was strong. *Invincible* was not returning to the Adriatic. For the first time since 1993, the plan was to deploy initially to the Mediterranean for joint operations and training with the RAF, 1(F) Squadron (Wing Commander Mark Leakey) also embarked, and with elements of both the Spanish navy and the Spanish air force. On completion of the Med training, two aircraft from 800 deployed via an air-to-air refuelling tanker trail to China Lake in the USA in preparation for the planned annual AMRAAM firing exercise out of Puerto Rico in early November. The remainder of the squadron sailed for the West Atlantic, bringing the helicopter squadrons for ASW training with the USN while 800 disembarked for a long period of dissimilar air combat training with elements of the US military in Oceana, Cherry Point, and Cecil Field.

Having enjoyed a thoroughly good work up with our 1(F) Squadron shipmates and with the Spanish forces, from day one in training with the United States military, it was apparent that the FA2 was a tremendous multi-role fighter asset, and with AMRAAM it was a world-beating air-to-air machine. Due to the RN/ US military exchange programme, we had a good understanding of the way to work with the Americans, and indeed they were excellent and welcoming hosts. Much mutual benefit was achieved through the many lessons learned as to how to fly and fight with our primary allies.

On completion of training with Cecil Field-based F-18s we were to perform for the base's final air show prior to closure. This event occurred on the last weekend in October 1997. After a very successful base families day and display practice on the Friday, I was woken relatively early on the Saturday morning by a telephone call from the duty lieutenant commander (DLC) on board our ship, which was now alongside nearby in Mayport, close to Jacksonville in Florida. The message he had was for me to gather in my squadron and return to the ship immediately. The DLC was relatively junior, and I didn't know him well, so it seemed natural to me that he was being put to the test by other influential parties (like the helicopter squadrons who were not at the air show) so I very politely told him I did not believe him and hung up.

About fifteen minutes later, the phone rang again, and this time it was commander air from the ship. He told me his call was "no duff" and that I mustn't ask any more questions over the phone, but I seriously had to bring the squadron back to the ship immediately. My squadron chief petty officers were an incredibly fine group of leaders, and once I gave the order everything was arranged and we were on our way within a few hours. The ground party reached the ship in time for lunch with all our deployment packs, and the aeroplanes flew to Mayport that afternoon. The ship sailed with my squadron embarked first thing Sunday morning. Once on board ship we were told the situation in Iraq was developing quickly. Saddam Hussein had evicted the UN inspectors looking for evidence of WMD, and the Security Council had agreed to deploy forces in order to re-affirm the international commitment to the containment of Iraq's military threat to its neighbours.

HMS *Invincible* sailed at speed with the initial destination planned to be Gibraltar where we would store ship for a major military deployment and embark the 1(F) Squadron ground party. There were several false starts as political activity reached frenzied levels and we found ourselves bouncing around the Atlantic for quite a few days as the allied governments postured and negotiated. During this period, I witnessed a feat of great bravery based on the operationally essential act of bringing the two aircraft detached for the planned Sea Harrier OEU AMRAAM shoot back to *Invincible*. Two excellent pilots, Lieutenant Commander Bill Dean of the SHAR OEU and Lieutenant David Lindsey, one of my junior officers, flew the aircraft on a multi-leg return to ship procedure leaving Puerto Rico early 2 November 1997. In launching from their final island staging post bound for the ship, they had no communications for nearly a day and had to fly to a rendezvous position hundreds of miles from land in any direction, completely dependent on the ship being where it said it would be when they left Puerto Rico early in the morning. They arrived safely on board late in the afternoon 2 November having completed an over-water leg of more than 800 nautical miles without any diversion or landing options other than the ship. The ship eventually arrived in Gib for a one-day visit 17 November 1997. Storing ship was completed very quickly and the ship sailed into the Med so as to enable 1(F) to embark.

My friend Wing Commander Mark Leakey was in charge at 1(F), and he came aboard raring to go. He insisted on night flying immediately on arrival, and this led to an unfortunate accident on their very first night on board. One aircraft was lost, and the pilot, Mark himself, was very lucky to survive. Nevertheless we pressed on with training and preparations as our new instructions came out, 'poise for action in the western Mediterranean'.

We practised heavily both internally with 1(F) and at Decimomannu in Sardinia, and the ship also sailed into the Adriatic where we performed useful operational missions over Bosnia. This programme of poise was maintained for close to two months. HMS *Invincible* (Captain James Burnell-Nugent) was ordered through the Suez Canal 18 January 1998. The first time a British carrier had deployed for operations east of Suez since the Aden withdrawal during the 1960s.

Operation Bolton, the British contribution to the allied containment of Saddam Hussein's regime, commenced with a night mission over Iraq 29 January 1998. A four-ship of FA2s escorted a four-ship of GR7s from 1 Squadron, and we were in a combined formation of over seventy-five aircraft mostly from the USS *George Washington* air group. Our recent travels to America really paid off, with our formations integrating seamlessly with the American embarked forces.

Invincible/800 NAS/1(F) stayed on station in the northern Arabian Gulf, carrying out both day and night sweeps most days in February 1998 and flowing into March. The tempo of operations increased as a showdown drew close. At night, it was easy to see our presence was opposed with occasional ground fire and missile launches observed. There was a brief respite around 23 February, when forces withdrew and an ultimatum was delivered to the Iraqi government by the UN Secretary General himself: "Re-admit my weapons inspectors or a bombing campaign will commence". Within a few days a tentative settlement was reached, and whilst the tempo of operations remained, the level of clear opposition declined. At that point, *Illustrious* steamed into view with our brothers of 801 NAS on board, and 3(F) Squadron. After a three-months training cruise had extended to a six-month operational deployment, *Invincible* and her reinforced air group turned for home. 18 March 1998, the squadron disembarked to Akrotiri in Cyprus. The ground party was picked up in a chartered airliner, and the Sea Harriers launched on the long tanker trail to Yeovilton, all arriving home to a rousing family and base welcome at sunset that same day.

After a period of leave, 800 NAS was back to work with normal peacetime training requirements. There was a period where we had two aircraft and support crews in Sardinia performing flight trials with the Sea Harrier OEU, two aircraft and crews on board with a pair of BAe development aircraft trialling new systems for the SHAR JTIDS upgrade, and two aircraft ashore undergoing maintenance.

When the squadron was all together, we participated in NATO exercises, were with the ship for a joint maritime course in the North West Approaches, went on a fantastic port visit to Gdynia in Poland, and topped off a busy year acting as red air for a tactical leadership programme exercise in the south of France.

Just prior to Christmas 1998 the commander of the UK Task Group (COMUKTG) notified me that a plan to visit the West Atlantic was confirmed, and that despite increased military tension and activity over Iraq, we would definitely not be deploying for a further period of operations over southern Iraq. My Christmas message to the squadron was to enjoy a safe and happy break with their families and to return at the end of leave ready for embarkation within a week. To that end, the squadron was fully ready to deploy prior to the Christmas leave period, and yet again we were at a very high state of operational readiness.

The day after the squadron departed on Christmas leave, the COMUKTG duty officer requested a full recall because the ship's plan had indeed been changed to return to the northern Arabian Gulf early in the second week of January. I had discussed the likelihood of such an event with Captain Burnell-Nugent and with my planning team, but the young officer seemed completely taken aback when I informed him we were ready to deploy immediately, so I would not recall my squadron because as soon as the ship actually set course for Iraq, we would be on board. In the meantime, I wanted my team to get a good break after a busy year.

This deployment to the NAG was much more planned than 1998. We left UK waters around 10 January 1999 and planned to leave the Arabian Gulf 29 March 1999. Operations in cooperation with the United States forces deployed in the region were planned throughout February and March. These operations included the aggressive containment of Saddam Hussein's forces with hostile activities observed and suppressed on a regular basis. The Sea Harrier role was exclusively offensive and defensive counter air, and in this role the RAF VC10 tanker force played a crucial part.

There were many memorable activities and occasions. Two come to mind, of which one became an apocryphal story, and the other was simply funny. The first instance was after a short break in Dubai, the ship was proceeding to our station off Kuwait, and I led a four-ship of my more junior pilots on a currency and orientation sortie to practise our four-ship fighter sweep tactics. After about half an hour of training, one of the young officers notified me on the chat frequency that he was hearing us being called on the international guard frequency. I switched to guard and identified my formation to a local national air traffic controller, and told him we were okay operating in international air space with due regard for other traffic because we had guidance from our ship's air traffic controllers, and we were also very capably equipped with our own on-board radars.

The local controller was quite clearly an expatriate British officer, and on hearing my call he became agitated. He threatened to launch a pair of armed F-16s to engage us and drive us out of his airspace. My response was polite and clear. I asked him where he would like us to move to, and he aggressively gave us a vector north 100 miles. Following that instruction would have taken us out of international airspace and placed us in Iranian skies. My next statement on guard was along the lines of, "We'll be finished here in an hour. We will not be flying into Iranian airspace, and if you wish to launch F-16s to drive us off we would love to see them. You should advise your fighters that we are armed and awaiting their arrival." Now whilst he didn't become apoplectic, he was most certainly angry despite my further reassurances that all would be well if he just let things be. I mentioned that I would switch the guard frequency off if he continued to interrupt our training. He then shouted down the radio, "What would you do if we parked an aircraft carrier in the English Channel?" I replied, "But sir, you don't have an aircraft carrier," and turned guard volume down. We completed our training and never heard another word about it.

The second event related to activity on board. During a busy operational period I was piped to attend a meeting in the admiral's staff briefing room. Captain Burnell-Nugent was there with some very serious-looking high-ranking admiral's staff officers. They briefed me on a new threat that had just been fielded. Saddam Hussein had broadcast in the media how his forces intended to take down a Sea Harrier. They had modified an old Soviet-era Ababil artillery rocket launcher to shoot rockets with altitude and proximity sensing warheads. The intention was to put a full salvo of rockets up through a Sea Harrier formation, cutting us to shreds. Captain B-N turned and asked me what I thought. My reply was, "Sir, I think he has about as much chance of hitting us as there is of a piece of falling space debris taking out a SHAR". Captain B-N appreciated my reassurance, although he did make me explain to the staff why I assessed the risk as negligible, and our show went on.

As *Invincible* withdrew from operations over Iraq on 29 March 1999, I was notified that we were fast transiting to the Aegean Sea to participate in NATO operations against Serbia in support of the independence of Kosovo. The Kosovo mission for 800 NAS was defensive counter air. Our combat air patrol stations were predominantly over Skopje (capital city of Macedonia) facing north and overlooking Pristina, or further west positioned over northern Albania facing Podgorica in Montenegro. The squadron was well equipped and trained to fulfil the mission, and again the RAF supplied tankers, this time in the form of TriStars, to enable useful four-hour windows on task. The airspace over Serbia and Kosovo was incredibly busy with NATO aircraft. The SHAR radar and weapon system was ideally suited for the mission in that we could easily identify friendly forces at high level at the same time as tracking others at low level.

All squadron pilots had incidents and events where enemy activity was observed, and where they faced up to the threat. The rules of engagement were such that no one ever actually got to shoot, but many of us were certainly placed in a position where engagement was very close. One such engagement happened during my last operational sortie in the navy, and as it turns out, it was 800 NAS's last mission of the war in Kosovo. My wingman, Lieutenant Nick Weightman, and I were positioned over Skopje when we detected a fast jet over Pristina operating at low level directly below a pair of friendly F-16s. We tracked north and both achieved high probability of kill firing solutions. Due to the proximity of the F-16s we were ordered to haul off. We turned south and tracked outbound back to our CAP station. When we faced north again we found the same picture, two F-16s now orbiting directly above the low level target, only now the target was declared as hostile. There was no response to a suggestion from me that the F-16s bug out and get out of our way, even though it was clear that at their vertical range above the bandit they were unlikely to get a sighting, let alone a shot. In frustration, I turned my formation towards the tanker and told the controller a little of how I felt.

As soon as we were on track for the tanker, we got a snap vector from the controller on board an RAF E3D AWACS aircraft. We had been facing north, so the vector 030° at 20 miles was an imminent threat. Both Nick and I picked up 'the bandit' immediately and we were cleared to engage. Both of us also realised that we were looking at a decoy or a bundle of chaff, possibly floating down range from one of the F-16s. Having flown up to the stationary threat and then flown through it, we realised the AWACS was gone, and there didn't seem to be anyone listening out at the airborne command, control and communications platform, so we notified the tanker we were inbound to them. Given the real proximity of the bandit, and the unknown nature of the target we were vectored for, the high value assets had performed survival manoeuvres, and we were quite relieved when they came back on air and found that all was well.

On the same mission, transiting back to the CAP station, AWACS directed us towards Podgorica stating that they thought there may be activity on the airfield. We steered west and picked up helicopters nearly immediately. The rest of our operation that evening was sparring with the helicopters, painting them with radar, watching them try to evade, and due to constraints placed upon us by rules of engagement, we strictly stayed outside the airfield-centred missile engagement zone (MEZ). The targets were already designated bandits, so we were chomping at the bit to get in amongst them with missiles. Several more visits to the tanker, and an hour spent awaiting the arrival of the SEAD aircraft which would have enabled entry into the MEZ saw our relief CAP aircraft arrive on station.

Our next day was planned to be a stand down from flying stations. The ship's executive officer surprised me with an early morning call to say I needed to talk to the captain. The message on 18 May 1999 was that an RAF Tornado squadron was deploying and that *Invincible* was cleared to go home.

I was honoured to lead 800 Naval Air Squadron during such an exciting period. We were called upon three separate times to stand up and be counted to perform armed operational missions over hostile territory, and no one on my squadron faltered. Our relationship with our ship, HMS *Invincible*, was first class, and we were very much a part of the finest Fleet Air Arm Carrier Air Group seen in modern times.

As a result of our participation in Operation Bolton in early 1998, the UK contribution to the containment of Iraq, the 1(F) Squadron executive officer (Squadron Leader Ian Cameron) and I were awarded MBEs in October 1998. I deeply appreciate the efforts of my entire squadron in coming with me on our exciting journey. Further, I am grateful to 1(F) for stepping right out of their comfort zone ashore and proving the STOVL concept as the answer to the future of naval aviation.

BRIAN JOHNSTONE
EMBARKED ENGINEERING

A squadron typically works a basic eight hours on/eight hours off watch-keeping system and a typical day for the maintainers would start at 0400 hours, with a 0400 to midday shift, a midday to 2000 shift and 2000 to 0400. Watch change times are coincident with meals except breakfast. In a two-watch system this means that over a two-day period each watch will work one of each shift.

The early shift consists of preparing the aircraft for the day's flying and movement of the flyers to the flight deck, followed by any required weapons loading and then a period of flight operations. Preparation is the carrying out of the before flight servicing (BFS) which consists of a walk round inspection to look for overnight damage or changes to the aircraft's condition such as landing-gear suspension extensions, tyre pressures, ejection seat emergency oxygen bottle charge and fuel at correct contents for intended flight (usually full).

Gaseous oxygen (GOX) packs had to be collected from the GOX charging bay which was accessed through a hatch in the hangar wall by the forward aircraft lift with the lift at hangar deck level. These were taken up to the flight deck and stowed in a locker at the aft end of the flight deck and waited until the aircraft were spotted at their allocated flight deck position before they would be fitted. It was not practice to fit GOX packs in the hangar. They were fitted and removed only with the aircraft on the flight deck.

The middle shift was mostly concerned with continuing daytime flight ops and any ongoing hangar maintenance, carrying out turnround servicing (TRS) inspections between flights. TRS is that which is required to get the aircraft back in the air as quickly as possible and consists of a walk around visual inspection, refuelling and only those replenishments indicated to be needed (engine oil, GOX etc). If systems are correctly serviced during an after-flight servicing (AFS) and rechecked at BFS then very few systems need further replenishment for a number of flights; fuel, water and weapons being the main consideration.

The late shift would continue flight ops, with TRS between each flight, including any night flying which would require an extra pre-night flying inspection called a night flying conditional (NFC) which basically checks all necessary lighting works and adds a colour filter to the head-up display projector. On completion of night flying they would strike aircraft to the hangar deck for AFS and any routine servicing requirements and fault rectification. An AFS inspection would be the most rigorous of the flight serving inspections and would return all systems back to full and require a thorough inspection of the aircraft. It is essential that the aircraft is fully inspected at this point in time to ensure any maintenance arisings can be dealt with prior to starting flight ops the following day. Some systems such as engine and gearbox oils must also be checked for levels within a specified time of equipment shut down or erroneous readings may be taken.

Securing of aircraft and all equipment is an essential part of life at sea. Even in the calmest of conditions the ship will pitch and roll due to sea swell or wave action and because of the ship manoeuvring, often violently, without notification. This requires that all equipment and aircraft when not being moved are chained or lashed to the deck using chains, nylon lashings or rope (GSE only). There are two conditions of lashing; normal (everyday weather conditions) or storm (when foul weather is forecast). With regard to aircraft, once a pilot has manned the aircraft and he has started the engine, and under the direction of the flight deck crew, lashings may be removed. Two types of lashing are used on aircraft carriers: chain and nylon webbing. In general, nylon was used for helicopters and equipment and chains used for aircraft.

Chains are threaded through the ship's deck fitting (ringbolt), secured to themselves with the end hook, and then attached to the aircraft's picketing point using a quick release coupling which can then be adjusted like a turnbuckle to tighten the chain. Nylon lashings are attached at the hook end to the deck ringbolt and at the clutch mechanism end to the aircraft's picketing rings. They are tightened by pulling on the free end of webbing and locked using the lever-locking device. One advantage provided by webbing-style lashings is that during rough weather you can leave the lashing connected at both ends and by releasing the locking mechanisms you can move the helicopter or aircraft using a technique known as 'running lashings', by allowing the webbing straps to extend and quickly locking should the situation demand it.

The biggest difference at sea was the conduct of an engine change. Ashore, the aircraft was placed on jacks and trestles and set in a level condition. Following disconnection of the various system connections the wing was lifted clear, using a mobile crane and placed on a wing stand and then the engine could be lifted out of the fuselage and be placed in a spare engine stand. On board ship this was made a good deal more difficult for several reasons. The equipment had to be far bulkier to stand the loads imposed by the ship's movement. The jacking and trestle equipment was bigger and to cater for the lack of roof clearance the trestle was fitted with its own jacks so that once jacked up and levelled, the trestle

could be lowered until its own jacks contacted the deck and then the actual aircraft jacks could be removed, and then the trestle could be lowered until the aircraft was just feet off the deck. We also attached 'goalposts' to the trestle which allowed the large embarked sling to be guided up the posts when lifting the wing and then when lifting the engine. The idea behind this was to prevent the large heavy

Engine change at sea. (Brian Johnstone)

wing or engine from swinging about as the ship rolled. When we lifted wing or engine it was normal practice to ask the officer of the watch on the bridge to steer a straight course for the period of the lift but although this helped prevent any sudden movement it did not cater for normal sea movement.

The other problem with an embarked engine change was that it took up the entire forward hangar, usually big enough to take four Sea Harriers. With the wing alongside on its stand then two engine stands, one with the new engine in it and the other for the removed engine, and stowage space for all the removed parts from the aircraft, a lot of space was required. A good amount of storage space, for all this equipment, was required when not in use, with some equipment (wing stand and engine sling) being broken down into parts and stowed on the first shelf, one deck up the hangar wall. These are still large and an evolution in its own right to be got down and assembled in readiness for the task. The sling alone when assembled weighed about 350 lbs. An engine change could take anything from three up to twelve hours to achieve, making maintenance on other aircraft more difficult because it may have to be carried out on deck, in the dark and in inclement weather. All the equipment and aircraft parts removed had to be secured to the deck and securing everything for sea exacerbated difficulties associated with maintenance. It just simply took longer to do things because of having to unsecure and re-secure things you needed to move and even under normal conditions once all the aircraft were in the hangar moving large items was impossible due to the closeness of the aircraft and chains leading from all landing-gear legs to ring bolts in the deck and from any GSE or tool boxes.

It is a requirement, when ashore, to foam wash the aircraft on a routine basis about every five-six weeks. When embarked it is reduced to weekly although it may just be a wash with fresh water, saving the foam wash for convenient non-flying days such as port calls. However, fresh water washing of engine compressors is carried out on a daily basis when the aircraft is used. This is to prevent a build-up of salt on compressor blades. It is usually carried out following the last flight of the day and it is achieved by positioning the flight deck tractor near where returning aircraft are marshalled to after landing. Once the aircraft comes to rest and whilst the chocks

A full CVS hangar. (Brian Johnstone)

and lashings are being fitted and the engine is still running an indication is made to the pilot, by showing him the water hose nozzle, that you intend to carry out a compressor wash. The pilot will select a few system switches to the off position (systems that take bleed air from the engine so that water does not enter them) and when he gives the thumbs up the water hose nozzle is offered up to the edge of the engine air intake and is turned on allowing a ten-second flow of water into the intake, the hose is then taken under the aircraft to the other side air intake and the process repeated. If an aircraft lands and the pilot vacates it, but it is subsequently declared unserviceable, then a ground run will be carried out by maintainers specifically to wash the engine compressor before the aircraft goes to the hangar.

CHAPTER 19

RESCUE AND FAITH

Mark Leakey had a very successful RAF career, but not without some trauma that would challenge a lesser man's determination. He arrived as a flight commander on 3(F) Squadron as I left, and was a neighbour during my subsequent tour in Harrier Plans. After that, we went our separate ways until 1997, when I was called out to head a Board of Inquiry into the loss of a GR7 in the Mediterranean. The pilot was Mark, who happily escaped, and indeed the aircraft was salvaged by the navy. The accident is also mentioned by Dave Baddams (my former Harrier student) in his chapter.

MARK LEAKEY

After university I decided to join the Royal Air Force in 1977 as a pilot. I flew Harrier GR3s in Germany, was a weapons instructor on the Hawk in Wales, and flew the F-16 on exchange with the USAF in Tampa, Florida. After that I went back onto Harriers – this time the new GR5 and then the night-attack GR7.

I had to be rescued on two occasions. The first was in the Falkland Islands, shortly after the war with Argentina. The engine of my Harrier failed on the approach to Port Stanley. I remember my flight leader suggesting that I eject as my jet plummeted towards Port Stanley harbour. Forty-five minutes later I was rescued from the sea by a Royal Navy helicopter. I sustained a number of crush injuries, or wedge fractures, to my spine. I was 'medically evacuated' back to the UK and spent a number of weeks in hospital – and several months off flying. This episode marked the start of a long road of rediscovery of my dormant faith – a road I'm still travelling on.

Fifteen years later, in the winter of 1997, I had a rather more dramatic Harrier accident – and had to be rescued a second time. By now I commanded 1(F) Squadron which deployed on Operation Bolton aboard the Royal Navy's aircraft carrier HMS *Invincible*, in the Mediterranean. This was the UK's initial response to Saddam Hussein, who had thrown the UN weapons inspectors out of Iraq. As the boss I had been pretty busy for some twenty days without a break, getting the squadron deployed operationally in some semblance of order. There was some considerable pressure to get 'night qualified' for what could have been imminent night operational sorties over Iraq; indeed we had only flown a small

number of night sorties off HMS *Illustrious* earlier that autumn. I remember
going up on the flight deck and making the fateful decision to launch on that
first possible opportunity – in spite of the distinctly poor weather. So I decided
that I would lead a pair of aircraft on the first night sortie. It was one of those
sorties I should never have flown. We flew a night low-altitude bombing detail
on the ship's splash target, at 100 ft and 480 kts, using NVGs and the aircraft's
FLIR system: reasonably challenging at the best of times. But the FLIR system
wasn't doing much for me, and I remember at one point my NVGs separating
from my helmet. Having dropped all our practice bombs, we recovered to
the ship – which was completely blacked out. The adrenalin was flowing fast
by now. I flew what was probably the worst approach I had ever made. I got
high on the approach to the hover and over-corrected. I remember becoming
increasingly disorientated. I could not stop the rate of descent and crashed into
the sea alongside the ship. I remember quite clearly thinking on impact: 'This is
the end...' Somehow I survived the crash; I briefly lost consciousness but came
to with a certain knowledge that now I was drowning. I was still in my ejection
seat; I thought I was still in the cockpit. Somehow, instinctively, I did the only
things that could have saved me – I undid the ejection seat straps, released the
parachute harness and pulled the life jacket toggle. I surfaced gasping for breath.
Some while later I was rescued – again by a Royal Navy helicopter.

What I did not realise was that the aircraft had rolled on its back on impact
and the ejection seat had fired me down into the sea. I quite clearly remember
the details of ejecting some 15 years earlier – but I have no recollection to this
day of pulling the seat-firing handle that night. I should not have survived the
impact; but having done so, I should never have survived being ejected down
into the sea.

I was sent back to the UK and had a routine scan of my back; there was concern
about possible further injuries to my spine. For some reason the radiologist
scanned my head as well. A short while later I experienced one of those sorts of
moments we all dread: the doctor sat me down and told me that I had cancer – a
brain tumour. I was instantly grounded, I lost my medical flying category and
two weeks after that I lost command of my squadron. I had been rescued – but
for what? The first prognosis was not comforting – I could be dead within nine
months. The maximum the neurosurgeon gave me was five to ten years. There
was nothing he could do for me.

I went to ground for six months. Why had God allowed all this to happen
to me? What would happen to my wife and two sons after I died? And more
immediately would I be court-martialled for flying an almost perfectly serviceable
aircraft into the sea? But actually it was an extraordinary time – a time of great
peace, knowing that God had my future in his hands. What happened next?

Well – instead of a court-martial, I was promoted into a pretty decent job in the Ministry of Defence. Then I was selected for the Royal College of Defence Studies. After that I was appointed to be the principal staff officer to a German general, and then a British general, in a NATO Headquarters in the Netherlands. I was then promoted to air commodore, the RAF's one-star rank, and I finished off as the chief planner for UK operations in the Joint Headquarters in Northwood – with responsibility for planning operations in Iraq, Afghanistan, Bosnia and Africa. After twenty-eight years of service in the RAF, I decided I had probably reached my ceiling and it was time to leave – in good measure because I wanted to do something more specific for God. For the next ten years or so I directed the Armed Forces' Christian Union.

Some 18 years after the doctors' diagnosis, I'm still alive and well. In fact, a few weeks before writing this piece, the consultants decided I did not have a brain tumour after all – but a dysfunctional blood vessel termed a 'cavernoma'. But we all must face death sooner or later. As Dietrich Bonhoffer – a German pastor – famously stated in a letter he wrote just before he was executed by the Nazis in 1945 for his opposition to Hitler: 'this is not the end but for me the beginning'.

Pilot Officer Cyril Barton captained a Halifax bomber that was badly damaged in a raid on Nuremberg on 30 March 1944. Three of his crew bailed out, but he pressed on to the target, brought the crippled aircraft back, and made a forced-landing on return when his fuel ran out. The remaining three crew survived – but he was killed. He was awarded the posthumous Victoria Cross[25]. He had written the following in a letter that was left for his mother:

'Except for leaving you I am quite prepared to die. Death holds no terror for me. I know I shall survive the judgement because I have trusted in Christ as my Saviour. All I am anxious for is that you and the rest of the family will come to know him…I commend my Saviour to you.'

The prophet Isaiah wrote many centuries ago:

'On this mountain the Lord Almighty will prepare a feast of rich food for all peoples,
'A banquet of aged wine – the best of meats and the finest of wines.
'On this mountain he will destroy the shroud that enfolds all peoples…
…He will swallow up death forever.
'The Sovereign Lord will wipe away the tears from all faces;
'He will remove the disgrace of his people from all the earth.'

(Isaiah 25:6-8)

---

[25] Bob Marston: Mark mentions his concern for his sons' future, and quotes this WW2 VC. In 2015, Mark's son Joshua was awarded the VC for his valour in Afghanistan.

This is a wonderful picture of what the God who rescues has planned for his people on the 'other side'. It is important, I believe, to be right with God today; as I discovered, we do not know what may come our way tomorrow.

BOB MARSTON

Mark has glossed over the details of his second accident, which was outlined in *Harrier Boys, Volume One*. However, readers may appreciate some amplification of the significance of the technology in the GR7. As is so often the case, the accident involved a long list of factors that made it more likely. In particular, two showed the impact of kit that had come with the new jet.

- The aircraft involved, ZD462, was not among the first aircraft chosen for the deployment. It had an engine that produced less thrust than any other. To decide whether the engine should be changed, a 'what if' calculation was conducted by inserting the details of another available Pegasus into the aircraft's electronic operating data manual (ODM) on a laptop computer. Because of the work involved, and the remote chance of this jet being used, it was decided not to change. When it did go, it was planned that if the ship reached the Suez Canal, then the engine would be changed prior to operations in the Gulf. On the night of the accident, the hover performance of all jets was calculated and checked using the electronic ODM. Unfortunately, the section for ZD462 still contained the details of the alternative engine, thus giving over-optimistic hover figures.

- That night, the ship was far from land, under a solid overcast of cloud, and the light level was around 0.8 millilux. Mark found that his FLIR gave him a poor picture, though fortunately for the investigation, the video recording direct from the sensor was good. Even if useable, the FLIR just looks straight ahead. This left Mark relying on his NVGs, which became detached from his helmet at one point. On the final approach, the Harrier pilot aims to decelerate to hover in formation with the carrier, on its port side. Looking through the narrow NVG tubes, the pilot has to move his head to point at what he wants to see, so in the final hover, he can either look forward to see his instruments, or to his right to see the ship. Struggling to slow down on that night, Mark had to divide his attention between the HUD, showing his height, speed, attitude and power available, and looking over his right shoulder at the mass of steel now towering above him. With multiple audio warnings and radio inputs from the ship assailing him, Mark faced an enormous challenge.

His escape was remarkable. The evidence recovered from the aircraft suggested that, having gone a little too far past the ship and uncomfortably close for a pilot struggling to keep it in sight, he descended slowly into the sea going backwards and to the left. This caused the aircraft to roll inverted, cracking the left side of the CFC cockpit wall and so misaligning the MDC firing mechanism. When he ejected, without MDC activation, he was fired through an intact canopy into water, hence his loss of consciousness. His well-rehearsed automatic actions soon saw him in his dinghy, ready to fire flares, as the carrier continued on its way, sorting out the other airborne aircraft. With the SAR helicopter still on deck, the AEW Sea King that had been acting as a substitute for the ship's unserviceable search radar came to his assistance. Not ideally equipped or crewed for the task, and with its own technical failures, this aircraft also came close to crashing, but great skill saved the day.

ZD462 being lifted from the Mediterranean. (Author)

CHAPTER 20

ALL AT SEA

For various military and political considerations, the struggle for the survival of the UK Harriers became tied to a policy of reinforcing and formalising the linking of the aircraft to the ability to operate from ships. This had proven useful at times over the years, but could detract attention from the major role of supporting army action on the ground. One by-product of this wagon-circling was a high level of banter between the RN and RAF, which was present from the days of the first ship-borne trials with the GR1 through to the disbandment of Joint Force Harrier. Many kept to a friendly rivalry, but some, on both sides, found jointery uncomfortable. Here are a couple of RAF viewpoints.

MARK ZANKER

Towards the end of 1997 Saddam Hussein was still in power in Iraq and the UN had deployed weapons inspectors to search for the rumoured WMD. Political tensions were high and eventually Saddam kicked the weapons inspectors out and things got very tense. The British government decided to send HMS *Invincible* to the Gulf and at that time it was cruising around the Med. I was with IV(AC) Squadron, based at Laarbruch, and as it was Christmas the station held its traditional Christmas Draw ball in the officers' mess. The next day I was nursing a humungous hangover and around lunchtime I set off for the NAAFI to buy some headache tablets and a large bottle of water. As I arrived I was met by my boss who told me that he needed to see me at his home immediately. It was Sunday and clearly something was up. So whilst I sat in the boss's lounge worrying whether I had perhaps misbehaved the previous night it was then that he broke the news to me that I was 'needed' on *Invincible*.

At this point I need to go back to the winter of 1981 when, as a young lad, I walked through the doors of the RAF recruitment centre in Bristol. There was a good reason why I went through the door marked RAF and not the one marked Navy. I had no intention of spending a career at sea and in 1997 I still felt the same way. However, 1(F) Squadron was already aboard *Invincible*[26] and they were short of a QWI and, since that was on my CV, I had been volunteered to go. I was to fly down to Yeovilton the next day, be subjected to the dreaded 'dunker' and do a couple of launches off the ramp in preparation for going aboard the carrier.

---

[26] This was shortly after the accident involving GR7 ZD462.

It was case of 'Do not pass go, do not collect £200 and forget about Christmas'.

As it turned out, my good friends on 1(F) saw sense and allowed me to at least enjoy my Christmas at home before flying out to the Adriatic in the new year. It was from there that we set off through the Suez Canal and the Gulf of Aden and then into the Arabian Gulf. For some reason the RAF personnel on that cruise did not gel with their navy colleagues and there was a fair bit of friction[27]. It may have had something to do with the fact that we insisted on calling their ship a boat and the portholes windows; cabins were rooms and hatches doors. They didn't take the banter very well and the more they reacted to it the worse we got. Our mission was to patrol the southern no-fly zone in Iraq and train for the possibility of something a bit more serious. Our weapon of choice would be the laser-guided bomb with TIALD, but it was brand new and we hadn't had chance to use it back home.

As the QWI on the squadron I was tasked with leading the first four-ship training mission into Iraq. I stress that this was purely for training and no actual weapons were being carried. Two of us had TIALD pods and I would be the first to launch. During flight ops on a carrier (which is most of the time) there is a pilot on duty up on the bridge who oversees everything that happens on deck. As TIALD was a new bit of kit, it had attracted a few more people to the bridge. The captain was up front and the navy chap in charge of flying, known as Wings, was there too. There was also a requirement for 1(F) Squadron to provide their own supervisor as the GR7 was significantly different from the FA2. At the allotted time Squadron Leader Ian Cameron arrived as the 1(F) Squadron supervisor, and with him he had a large box. He placed the box on the table and without saying a word he removed a pair of glasses from the box and put them on. These were orange tinted and specifically designed to filter out laser light. As a safety precaution the pilots flying with TIALD had to wear them. The navy chaps on the bridge stared at him and after a while someone said, "What are those?"

"These are laser specs," said Ian. "You know.....just in case."
"Just in case what?" inquired the navy.
"Just in case there are any stray laser beams. We don't want to get blinded. Would you like some?" and he handed out more specs.

Ian proceeded to describe the TIALD pod as some sort of futuristic laser weapon that fired an extremely powerful beam that could cause significant eye damage and that, as this was a new bit of kit, it would probably be shooting laser beams

---

[27] Bob Marston – After ZD462's crash, I disembarked, with the jet, in Barcelona. At about 0200 hours on the first night in port, 1(F) Squadron ground crew who knew me confronted me in the Hard Rock Cafe, leaving me in no doubt about their feelings for life at sea.

all over the place. He said it fired as soon as there was power to the pod and the gimballed eyeball that contained the laser would probably bounce all over the place during a Harrier launch. Of course it was all total rubbish but Wings took it all in, hook, line and sinker. He exploded with rage and ordered the mission to be scrubbed. Behind him, the captain was desperately trying to contain a fit of the giggles (he was in on the joke). Meanwhile I was strapped into my Harrier, engine running, lined up on deck, waiting for the green light to launch. I had no idea what was going on up on the bridge. Ian strung it along for as long as he dared but eventually he came clean and explained that the whole thing was a wind up; Wings was in such a rage that it took some time for him to come down off the ceiling. The mission finally went ahead and thankfully we never had to use TIALD in anger on that deployment. After my free three-month cruise I was very happy to get back to dry land.

STEVE LONG
OCU MAGGOT

When I joined it, the Harrier Force had a pretty fearsome reputation for being populated with over-achieving, excessively hard-working bullies. Not everyone lived up to that reputation, but I suppose there were a couple of folks that came close. For me the OCU was an endurance course that just had to be tolerated and survived; I didn't enjoy it at all. It was also a serious time to join the force as there had been a rash of crashes recently – one fatal (a low-level toss attack that went wrong), one in which the pilot had been extremely seriously hurt (an ejection at 450+ knots and 150 ft, slightly inverted, which was probably outside the seat's limits and by rights the guy was lucky to be alive at all) and a third in which the pilot got out ok (on an air test).

Ground school on every other aircraft I flew before or since was a leisurely affair with lots of time between classes to read the aircrew manual, to sit in cardboard cockpits and learn checks, simulators, perhaps the odd survival course thrown in there too. But the introduction to the Harrier was a bucket of cold water in the face. On day one the boss burst into the classroom precisely at the designated time, told us that we were worthless to him and had a lot to learn as war was breaking out in Serbia/Kosovo and we were going to be late to the fight, and then he swept out of the room. We had two weeks to get our shit together and then we'd be starting flying. That first morning we went up to the crewroom to grab a cup of tea between lessons and paused to watch a T10 taxi out, line up on the runway and burst into flames. The crew had started the APU for some reason and it failed catastrophically, forcing them to do an emergency shutdown and egress. That certainly focused the mind even more on the next lecture.

The second half of the course, after we'd been taught by the QFIs how to fly the jet, navigate, land and do rudimentary 1v1 air combat, was where the really serious stuff started. The QFIs of B Flight handed us over to the 'qualified weapons instructors' of A Flight to be taught weaponeering and tactics. I can't help but put 'QWI' in quotes because the number of QWIs that could actually instruct was much less than half. If you were to draw a cartoon of the average Harrier GR7 QWI he'd be guarding the knowledge imparted to him on the QWI course like a sorcerer guarding his favourite spells. Knowledge is Power. You could have saved the RAF hundreds of thousands of pounds by sacking half of all the QWIs and putting a continuous loop recording in all the debrief rooms, endlessly repeating the QWI chant – "What you did was fine, but I would have done it better and you needed to grip it more. Sharpen up."

FIRST TOURIST

Six months into my first tour I found myself aboard HMS *Illustrious* in the Mediterranean. We each had five flights to become carrier qualified (day) and the whole squadron was 'done' by the time we sailed through the Straits of Gibraltar and up into the Bay of Biscay. After a brief port call in Brest we were scheduled to take part in a naval exercise as part of the flag waving involved with the recently formed Harrier Joint Force 2000. We were suddenly supposed to be bosom-buddies with the RN's Sea Harriers and were expected to do a lot more work together in the future.

About that time though, Tony Blair, emboldened by his experience with Serbia and Kosovo, decided that the 10-year-old simmering civil war in Sierra Leone was a perfect place to exercise his moral foreign policy ideas. So one day we were busy studying maps of the air-ground bombing ranges in France, and the next thing we knew all the communications lines went dead and the ship went to vibration speed. I've no idea how fast Lusty did flat out, but it was like living inside your washing machine on the spin cycle for 3-4 days. A quick look at the sun and we could tell we were heading south, with absolutely no idea why or where. As we finally decelerated from vibration speed it was announced triumphantly to us on the 1MC – "We are now sitting over the radar horizon from Sierra Leone, ready to do our government's bidding". Luckily it was announced over the loudspeaker system because if it had been in a briefing room then I'm afraid I'd have had to stick my hand up and ask the stupid question of exactly how many hostile radars the second poorest nation on earth possessed and quite why we were hiding from them after we'd come all this way. There were other questions on many people's lips too, such as why send an aircraft carrier when there was clear host nation support and an airport there so any squadron of jets – Harriers, Jags or Tornados – could have been there within 24 hours? But from my worm's eye view the whole of Operation Palliser, as it was officially called, was from the very start, a total political and inter-service farce.

The Joint Force Air Component Cell (JFACC) had recently formed. At that time there was a frenzy of re-naming every single unit in the armed forces to include the word 'Joint' somewhere in its title. It was the in thing to do and if you weren't 'Joint' then you'd have your budget cut. So the JFACC was flown at great expense to join us on Lusty and set about drawing up an airspace coordination plan (ACP) for us. We were all fresh from flying over Serbia and Kosovo where the ACP had essentially had three corridors in/out of Serbia and another one for Kosovo. That seemed to have worked pretty well for deconflicting a NATO-wide air campaign. After working countless hours, the beloved JFACC produced a tome of knowledge that defined over ten corridors in/out of Sierra Leone, a country which was about a third of the size of Serbia. It was a dog's breakfast. And oh-by-the-way the only aircraft flying in Sierra Leone were us, 801 NAS who we could walk down the corridor to talk deconfliction plans with, and a solitary Mi-24 Hind helicopter flown by a South African mercenary. It smelt a little like some people were trying to justify their existence.

So then came the great SHAR game of Top Trumps. Having sailed at high speed all that way no one seemed to know quite what to do with sixteen or so Harriers. The squadrons were invited to declare their capabilities up the tasking chain. The GR7s declared they had the capability to bring back to the ship a single unexpended 540-lb bomb on an average hot day. The SHAR boys crunched their numbers and said they could bring back 1,000 lbs of bombs (working to some obscenely low fuel state, but they had to show they were better than the RAF). The GR7s declared no precision-guided weapon capability as we didn't have any TIALD designator pods aboard (they were all still being used to support the Kosovo operation). The SHAR boys declared they were LGB capable; when asked how they intended to designate their precision weapons they declared the GR7s would, or someone on the ground would, but they were definitely LGB capable. When asked for night combat-ready status the GR7s declared a handful of pilots had completed the thirty-plus flight syllabus to learn night low-level attack in all its forms. The SHAR boys didn't have any night ground-attack qualified pilots, so they pushed a flare pack into the sea one night, launched a four-ship of guys who then threw eight practice bombs at it – with no idea if they hit or missed – and on landing declared themselves night-attack qualified. On and on it went, with the navy appearing to be playing Top Trumps with their military capability and taking any opportunity to take a swipe at the RAF and the GR7. It was a great introduction for me to the concept of jointery.

I only flew a handful of sorties over dry land into Sierra Leone and they were all non-events. The most scary part of it was that there were a lot of big birds in the jungle and the thought of taking a bird strike from one of them was the biggest threat to our lives. There were tales of what the rebels liked to do with government forces that they captured – limbs machete-ed off, chained to a tree and skinned alive etc – so the thought of taking a bird in the engine and having to eject over rebel territory was a distinctly unattractive proposition. The first few flights we made were at ultra low level. All the guys who were 'operational low flying' qualified, which meant they could fly down to 100 ft above the ground in peace time, were cleared to fly as low as they wanted without restrictions. As the most junior pilot aboard, I hadn't done that course so the initial plan was for me to float around at the back of the formations and up at 250 ft. I had two words for that idea, and managed to persuade folks that I'd work myself down to ultra low level carefully and progressively. As we approached the shoreline on my first trip inland, flying as number four of a four-ship, we all dropped to 20-30 ft on the radio altimeter and accelerated to 480 kts. I saw some unsuspecting fishermen working from their boats close to shore as we charged right over their heads and from what I could see they were quite surprised by the front pair of jets. We pulled up a few feet to clear the trees and headed for rebel territory. Having deployed us all that way, it appeared the politicians got cold feet about the whole idea and wouldn't give us authorisation to do anything. All we could do was fly 'presence' sorties which was a posh way of saying that we flew around making noise so that the rebels knew we were there, and also so that the UN troops knew we were there to support them too if needed. I suppose we may have done some good.

One night the call came through from the Paras who were ashore securing Lunghi airport that they wanted air support. Pathfinder platoon had an OP a few miles up the only access road to the airport and had seen rebels crawling up the road towards them. This was it. This is what I'd done all those years of training for – to fly in direct support of ground troops in trouble. The squadron was buzzing with excitement and even though I wasn't even close to being night combat ready I loitered in the ready room waiting to hear the call come through that would scramble my squadron buddies. But the call never came. As I understood it, the request for air support had come through to Lusty, was relayed to HMS *Ocean* (the 'command ship'), bounced off satellites to the Permanent Joint Headquarters in the UK, relayed to Tony Blair himself and then … nothing. At some point later that night, after Tony had ruminated on it, had a cabinet meeting, discussed international law, or maybe he was just watching TV, the decision was sent back that we were not allowed to launch and absolutely forbidden to employ weapons on another nation's soil as it would be an unforgivable escalation. Meanwhile, about 10-15 minutes after they'd made the call, the boys of Pathfinder platoon had taken care of business and half a dozen dead rebel soldiers were being carried back into the jungle by their compatriots. The feeling of frustrated impotence I had was indescribable. I couldn't understand for the life of me what we were doing. Lunghi airport was almost a tailor-made example of a Harrier austere operating base – the GR7s could have sat there on strip alert indefinitely, with a full warload on the wings, and been able to support the Paras at will. But our lords and masters required us to stay on board the ship where our operational ability was severely hampered by our ability to hover alongside with bombs on in tropical temperatures and our ability to operate at night was severely restricted due to a lack of experience and training.

Salt was rubbed into the wound even more when we sailed out of theatre at the end of June. Operations were still continuing on the ground in Sierra Leone but the ship's captain had a new posting and wanted to sail his boat home for a change of command ceremony. So Lusty sailed home to make the captain's cocktail party schedule work, leaving the troops ashore without our (albeit hamstrung) firepower. As we sailed home there was a dinner night held in the wardroom to say farewell to the commanding officer of 801 Squadron. He took plenty of time in his speech to remind everyone in the room that the RAF were all chicken shit yellow-bellied cowards and that the GR7 was rubbish compared to the SHAR. It was a fine way to make sure every RAF pilot in the room understood what senior officers of the Royal Navy thought about 'jointery'. Anyway, a few weeks later eleven British troops were taken hostage not far from Freetown by a rebel faction who called themselves the 'West Side Boys' and a UK Special Forces hostage rescue operation was launched under the title Operation Barras. They did the job just fine without us and used Lynx gunships and the Chinook door guns to great effect against a determined foe, but it was a textbook example of something we could have helped out with – except we weren't there.

EXCHANGE WITH THE USMC

I keyed the mic switch and screamed, "Break right! Break right! Missile right three!" It was dawn on day two of Operation Iraqi Freedom (Gulf War Two) and my wingman and I were just north of Basra when I saw my first SAM launch. We'd had a frustrating start to the fight. I was serving as the RAF exchange officer on a USMC squadron, VMA-311 'Tomcats', embarked aboard the USS *Bonhomme Richard*. The day previously, we'd both spoken to our buddies returning from the first night strikes and were engines-running on deck, about to launch for our own first trip 'across the berm' into Iraq. My plane captain did his final checks of my airplane, went out in front of me and gave me the hand signal to tell me my jet was 'down' (broken) and I should shutdown. There were no spare airplanes that I could take instead; we were launching every serviceable jet. I frantically indicated I needed him to plug in his headset and talk to me as I was aware our launch time was looming and the ship wouldn't sail into the wind forever. He came on and told me I had a weeping hydraulic leak in the nose-wheel bay. I was furious and told him all the indications were fine in the cockpit and I wanted him to strip the chains and let me go. We argued back and forth for a few minutes but all credit to the guy – he stuck to his guns and refused to let me go. So my wingie and I had to sit out the first day of the shooting.

Day two started better. We topped off with fuel from a C-130 over Kuwait and were just about to enter the close air support stack when our controller, Blacklist, gave us an urgent task. A Seersucker surface-to-surface missile had just been fired from the Basra area and we were to go find the launcher and kill it. Exciting stuff and a juicy target to get us started. But when I entered the coordinates and looked through my Litening II targeting pod I couldn't see anything remotely resembling a military vehicle, let alone a missile launcher. All I could see were people going about their daily lives in an urban neighbourhood. I re-confirmed the coordinates with the controller, double-checked everything and looked again, this time scanning around, zooming in and out, using infra-red to look for the heat signature that a rocket launch would undoubtedly leave – everything I could think of. I spent an unwise length of time with my head in the cockpit, staring at the screen, getting increasingly desperate. When I looked up I realised I'd been a terrible flight lead and had spat my wingman out in front of me.

There he was, about half a mile in front of me with a steady trickle of flares firing out of his top and bottom buckets. He'd activated one of our pre-emptive flare programmes that would put out a 30-second firework show, designed to defeat just about every known hostile heat-seeking missile. I was alarmed and called on the radio – "Dude, are you getting shot at?" "No." "Well you're flaring. Quit it!" I guess our impromptu firework display highlighted our position to the guys on the ground as we suddenly started getting sniffs of the SA-3 system that we knew was in the area on our radar warning gear. We'd just decided we thought we'd better bug out for the time being and let the place cool down when I saw the plume of smoke to our right. It didn't seem to be guiding but our break turn towards it would/should have made its endgame tracking manoeuvre (if it were to do one) that much harder. After that, we'd definitely had enough fun for one day and headed for Al Jaber in Kuwait for another splash of gas, re-tasking and a productive morning's work killing armoured vehicles at the Republican Guard barracks just outside Al Kut.

Being on exchange with the USMC was a truly eye-opening experience and gave

AV-8B+ Harrier. (McDonnell Douglas)

me a very different perspective on the RAF. My transition from one to the other had been a fast and furious baptism of fire. I arrived at Marine Corps Air Station Yuma at the end of November 2002. My arrival chat with the commanding officer was short and to the point – "don't unpack, we're off to war next month". I had five flights in the AV-8B Harrier II+ and trip six was to embark on board the USS *Bonhomme Richard*, already sailing west out of San Diego with a full amphibious readiness group of nine or so ships. It was just enough time in the jet to realise that just about everything that could be different, was different – the software, the weapon-aiming techniques, the weapons themselves, their radar warning gear, the radio calls, the hand signals, the HOTAS. Oh, and for the first time in my life I had a radar on the nose of my jet to figure out how to use. In US eyes I was a dirty foreign spy and wasn't allowed to read any of their manuals (all stamped with the caveat SECRET – NO FORN in unfriendly red ink), so it was a little tricky to find out what I wanted and needed to know.

The day we were due to fly the jets onto the Bonnie Dick, which had already sailed, I was dressed in my flight gear and about to head out the door when the British embassy in Washington phoned wanting to speak to me urgently. Approval hadn't yet come through from the UK for me to deploy with the USMC and I was to stay in Yuma. I had to take a deep breath and count to five before replying to my superior officer at the other end of the line. I explained that the ship had sailed, and there were no spare pilots left at Yuma to take the jet I was fragged to fly; I stated that I would be flying aboard the USS *Bonhomme Richard* and deploying with my unit and that if formal permission was still not forthcoming as the ship sailed past Hawaii then I'd try to figure out a way to get off on one of the mail runs. Fortunately the admin and political scribblies ironed everything out by the time we got abeam Hawaii, but it was a taste of what was to come.

As we approached the Persian Gulf I fired off a string of emails to the British embassy in DC who were supposed to be supporting me. I needed clarification on what rules of engagement I was to operate under – UK or US. They weren't vastly different, but there were a few significant differences such as the UK's aversion to dropping cluster weapons and firebombs. I had a short list of requirements: a UK 'goolie chit' – the piece of paper that said 'please don't cut my balls off; hand me over to the British authorities' in a number of Iraqi languages, a Union flag to wear on my flight suit, UK dog tags etc. My thought was that if I got shot down and captured I wanted to have my nuts cut off for being British and not because they thought I was an American. There'd be nothing worse than being castrated for the wrong reason. But the embassy proved incapable of doing anything at all for me apart from reminding me of my obligations to refuse any US medals that might be awarded to me. All good morale-boosting stuff.

The US pilots had such a totally different mindset on fighting than we'd had back at Cottesmore. I'd been the combat survival and rescue officer on

3(F) Squadron at Cottesmore and had been on a bunch of survival and evasion courses. It had always been emphasised that our personal weapon, the mighty Walther PPK of James Bond fame, was pretty useless. Some said, and not terribly tongue-in-cheek, that instead of trying to shoot anyone with it we should take the magazine out as at least then we'd have two lumps of metal to throw at someone and have more chance of doing some damage to them. If we got shot down we'd try to go to ground and wait for a pickup and the PPK was a psychological boost. But the USMC chaps went looking for a fight. If they could have figured out a way to get their M-16 onto the ejection seat then they would have. But without a rifle they all flew with the issued Browning 9mm and at least four-six clips of ammunition in one armpit. Most guys flew with a K-bar, the marines' standard issue bayonet, stuffed into one boot; a 'Saturday Night Special' or 'boot gun' pistol jammed into the other boot; and their own weapon of choice in another armpit holster – a Magnum .357, a Colt .45 or some other huge hand cannon. If they got shot down and they lost their primary weapon system, the marines' mindset was to use one of their handguns to shoot a guy with an AK-47, use that to take over a T-55 tank and then keep heading for Baghdad in the tank until they got to Saddam's palace. As I said, they thought of things differently from the RAF.

My most memorable day of Iraqi Freedom, other than the one mentioned previously, was in mid-April, as the ground troops were approaching Baghdad. By that time the air tasking order that arrived every morning hardly seemed worth the paper it was printed on. My take-off time was always determined by the success of the night wave's sorties. If they'd had good luck finding targets they'd keep hitting them until they were 'Winchester' (out of bombs); if they hadn't found anything they'd keep looking until they were 'Bingo' (out of gas). But either way it was impossible to predict when they'd get back or when the jets would be turned around and ready for us to launch on the dawn/morning wave. Anyway, on this particular morning we launched late, with a tanker's call sign to try to take gas from, but we were way outside the time window, and a killbox to aim for that we were pretty sure had been worked over already. Sure enough, after making our way through all the various radio channels to get from the boat and into Iraq without getting schwacked by an over-enthusiastic Aegis cruiser or Patriot battery, we checked in to try to find our tanker and were told that it had gone home. Plan B was to try to 'bootleg some gas' so I asked around for any tanker airborne that had some spare gas they could give us. No joy. Hmm. Without any gas we'd have only a few minutes on station up at Baghdad (over 350nm from the Bonnie Dick). We'd been briefed recently that a helicopter forward refuelling point had opened at An Numaniyah, just outside Al Kut (where we'd been dropping bombs just over a week before). I thought I'd give it a try and see if they could give some gas to a couple of thirsty jets. My wingman recognised the voice of the guy who answered at 'Three Rivers' – he was a fellow USMC Harrier pilot who was on a ground tour at the time and was running the radios at the FRP. He was only too happy to give us what we needed as they had plenty of gas and seeing us arrive would be a great demo to the ground troops that they were being supported.

The USMC Harriers had had a bit of a bad experience in Gulf War 1 with heat-seeking missiles and I was mindful that the locals might not be too friendly where we were about to land. So I made sure my wingie was happy with the idea and we did an idle descent from altitude, both only goosing the power on short finals to cushion our landings. Taxiing to the refuel point we passed a number of burnt-out tanks and APCs – evidence of the work we'd been doing only a couple of weeks previously. The engine-running refuel went smoothly with lots of grunts grinning at us and our next problem was how to take off again without exposing ourselves unnecessarily to IR missiles. The USMC didn't have a procedure that I was aware of so I relied on an RAF technique that I'd read about. Instead of a normal climb out, we stayed at less than 100 ft after we got airborne and accelerated as fast as the jet could on the deck with a full warload. Once we had a bag full of knots in hand and we were over a barren bit of desert, we selected a pre-emptive flare programme and pulled skywards, zooming as quickly as we could up to 10,000 ft and out of the threat zone.

As soon as we got to the top of climb and checked in with our controller we were tasked. An 'asset' had detected armour in a clump of trees between Baghdad and Tikrit to the north and we were to investigate. We side-stepped Baghdad, just to be on the safe side. At the start of the war there were dozens of surface-to-air missile sites understandably positioned in and around the capital city, so it had been dubbed the 'Baghdad Super MEZ'. As the days wore on those SAM sites were obviously targeted by coalition forces but we never really got any intelligence to confirm that they were getting hit. At one point we were ordered to desist from referring to the 'Super MEZ' so we had to re-name it amongst ourselves as the 'Really Quite Good MEZ' instead. It was probably all cleaned out by this point, but I didn't want to tempt fate. Anyway, sure enough, when we got to the allotted location and I got the Litening pod uncaged I could see half a dozen APCs dug in, in what appeared to be an orchard. We set up for a standard attack, flown in 'combat spread' and my wingie dropped his first GBU-12. Seconds before impact though a line of high trees obscured my line of sight to the target I was lasing and the bomb missed. I was very frustrated with myself for rushing the attack and wracked my brain for a profile that would work in this situation, but none sprung to mind. Time to improvise.

I had a quick chat with my wingie to make sure he was happy with flying without mutual support for a few minutes, given the pretty low threat situation we were in. He was cool with the idea so we lined up running down the neat lines of trees in the orchard and I dropped into trail a couple of miles behind him as he ran in to drop his next GBU. I locked my radar to him so I could find him later after all my heads-in time working the targeting pod. As soon as I heard

F35 test pilot. (Steve Long)

the tone on the radio that signalled his weapon was in the air I selected idle and climbed to slow down to just above the stall speed, area track, laser on. It worked like a charm and his weapon impacted seconds before I overflew the target and the pod started to hit its gimbals. A quick in-place 90° turn and we were back in a wide spread formation and setting up for the next attack. After we'd dropped our ordnance I marked the location of another couple of pieces of armour and gave a full report to the controller as we checked out. All in all, it was a good day out.

CHAPTER 21

TRANSITION

JIM ARKELL

The Harrier Integrated Project Team (IPT) was responsible for supporting, maintaining and upgrading the fleet of Harrier aircraft throughout its life. I joined the IPT in 2002 as the requirements manager (RM) at an important time for the upgrade to the Harrier GR9. Previously, the IPT had relied on the resident release to service authority desk officer for advice on operational matters and had employed a Royal Navy helicopter engineer as the RM. I felt that, with my background as a Harrier GR3 QWI and experience flying the FA-18 on exchange with the USN, I could make a difference to the project.

My responsibilities were to define the system requirements for the various upgrades and ensure that what was delivered met the operational needs of the front line. I was also responsible for progressing urgent operational requirements for the GR7 (my successor doing likewise for the GR9). My first such UOR was for Enhanced Paveway II, a laser/GPS-guided bomb for Operation Telic, with work commencing in late 2002. The UOR included the installation of a control unit mounted next to the HUD through which target coordinates were passed to the bomb. I quickly gained an insight into the workings of the IPT and its relationship with external agencies and the MoD.

The GR7 had represented a huge leap in capability compared with the GR3. Foremost amongst the improvements was the ability to operate at night using night-vision goggles and forward-looking infra-red sensors. And whereas the GR3 could only realistically operate at low level, the GR7 was equipped with improved navigation, attack and defensive aids to effectively be employed at medium level with increasingly modern weapons and reconnaissance sensors. There

GR7 cockpit with UOR modifications.
(Jim Arkell)

were, however, a number of limitations with the equipment. To use frequency-hopping HAVEQUICK communication modes, pilots had to operate the radios looking 'head down' inside the cockpit, with implications for flight safety. The TIALD pod could not be used concurrently with the ground proximity warning system (GPWS) due to GR7's lack of computing capacity. Reconnaissance from medium level required careful pre-planning and accurate navigation to capture the required imagery using a pod controlled via a unit mounted on a panel inside the cockpit. The proliferation of ad hoc modifications being applied to limited numbers of aircraft exacerbated the 'fleets-within-fleets' situation resulting in an ever-decreasing number of fully capable aircraft being available for operations. An upgrade for smart weapons and sensors could overcome such limitations and enable the aircraft to operate in the early 21st century until replaced by the Joint Strike Fighter.

The MoD had decided in early 2002 that there were insufficient funds to upgrade both the Harrier GR7 and the Sea Harrier FA2 variants and that priority would be given to the UK's ability to mount offensive operations from land and from the sea. To achieve this aim, the air defence variant (FA2) would be phased out early (by 2006) and the GR9 would replace the GR7 in 2006. In concert with this change, RAF and RN Harrier personnel and equipment would amalgamate to form Joint Force Harrier (JFH), which would provide centralised command and control and delivery of operational capability. In addition to the new capabilities, the GR9 programme had to take account of the need for enhancements for carrier-borne operations, including fitting the more powerful Pegasus engine, ensure that 'obsolescence' issues with the airframe were addressed and, additionally, upgrade the Harrier T10s to the T12 version, minus full weapons clearances and secure communications modifications. Finally, the IPT also had to implement cost-cutting changes to the way in which the fleet of aircraft were serviced and modified to reduce overall support costs.

The MoD approved the GR9 upgrade towards the end of 2002, shortly after I had joined the IPT. The head of the IPT formed a team focused solely on the GR9 programme, led by Group Captain Ian Thorne. His remit was to deliver the new capability to the required standard, on time and within budget. He developed a strong partnering arrangement with BAE Systems, a number of whose staff were embedded at RAF Wyton as full-time members of the IPT, and broke down barriers particularly between people in 'Defence' and 'Industry' by novel methods to create trust at all levels of the programme. Later, as 1-star IPT leader during one such team-building event, one of Ian Thorne's senior management team members came off second best in a wakeboarding collision with a BAE Systems colleague; Andy Ebdon's battered and bruised face telling its own story for several weeks after.

The main improvements to the GR9 involved wiring changes inside the aircraft and other hardware and software changes to support smart weapons, data links and recce sensors. Hardware changes included a new open-system mission computer with dual processors providing increased storage and processing capacity, a new MIL-STD-1760 stores management system and associated wiring to the weapons pylons to allow communication with smart weapons, a new inertial navigation unit/GPS and upgrades to the display computer (DC). Structural changes included new power distribution panels, modified pylons and relocation of a new weapon load-out panel to the port-nozzle fairing. Software changes included a new operational flight programme (OFP) written in ADA higher order language to ensure future maintainability and upgrades to the DC software to support new symbology for the Brimstone missile and Paveway IV precision-guided bomb (PGB) and data links. New radios were fitted and better integrated to allow operation of HAVEQUICK and secure modes via the up-front controls.

Ahead of the delivery of the Harrier GR9 and as a de-risking measure, the IPT had been given approval to fit the bigger engine to the GR7, which would then become the GR7A. Although in some quarters its main justification was to improve hover performance for carrier (CVS) ops, the Pegasus Mk107 had obvious benefits for hot and high airfields and pilots particularly liked the enhanced thrust available at take-off, in the climb and during air-combat manoeuvring (ACM). Aptly, the first Harrier deployment to Kandahar (a hot and high airfield) was with GR7As in September 2004. The new engine, which was also easier to maintain, had lower whole-life costs than the Mk105 and so the IPT presented a case for full-fleet fit with the Mk107 engine; however, as the sums did not produce sufficient savings based on the expected out of service date (OSD) of 2015, the Harrier Force had to make do with the thirty or so Mk107s available to it. When the OSD was subsequently extended to 2018, full-fleet fit could have been financially advantageous; however, the production line had by then been mothballed and would have been too costly to reopen. The T12 also received a modification to fly with the bigger engine to enable the OCU to teach VSTOL manoeuvring on a typical UK hot summer's day. I was reminded by the IPT leader that this was funded by the defence logistics organisation (DLO) and not by defence equipment capability (DEC) and was therefore a modification, not an upgrade.

In order further to reduce risk, the programme was broken down into manageable 'chunks' of upgrades delivered sequentially with the in-service date (ISD) formally set for 1 September 2006 with twenty-four modified aircraft delivered with the Brimstone anti-armour weapon (capability B); however, because of missile susceptibility to Harrier vibration and concerns over the integrity of the rocket motor, integration of Brimstone was delayed; instead, the GR9 was delivered with the legacy Maverick missile-weapon system at ISD and CRV7 rockets, with PGB following on a year later and Brimstone to follow after that. Originally regarded as a legacy capability, CRV7 was not a candidate for the GR9 upgrade; however, the need for a forward-firing weapon for ongoing operations in Afghanistan allayed any lingering objections and the capability was restored at minimum cost to the MoD because of the IPT's foresight in retaining CRV7 coding in the GR9's 'baseline' software capability.

With a background in operational evaluation, I felt it was important that front-line operators should have a strong voice in defining the Harrier GR9 human machine interface (HMI). In addition, the GR9 programme manager strongly supported the concept of combining the various testing activities not only to reduce delays and costs but also to improve effectiveness in the round. BAE Systems and QinetiQ test pilots along with staff of the SAOEU subsequently formed a joint test team so that any problems which, more often than not, were software related could be identified as early as possible and remedied either as a software 'patch' or added to a new software release at a later upgrade point. Regular 'pilot working groups' were held with all the relevant parties to define and agree the HMI. I relied heavily on the staff of the OEU to comment on BAE Systems' proposals to ensure that the front line got what they needed rather than what non-aviators thought they should have.

PGB was originally intended to be rolled out on the Tornado as 'lead' platform; however, with Tornado integration proving complex and costly and Brimstone on Harrier now delayed, the MoD opted for the Harrier to be the lead aircraft for PGB with delivery of capability in 2007. The PGB was a new 500-lb bomb equipped with an inertial navigation unit to 'fly' itself to the nominated target and a laser seeker to home onto marked targets. PGBs could therefore be used in all weather conditions, unlike laser-guided bombs, which required clear line of sight between the laser returns from the target and the weapon. Via the 1760 SMS pilots could programme the weapon with target coordinates, desired impact heading, impact angle and fusing to achieve optimum effect. Thus, pilots could select the parameters required to minimise collateral damage, for example by choosing a short-delay fusing and vertical impact through the roof of a structure so that detonation would occur inside the building; these were important considerations for the Afghanistan mission. The ability for each of six bombs separately to 'fly' to independent targets required the development of a bespoke airborne planning facility tailored for the single-seat aircraft. Staff of the SAOEU, working with specialists from BAE Systems and the PGB IPT, devised the means by which a single-seat pilot could arrive at the correct point in space to achieve the desired result. Significant upgrades to the Harrier mission-planning aid became necessary and cockpit workload was deemed manageable only if colour was available on the multi-function displays, which led to the purchase of multi-purpose colour displays (MPCDs), both initiatives being funded in part by the PGB programme.

Unlike the QinetiQ Harrier software maintenance unit's (HSMU) support for the GR7/T10, which was service manned and based at Boscombe Down, the GR9 programme called for a new approach because of the unique ADA language used in computer programming. The new software team comprised BAE Systems staff with embedded military personnel working on rigs based at BAE Systems Farnborough. Although people initially thought that such a set-up would be expensive and unresponsive to front-line needs, this proved not to be the case, possibly because of the evident change of culture within defence and industry as a result of the new partnering arrangements in place at the time and recognition that the heart of the aircraft – its software – was crucial to mission effectiveness.

As stated earlier, the Harrier GR9 was delivered on time by 1 September 2006 with an additional two aircraft above the required twenty-four at the capability B standard, albeit without Brimstone. All front-line aircraft were now fitted with a highly accurate IN/GPS with GPWS, new TALON radios, one of which could be operated in the secure mode, and improved Maverick HMI to exploit tracking features not available on the GR7. Aircraft could continue to operate with the joint reconnaissance pod and with an improved version of the TIALD 500 pod. In addition, CRV7 rockets could now be fired individually or in salvo, with the number or rockets being pilot selectable. Previously, the GR7 had to carry training pods for single-shot firings and operational pods for eighteen rocket salvos for 'tuned effects': single rockets would usually be sufficient as 'warning' shots to encourage the Taliban to desist from attacking friendly forces, otherwise a full pod of rockets would follow.

Although many of the software gremlins had been identified by the SAOEU and either fixed prior to service release or nominated for the follow-on software update, a system was put in place for any anomalies to be 'captured' and rectified at the next opportunity. Additionally, front-line requests for software changes (RSCs) were formally recorded, prioritised and costed and incorporated in subsequent releases if deemed necessary and affordable. Again, staff of the SAOEU and STANEVAL, along with the RM and IPT specialists, were fundamental to the process. It became apparent that the software support team could include minor changes relatively quickly and cheaply using the ADA programming tools at its disposal.

While the GR9 'team' were busy managing the upgrade other parts of the IPT had to devise and implement new ways of maintaining and upgrading the fleet whilst supporting ongoing operations, the aim being to significantly reduce support costs to defence. Four traditional 'lines' of maintenance were replaced by two known as forward (for the flying squadrons) and depth. Engineering establishments such as St Athan, where major modifications were carried out, were closed. Second-line servicing was combined with major upgrades at the front-line base at Cottesmore. This required civilian BAE Systems staff to relocate to Rutland and work in the joint upgrade and maintenance programme (JUMP) hangar. Former engineering bays were replaced with a 'pulse line', adopting best practice seen in manufacturing industries such as for cars and vehicles. Watching a jacked-up Harrier being moved on a hover pad by an engineer (admittedly at only a few inches per minute) was nerve-wracking to say the least. The changes resulted in huge benefits: modifications and upgrades were completed more quickly and aircraft availability was improved – an important factor given the relatively small fleet of some seventy GR9s.

On 27 January 2007, barely four months after ISD, the first two Harrier GR9As arrived in Kandahar followed by a further four in September. At the time, the front line were eagerly anticipating delivery of capability C with PGB; however, problems with the fuse led to delays and further improvisation by fitting a Paveway IV seeker to the 1,000-lb Paveway II bomb and tail, an interim modification known as Enhanced Paveway (EPW) II+. This allowed pilots more effectively to employ laser/GPS-guided weapons via the aircraft systems rather than through a box mounted to one side of the HUD. Capability C was thus delivered in April 2007 with EPW II+, Paveway III dynamic weapon aiming and a number of avionics upgrades such as Successor IFF (SIFF) and improvement to rangeless airborne instrumentation and debriefing system (RAIDS) to improve the effectiveness of air-to-air training.

Despite the TIALD pod improvements, its deficiencies for the Afghanistan operation were stark compared with the performance of the equipment available to other air forces. TIALD had been designed for larger objects such as tanks and hardened aircraft shelters whereas the Afghanistan theatre called for the ability to discriminate between much smaller objects such as people and equipment, for example mortar tubes. Now coming to the end of my tour and retirement from the RAF in June 2007, it was left to my successor (Wing Commander Paul Wharmby) to progress the first of a number of significant UORs to go onto the GR9. The first of these – the Sniper targeting pod – stemmed from a BAE Systems private venture funded rapid technology insertion programme in 2006. The Fast Jet Weapons Operational Evaluation Unit (FJWOEU) – formerly the SAOEU – was quickly able to evaluate Sniper on GR9 using TIALD functionality clearing it for use in record time. The integration included transmission of live video to the man equipped with a Rover terminal on the ground. The other UORs were for the helmet-mounted cueing system using legacy hardware from the Jaguar and the Terma EW pod fitted to the starboard gun station. These were released to service in June 2007 along with the 500-lb Paveway IV (at capability C+), providing the Harrier GR9/9A with a significant operational edge compared with the GR7.

When Paveway IV was down-selected for the PGB programme, very little funding was available to meet front-line training requirements. PGB staff felt that a dozen or so inert warheads over the lifetime of the aircraft would suffice. The problem was that a bomb (live or inert) had to be strapped to a pylon in order for the pilot to access the weapon-performance envelopes known as launch-acceptability regions. A similar situation applied to Brimstone. The solution was to provide a software emulation of the weapon-performance characteristics and modify the stores-management system with training modes. The upgrade, delivered in 2009 (capability EA) also included control of the digital joint reconnaissance pod (DJRP) through the mission computer, with Jaguar Force expertise helping to define the HMI. Integration via the MC resulted in the removal of the recce control panel with control through the MPCDs allowing the pod to be pointed in the right direction irrespective of aircraft height and speed and switched on and off (automatically if required), thus reducing pilot cockpit workload and increasing mission effectiveness.

Although Brimstone was designed to find and destroy targets autonomously using a millimetric wave radar seeker (known as 'legacy' Brimstone), this presents difficulties with rules of engagement in certain theatres such as in Afghanistan. The missile was therefore modified with a laser seeker to guide to a target being marked by a laser – the dual-mode seeker (DMS) Brimstone. Brimstone has a small warhead, which is an advantage when attempting to minimize collateral damage. At the time of my departure from the IPT, legacy Brimstone was due to be released by the turn of the decade and DMS Brimstone would probably have followed soon thereafter. Two other systems were under consideration at that time. The first was for the provision of tactical information exchange capability (TIEC). This consisted of two data links: a terminal to provide Link 16 and an integrated data modem (IDM). Link 16 would provide a secure data link with other Link 16 users and significantly increase pilot situational awareness in hostile air-to-air and surface-to-air environments thereby improving aircraft survivability. IDM would provide a link to other users predominantly for the close air support task. Although choosing and manipulating the right messages and transmitting IDM messages securely were challenging, TIEC was due to be delivered in the summer of 2011 (capability EB). The second system requirement was for a collision warning system (CWS), which arose from numerous flight-safety recommendations. Like the Tornado Force, the Harrier community felt that an IFF-based TCAS system would not be effective because of the high rate of false alarms likely to occur in tactical formation situations; however, such a system was fitted (inexpensively) to the Tucano and has nevertheless provided the solution for Tornado too. Installation of CWS on Harrier would no doubt have been possible before disbandment intervened.

One final requirement that caused some angst during the early life of Joint Force Harrier was whether the GR9 should be fitted with a landing recovery aid and if so what. Advocates of deployability suggested that ILS would allow suitably equipped airfields to be used as staging posts or diversions in poor weather. Others extolled the virtues of the microwave airborne digital guidance equipment (MADGE), which had allowed the Sea Harrier to recover semi-autonomously to CVS in poor weather. MADGE on GR9 would have required a completely new set of hardware and software and was deemed too expensive. BAE Systems also costed a number of ILS installations including one fitted to Spanish navy AV-8Bs, which used a display unit mounted next to the HUD. As the limited funding available had to be justified by its ability to enhance CVS operations and not by arguments concerning deployability, the CVS were fitted with radar to provide carrier controlled approaches to the ship and TACAN (as an approach aid), which benefitted rotary wing operators too.

It has been a fascinating journey witnessing at first hand the changes over the past forty or so years. Gone are the cluster bomb units, which were the staple weapons during the Cold War. Gone are the days of flashing around in daylight at low level in poor weather with the help (or hindrance) of Mr Ferranti's navigation kit giving 4-5 miles errors after 45 minutes. The QWI's mantra of 'Go REV[28] early' are words from the past. Today's operators no longer put up with a single, appalling radio whilst enduring one and half second timing 'pips' listening out for threats on the radar warning receiver[29]. But the spirit of endeavour and improvisation has endured. Fitting Sidewinders to GR3 weapons pylons as a UOR for the Falklands War is just as impressive as temporarily fitting a PGB seeker head to a 1,000-lb bomb on GR9s whilst sorting out a fusing problem. Arguably the customers' satisfaction at the rapid sensor-to-shooter response times achievable over Afghanistan in 2008 were matched by those achieved by the 1980s RAF Germany Harrier Force's ability to respond quickly to requests for support through forward deployment, cockpit tasking and high sortie rates. Although the missions of close air support and reconnaissance have changed little, the means have altered radically and will no doubt continue in the future with the arrival of Lightning II. Happiness is vectored thrust.

---

[28] Reversionary mode, using a fixed sight rather than a computed one.

[29] The first GR3 RWR scanned three frequency bands, each for 0.5 seconds in a continuous cycle, a high-pitched tone marking the end of a cycle. If a threat was detected, it was represented by a tone that the pilot had to recognise and react appropriately.

CHAPTER 22

THE FINAL PRODUCT

The last operational deployment of the UK Harriers turned out to be the longest of all. In September 2004, GR7As flew out to Kandahar Airfield to support the International Security Assistance Force (ISAF) and to fight against terrorism as required. This was seen as a relatively short-term task, just until Afghanistan stabilised with a new government. Five years later, and at considerable cost, the task was finally handed over to the Tornado Force.

During those five years, Afghanistan became far from stable, and all forces, including the British army and the UK Harriers, were called upon to undertake ever greater fighting tasks. Unfortunately, this narrow focus of effort made it difficult for the Harrier Force to maintain currency in the flexibility for which it was renowned. However, by 2009, the Harrier, both American and British, had become the most trusted air support platform for troops on the ground in Afghanistan. Here, one of the final senior British pilots summarises the overall achievement.

JAMES BLACKMORE
After five years, 8,500 sorties and more than 22,000 hours airborne, the Harrier finally returned from operations in Afghanistan. During this busy time for the Harrier I was privileged enough to serve during Operation Herrick with both 1(F) and IV(AC) Squadrons under the umbrella of Joint Force Harrier (JFH) and this piece is a look back at my time there, focusing on the capabilities of the GR9 and our role in Afghanistan.

It is my intention to concentrate on the Harrier GR9 as this is the capability with which we eventually finished the operations in Afghanistan and this variant is a very different beast compared to the GR7. Crucially, when compared with the GR7, the GR9 is essentially digitally wired, meaning that the pilot can communicate directly with the weapons on the pylons; consequently this has seen the introduction of the Paveway IV (PWIV) 500-lb laser and GPS-guided bomb along with a number of other significant upgrades.

The aircraft's most common war-fighting fit during operations in Afghanistan was, working from the left-hand pylon:

GR9 in Afghanistan. (J Boothe)

- PWIV – Fundamentally this weapon changed the way the Harrier operated; not only can the bomb be guided to its target using a laser from either the aircraft (Sniper advanced targeting pod) or from the ground, it can also be delivered onto precise GPS coordinates. At 500 lbs it is also a lighter weapon when compared to some of the more traditional 1,000-lb variants; this therefore gives the added benefit of reducing the overall launch and recovery weight of the aircraft – crucial when you consider CVS operations. The fuse is cockpit programmable allowing the pilot to tailor the effect of the weapon depending on the target and the requirement of the soldier on the ground. It can, for instance, penetrate through layers of concrete before exploding thus allowing the pilot to accurately target the precise part of the building to be destroyed.

- CRV-7 – The pod contains nineteen individual rockets; giving a total of thirty-eight per aircraft. In many ways these mitigated the lack of a gun (a subject which is open to a much bigger debate) and with this standard of Harrier we could again make selections in the cockpit that allow us to fire one rocket, thirty-eight rockets or any multiple in between. Once again this is crucial when considering the effect required on the ground and proportionality. Why fire thirty-eight rockets when one as a warning shot would have the desired effect?

- Fuel tanks – When fully fuelled the aircraft sits with 11,700 lbs of fuel with two tanks. Over Afghanistan this would quite often give us in excess of two hours airborne without the need to air-to-air refuel (AAR), but with the AAR capability our time on station could be dramatically increased, sometimes missions lasting well in excess of six hours.

- Terma – This pod was a new addition to the Harrier for Afghanistan and provided us with many more defensive flares than the usual internal load; it also provided a missile launch cue to the pilot.

- Digital Joint Reconnaissance Pod (DJRP) – Whilst many would imagine that our time in Afghanistan was all about dropping bombs, this couldn't be further from the truth; in fact the vast majority of the time we would be tasked with taking high-resolution imagery for the ground commanders and their soldiers. This could be anything from looking at changes to patterns of life, building construction and layout, or in the hunt for improvised explosive devices (IEDs). Crucially, carrying this pod did not affect our weapon load-out and therefore we could 'swing' from a reconnaissance mission to close air support at the drop of a hat depending on the circumstances and the requirements of the soldiers on the ground. Although the product is in black and white, the resolution is exceptionally high and with correct equipment, 3D images could be developed and intricate graphics produced thus providing an excellent tool in intelligence gathering.

• Sniper advance targeting pod (ATP) – This replaced the TIALD 500 and offered a huge leap forward in capability. Essentially Sniper allowed us to view the ground from altitude and stand-off with incredible resolution in both TV and infra-red, which crucially allowed us to operate to the same effect at night. With the ability to zoom, the pilot has the potential to observe persons on the ground and in some cases distinguish between adults and children. Other enhancements on the pod allow the pilot to generate GPS coordinates from what they are viewing or fire a laser to guide bombs to their point of impact. At night an infra-red pointer allows aircraft to operate together and point out ground features to each other; rather like using a Star Wars-style lightsabre when viewed through night-vision goggles. Finally we were able to broadcast the image we saw directly to the soldier on the ground or back to the operations centre; crucial when having to make quick decisions. All of this imagery is recorded for analysis post the mission and also affords us a second reconnaissance sensor, again increasing the ability of the aircraft to gather intelligence.

Finally, moving on to the pilot and the cockpit. For the final six months we operated with a helmet-mounted cueing system (HMCS) which allowed the pilot to quickly identify coordinates on the ground using a red diamond that is projected over it on a reticule placed over the right eye. This is an excellent tool in increasing spatial awareness and takes away the need to spend vital minutes using binoculars to identify features from a map. Equally, in reverse the pilot is able to look around the battle space and if he sees something of interest, he simply looks at it, designates it using controls on the throttle and immediately the Sniper ATP will move to look at that same point on the ground. At night, the pilot wears NVGs and these are fully integrated with all the systems meaning the way we did business by night was exactly the same as during the day, including flying at low level, something the Harrier Force is well trained in and extremely proud of.

The cockpit itself continued to be busy with two TVs displaying anything from Sniper imagery, through to weapon programming, engine performance data or a moving map. We simultaneously used two radios to keep in contact with the ground forces, our wingman or the various control agencies that help make the tactical decisions. We also carried many maps to help us orientate ourselves with the forces on the ground or to find points of interest. Put simply, we were the pilot, navigator, engineer, communicator, weapons officer and lawyer whilst operating the Harrier; this certainly is testament to the training each pilot is given.

THE ROLE OF THE HARRIER ON OPERATION HERRICK

Joint Force Harrier (JFH), a combined RAF and RN Fleet Air Arm unit, first deployed to Kandahar in 2004 in support of the NATO-led International Security Assistance Force (ISAF). Under this umbrella Harriers operated continuously day and night over five years and its contribution of close air support and reconnaissance was crucial to the ISAF mission. During this operational period JFH provided eight Harriers continuously available in theatre with eleven pilots and around 100 engineers and support staff. We always planned and flew missions in pairs with two pairs being tasked during the day and a pair at night. Equally, during the day we kept two further Harriers at Alert 30, i.e. 30 minutes notice to get airborne and at night this was extended to Alert 120 although the CAOC (Combined Air Operations Centre) could reduce those times depending on the tactical situation; quite often aircrew would be airborne in well under these times. This stance was maintained throughout the five-year period. Harriers never once lost a mission due to an unserviceable aircraft, often there would be numerous spare aircraft if one unusually developed a problem on start. The only times that Harrier failed to get airborne in the five years of operations was if the weather curtailed flying operations.

Unique to the Harrier was its short field capability, which proved to be extremely worthwhile throughout the five-year period. When Harriers first deployed the runway at Kandahar, it was a narrow 3,000' strip only suitable for VSTOL aircraft. Latterly, there were times when the runway became blocked and only a few thousand feet were available, not enough for the other fast air to operate from. This occurred during one of my day missions when crucially, the US carrier with its F-18s was in port, thus unable to get airborne, and Bagram and Kabul airfields were iced in; as such the Harriers were the only aircraft helping to support the troops at this time.

The main area of operations for the Harrier was over the Helmand valley supporting the UK army and Royal Marines as well as all the other coalition troops. At 90 nm from KAF, flying time was usually about 15-20 minutes. However the Harrier was often tasked or re-tasked all over the country with jets operating over places such as the Khyber Pass and alongside the neighbouring countries of Pakistan, Iran, Turkmenistan and Uzbekistan, showing its full reach.

As for the role that Joint Force Harrier undertook it could perhaps be summarised as shape, clear, hold and build. This was achieved through a graduated response. It must be stressed at this stage that this was through a mixture of kinetic and non-kinetic effects; indeed the latter was how the pilot often tried to resolve any situation.

Shaping could best be described as missions that undertook the role of NTISR, (non-traditional information surveillance and reconnaissance). In this respect we would use our sensors to provide an overview of the battle space. Equally it may also have been appropriate to provide a 'show of presence' where the aircraft were positioned such that a visible or audible presence would be observed on the ground. Finally, if the situation dictated, a deliberate 'surgical' strike might be called for in order to provide ground forces with a tactical advantage.

Clearing was where we brought the Harrier into the close air support role providing armed overwatch. Utilising shows of force, the aim was to deter or disperse insurgents; if that failed then a kinetic response could be brought to bear. The important point to stress at this juncture is that this effect had to be precise, discriminate and proportional, something that the Harrier became known for; if an effect could be achieved through firing one rocket then that was what was delivered, equally if soldiers' lives were at risk then a PWIV might equally be the most appropriate weapon.

Holding, in many ways similar to shaping, would see the pattern of life monitored as well as a continued presence being maintained both audibly and visually. Equally the continued hunt for IEDs took place whenever the sensors could be spared, ensuring that the key ground gained was then held.

Finally building through support to the local populace, this could include providing presence on voting days, deterring the placement of IEDs and a demonstration of a continued commitment by maintaining presence overhead both audibly and visually.

Looking back, I can honestly say that JFH made a huge difference on Operation Herrick; undoubtedly the lives of many Afghanistan civilians have been saved along with the lives of our own and coalition troops. In many ways, the statistics speak for themselves: missions flown: 4,500; close air support missions: 2,000; sorties: 8,557; hours: 22,771.

I was fortunate to fly the last mission for JFH over Afghanistan, a night-into-day sortie, and then fly one of the aircraft back to the UK, aircraft thirteen, ZD346, with my name on its side. I feel extremely privileged to have served in and over Afghanistan on Operation Herrick.

CHAPTER 23

THE END OF AN ERA

GARY WATERFALL

As a young twenty-one year old arriving at RAF Wittering in the summer of 1988, little did I realise that some twenty-two years later, I would be called upon to close a most remarkable chapter in the history of British military aviation. Young, fresh-faced (everything in life is relative) and very afraid of 21,500 lbs of raw Pegasus, passing the OCU wasn't easy and only achieved once I had the same level of belief in myself that others had in me. I know that I will always live in the debt of the patient blend of instructors and mentors that encouraged me to arrive at RAF Gütersloh for my first tour and join the much coveted ranks of 3(Fighter) Squadron. Like many, I could fill this book with my own tales of friendship, excitement, danger and humour from worldwide Harrier adventures, but alas my task is to focus on the closing chapter.

Much to my surprise (and that of many I'm sure), I found myself in command of RAF Cottesmore and Joint Force Harrier (JFH) in late 2009. The force had just returned to the UK after a continuous five-year operational tour in Afghanistan, where all involved had served with distinction, undoubtedly saving many lives throughout the course of their selfless duties. The MoD had made the decision to rest the Harrier Force and allow it to enter a period of regeneration and to concentrate on broader war-fighting skills including carrier operations. Meanwhile, the mantle was taken by the Tornado Force who deployed until the end of operations in Afghanistan. The removal of the Harrier from Afghanistan was not universally popular, and many in the Harrier family had, and will still have, various conspiracy theories or views on inter-service agendas between the RAF and RN as the RAF sought to sustain combat air at any cost. Meanwhile, the Royal Navy was keen to secure the future of two aircraft carriers with embarked fixed-wing aviation at their very core, able to deploy global airpower.

In 2009, barely three months into my tour at Cottesmore on a very snowy day of the pre-Christmas grant, Liam Fox announced that JFH would shrink to leave two operational squadrons and that Cottesmore would close and the force would relocate to the home of the Harrier – RAF Wittering. The stage was set. 2010 brought the General Election and the strategic defence and security review (SDSR) loomed on the horizon, timetabled for late October. Those who lived through the period will remember much conjecture around the future of the Tornado and Harrier fleets, as it seemed certain that the UK's combat air mass would shrink to help reduce overall defence spending. Leading the station through closure and supposed relocation of the Harrier Force to Wittering was a complex task; but even today I still marvel at the gusto and spirit of the Joint Force who maintained a level head and humour throughout.

The conjecture reached a crescendo as October approached and it was seemingly impossible to see which way the decision would fall whilst the media ran conflicting tales dependant on the source. CAS pulled me to one side during an evening function at the start of October and told me it was all over and that JFH would be, in RAF vernacular, 'chopped'. That news allowed me to plan with a degree of certainty. However, it was all set against a backdrop of secrecy and an inability to discuss with anybody apart from my most loyal lieutenant – Commander Tony 'Stinger' Rae, the deputy force commander. The decision continued to see-saw until the end. It really was that close.

Monday 18 October 2010 – all air rank officers and station commanders were summoned to RAF High Wycombe for an address by CAS that laid out the outcome of SDSR behind closed doors; his plan was to allow preparation from those officers that would need to lead their personnel through the challenges that lay ahead. Early in the brief he announced that JFH would disband and the iconic Harrier would retire from service. The death of an icon. There was an embargo placed on any public announcement until the Secretary of State for Defence made the announcement in the House of Commons at 1530 hours the next day; until such time I was sworn to secrecy. I drove back to Cottesmore with a heavy heart and feeling the enormous burden that now rested with me; the next ninety-six hours would be crucial to ensure that information flow was managed and that our people were looked after. Too many questions lay ahead; not least was what would happen in the coming months to the community. Already there was a swell of perception that all Harrier flying might cease with immediate effect. On arrival back at Cottesmore I drove straight to the pan to greet OC 1(Fighter) Squadron and award him his 2,500 hours+ badge after he landed from a night sortie. In my heart I knew that it was his last-ever night flight and it may have been the last-ever UK Harrier flight for us all. I arrived home just in time to see rampant conjecture mixed with political leaks on the BBC 10 o'clock News, already suggesting that UK carriers would be retired from service.

After a fitful night's sleep, I dressed to the accompaniment of Liam Fox on the BBC news and at 0722 (it's odd what you remember) he announced, in advance of his formal announcement to the House, that the United Kingdom would accept a gap in her carrier strike capability until the arrival of the Queen Elizabeth Class carriers at the end of the decade. After a phone call with my very supportive AOC, I was granted permission to prepare the force for the formal news. After a short brief using the station tannoy at 0930 hours, all flying was stopped and we awaited the formal announcement that afternoon. There was a sombre mood across the whole station as all personnel – military and civilian – pondered what the future would hold. The AOC arrived with his RN 2* counterpart, and all gathered in the MT hangar to learn of their fate from the chain of command at 1500 hours – thirty minutes before the Defence Secretary's address to the House. Immediately after the AOC finished speaking, I gathered all of the current OCU students together to let them know that, regardless of the immediate future for Harrier flying, they were suspended from training with immediate effect; of all of the difficult briefs I had to give, this was undoubtedly the hardest. The emotional pain was clear on their faces. However, the route to force closure was uncertain for all; the RAF had not decided if we should carry on flying. Many outside JFH were keen to cease operations straight away and it took much negotiation to convince the leadership that flying should continue. My strategy was twofold: Firstly, I was keen that all those who were able, gained qualifications and competencies in the time we had left. This ranged from combat-ready work-ups and ATC 'tickets', to crucial engineering experience and qualifications that would give everybody the best possible chance of moving on to pastures new. Secondly, I was determined that the Harrier family, stretching across four decades, had the opportunity to say farewell to the old girl with respect and dignity. After much negotiation and setting a realistic balance of risk against benefit, day flying resumed a week later with plans that all flying would cease on 18 December, less than two months away.

The weeks that followed were short and packed with highs and lows, with all having a view and input into the plans for the retirement event. The retention of Tornado and the loss of Harrier and carrier-strike capability meant that relations between the Royal Navy and the Royal Air Force were complicated. However, as would be expected, the tactical JFH relationship remained strong and resolute.

Overall, it was uneventful and in quiet moments I occasionally struggled with the enormity of the situation we faced. There were several amusing rumours of extension of service, immediate cessation and Royal Naval undercover actions to steal aircraft and form a new Phoenix-style squadron at Yeoviltion; some rumours were a welcome distraction and most of the latest could be obtained from a quick chat at the main gate. In the main all respected the privilege to carry on flying. Upon request, JFH deployed aircraft to HMS *Ark Royal* for an extended weekend to undertake the last embarkation. Whilst the humorous 'For sale' sign in the windscreen of one of the aircraft onboard didn't quite amuse all within the senior echelons of defence when it appeared in the newspapers, it was nevertheless an important moment to salute another halt to fixed-wing embarked aviation through the life of the Fleet Air Arm. In true JFH style, the last launch was flown by a RN pilot flying on an RAF squadron. Likewise there were several overnight stops around the UK, including Yeovilton, as all maximised the opportunity to show our military colleagues what would soon be gone for good.

As the day of the last flight got ever closer, the winter weather decided to throw a few rolls of the dice to ensure things would not be easy. Heavy snow markedly reduced the amount of flying in the December and all Wittering Harriers had to be moved to Cottesmore on the Friday prior to the last week. With seventy-nine Harriers bulging in hangars, the stage was set for an emotional finale.

My superiors were concerned that holding such a send-off carried reputational risks, but I convinced them that it was worth it. The remaining two days before the final flight were dogged by more winter weather, including yet more snow. However, we managed to launch a sixteen-ship rehearsal on the penultimate day, which included a fly-past over RAF Wittering that was immortalised forever by my good friend Jamie Hunter.

So, in a freezing northerly wind and a solid green cloud base, sixteen Harriers, with a photo chase in tow, launched to mark their retirement. The whole formation, Kestrel, was made up of four, four-ship elements, each led by a specially painted aircraft to mark the occasion. I led the formation and front element in ZG506, resplendent in her retro scheme denoting the life of the Bona Jet, with Wing Commander Dave Bradshaw – OC Ops from Wittering – as my deputy. The 1(F) Squadron element were on the right wing, ably led by Wing Commander Dave Haines; the 800 NAS element were on the left wing, led by Commander Dave Lindsey; and, at the rear, the 4 Squadron element led by Wing Commander Simon Jessett, which included three T10s. Thirty serviceable aircraft were prepared on the pan but not a single spare was needed on the day due to the exceptional work of OC Eng, Wing Commander Scott Wray, and his fine team. The weather was so bad we all took off in a sixteen-ship 'snake climb' as pairs, and for the first time in history it actually worked.

We joined on top into close formation for the last dance together above a winter landscape. The professionalism of all the pilots involved was exceptional; all sitting rock steady on their references and having their own final and quiet moment with the old girl. All too soon it was time to split into individual four-ships for a 'finger four' radar to visual recovery. Air traffic control played a blinder, feeding us all into Cottesmore in 'legal' weather conditions for the final run and break. On the ground the noise rose steadily as, one by one, each four-ship came to the hover over the three VL pads and main runway with precision and unison. As three of each element landed vertically together and the leader RVL'd ahead, the next four-ship could be seen breaking overhead with tails slicing through the low grey cloud base. Even CO 800's brief 'curtsy' couldn't detract from the aerial coordination, giving ultimate truism that you're only as good as your last bow. Last was my four-ship; I was to have the honour of the final bow and landing of a UK Harrier in service. The 15 kt on-crowd wind certainly kept my attention to the task at hand with a feeling of enormity and respect for everyone in the

Harrier family that had been privileged to fly, work or just be associated with such an icon. And yes, of course the stick reached the backstop as I arrested the bow in a 15 kt tailwind after a sporty cross wind decel to crowd centre. However, on reflection it was just how it should have been – testing to the last.

Bringing the undercarriage up in the hover saw the nose-wheel light extinguish in the murky December gloom which provided an emotional signal that the lights were indeed going out on the Harrier Force. As ever, the Pegasus had the last word as a short lift wet exploded in the ear drums of the many that had braved the conditions to watch, as I accelerated away from the hover and then raised the nose to climb to the low cloud base. It was then good to explore the other end stop of the control column as I pitched over with the tail scraping in the low cloud base. Finally, at 1542 hours on Wednesday 15 December, I VL'd on the MEXE Pad (almost on the markers) and an iconic chapter in British aviation history was complete. I taxied back in to join the other fifteen jets with the four painted jets formed at the front in a semi-circle. After declaring the chapter was closed and thanking ATC one last time, all sixteen Pegasus engines were shut down simultaneously. It was an eerie silence that followed and a moment truly symbolic of the death of a remarkable capability. All the pilots shook hands with their ground crew and each other before walking through an honour guard of bagpipes and a fly-past by three Red Arrows, all flown by former Harrier pilots.

The rest of the day and evening became a blur as the wake kicked in. Events on the ground were organised with ruthless efficiency by the media and communications officer, Paula Wilmot. The next month or so for Joint Force Harrier was a sombre one for us all. The engineers carefully placed the aircraft in a state of storage to be ready for an uncertain future. The odd private sale was mooted, together with numerous countries declaring an interest; ranging from extant Harrier users to potential new customers. In the end, the aircraft were sold to the USMC for spares and eventual storage in the desert in Arizona but a few survived to go on show and be immortalised in museums. Luckily, ZD318 was spared and now sits in the Wittering Station Heritage Centre together with a GR1, GR3 and T4 as a lasting legacy. ZD318 was of course the first Harrier II built and transitioned through all guises, ending up as a GR9A.

On 28 January 2011, Joint Force Harrier was officially disbanded at an emotional parade in the OCU's hangar at Wittering. The First Sea Lord and Chief of the Air Staff both came and spoke with passion about the loss of such a revolutionary capability. Symbolically, but against traditions of seniority and service, 4 Squadron, 1 Squadron and 800 NAS standard parties slow marched in line abreast out of the hangar into the cold crisp January air. I then led the parade out of the hangar to a medley of Heart of Oak and the RAF March Past, as JFH paraded in front of the dais one last time. As we passed the dais, heads held high saluting our seniors, the assembled crowd rose to their feet in rapturous and symbolic applause, many with tears in their eyes. It was over.

GLOSSARY

AAR	air-to-air refuelling, or after action report	BAE Systems	the conglomerate that subsumed BAe
abo	ab initio (from the beginning) trainee pilot	Balbo	large formation of aircraft, named after Italian General Italo Balbo
ACE	allied command Europe		
ACI	air combat instructor	BFM	basic fighter manoeuvring – air combat
ACL	air combat leader		
ACM	air combat manoeuvres	BFPO	British forces post office
ACMI	air combat manoeuvring installation	Bingo	a pre-briefed fuel quantity, usually called by radio as formation progress check
AH	artificial horizon		
AI	attitude indicator		
AoA	angle of attack	BoI	Board of Inquiry
AOC	air officer commanding	BVR	beyond visual range – radar-guided air-to-air missiles
AOCC	air operations co-ordination centre		
AOR	area of responsibility		
AMRAAM	advanced medium-range air-to-air missile	CAOC	combined air operations centre
APC	armament practice camp (or armoured personnel carrier)	CAP	combat air patrol – a fighter screen to stop offensive aircraft
AR5	aircrew respirator no 5	CAS	Chief of the Air Staff
asap	as soon as possible	CAS	close air support
ASR	air staff requirement	CBF	Commander British Forces
ASRAAM	advanced short-range air-to-air missile		
AST	air staff target	CBFFI	CBF Falkland Islands
AUW	all-up weight	CBR	California bearing ratio, a measure of surface hardness
AVTUR	fuel for jet engines (aviation turbine)		
		CFC	carbon fibre composite
		Chicken	minimum fuel state for return to base
BAe	British Aerospace, which subsumed Hawker Siddeley Aviation	Chinagraph	a wax pencil with plastic case and screw-out lead

CR	combat ready	
CRBN	chemical, radiological, biological, nuclear	
CRV 7	Canadian rocket vehicle 7, an unguided rocket weapon	
CTTO	central trials and tactics organisation	
CWP	central warning panel	
DJRP	digital joint reconnaissance pod	
ECM	electronic countermeasures	
EO	electro optical. In the Harrier context, using FLIR and NVG	
F540	the official diary of each RAF unit, compiled monthly	
FAC	forward air control	
FINRAE	Ferranti inertial navigation rapid alignment equipment	
FLM	flight-line mechanic	
FOD	foreign object damage	
Fragged	tasked, listed on fragmentary order	
FRI	fighter reconnaissance instructor	
FWOC	forward wing operations centre	
GCA	ground-controlled approach – a radar talk-down	
GLO	ground liaison officer	
GPMG	general-purpose machine gun	
GSE	government supplied equipment – official kit	
Guard	the standard radio emergency frequency –	

243.0MHz for military aircraft

HARM	high-speed anti-radiation missile
HE	high explosive
HEFOE	a system of hand signals to indicate an aircraft emergency without using radio. The number of fingers extended indicates, in order: Hydraulics, Electrics, Fuel, Oxygen, Engine
HOTAS	hands on throttle and stick
HQ	headquarters
HSA	Hawker Siddeley Aviation
HUD	head-up display
IFF	identification friend or foe – a transponder to identify aircraft
IMC	instrument meteorological conditions
INAS	inertial navigation attack system
IP	initial point
JP	junior pilot
JTIDS	joint tactical information distribution system
LERX	leading-edge root extension
LFA	low flying area
LOROP	long-range oblique photography – a pod with a single long-lens camera
LRMTS	laser ranger and marked target seeker
LSL	landing ship logistics

		PMC	president of the mess committee, the officer in charge of the mess
1MC	l main circuit – a ship's public address system		
M-16	assault rifle	PNB	power nozzle braking: use of engine thrust to slow down on the ground
MDC	miniature (or mild) detonating cord, used to shatter aircraft canopies		
		PSA1	prefabricated surfacing aluminium no 1 (possibly PSA interlocking), the planks used to build operating surfaces
MEXE	military engineering experimental establishment, whence came the design for Harrier strips and pads		
MO	medical officer	PSP	personal survival pack
MoD (PE)	Ministry of Defence Procurement Executive, the interface between the forces and industry for new equipment	QFI	qualified flying instructor
		QWI	qualified weapons instructor
MoD	Ministry of Defence	RAFAT	RAF Aerobatic Team – The Red Arrows
MT	motor transport (vehicles)	RAFG	RAF Germany
		R & R	rest and recuperation
		RBL755	the BL755 cluster bomb with a radar altimeter for delayed opening
NAS	naval air squadron		
NBC	nuclear, biological, chemical	RE	Royal Engineers
no duff	true, operational, not exercise	RIC	reconnaissance intelligence centre
		ROE	rules of engagement
OBOGS	on-board oxygen generation system	RTB	return to base
		RV	rendezvous
ODM	operating data manual	RVL	rolling vertical landing
OLF	operational low flying	RVTO	rolling vertical take-off
OP	observation post	RWR	radar warning receiver
OR	operational requirements		
orbat	order of battle – military line-up	SACEUR	supreme allied commander Europe
		SAOEU	strike attack operational evaluation unit
PAR	precision approach radar		
Paveway	a laser-guided bomb system	SAP	simulated attack profile
		Sappers	Royal Engineers
Pickle	press the button for weapon release	SARBE	search and rescue beacon, a small emergency radio

SASO	senior air staff officer		
SDSR	strategic defence and security review	V/STOL	vertical/short take-off and landing
SEAD	suppression of enemy air defences	VIFF	(thrust) vectoring in forward flight
SL	slow landing	VL	vertical landing
SMS	stores management system	VMC	visual meteorological conditions
SNCO	senior non-commissioned officer	VSI	vertical speed indicator
		VTO	vertical take-off
SNEB	from Société Nouvelle des Établissements Edgar Brandt, a podded unguided rocket weapon	WAC	weapon aiming computer
Sniper	an advanced targeting pod, with sensors and laser designator	XO	executive officer – the second in command of a squadron
SOF	supervisor of flying	Zulu	Option Zulu – pre-planned attack plans for countering Soviet aggression
SOP	standard operating procedure		
STCAAME	Strike Command air-to-air missile establishment		
STO	short take-off		
STOVL	short take-off, vertical landing		
Taceval	tactical evaluation		
TACP	tactical air control party: FAC and support		
TACSOP	tactical standard operating procedures		
Tally	or tally ho, radio call meaning I can see the target and need no further assistance		
Terma	an infra-red countermeasures (flare) system		
TOT	time over target		
TRU	transformer/rectifier unit		
TWU	tactical weapons unit		

INDEX

PLACES